To my two children,
Victor and Sonia

SEEKING WISDOM
From Darwin to Munger

By Peter Bevelin

First Edition

For permission to use copyrighted material, grateful acknowledgment
is made to the copyright holders on next page, which is hereby
made part of this copyright page.

Published by Post Scriptum AB
Stora Nygatan 25, S-211 37 Malmö Sweden
Fax + 46 40 97 42 66

Printed in Sweden by Printing Malmö AB

ISBN 91-631-3685-6

For more information, please contact Peter Bevelin, AB Possessor
Stora Nygatan 25, S-211 37 Malmö, Sweden or by e-mail to
p.bevelin@possessor.se

— ACKNOWLEDGMENTS —

Thanks to Charles Munger and Warren Buffett for their kind permission to quote extensively from their work. Thanks to Charles Munger who generously took the time to read the whole manuscript. Thanks to Warren Buffett for his early encouragement of my first private memorandum – the foundation for this book. Thanks to Henry Emerson who permitted me to quote from *Outstanding Investor Digest.* Thanks to Ralph Greenspan at the NeuroSciences Institute for many fruitful discussions. Many thanks also to Edward Beltrami, Charles Brenner, Peter Gärdenfors, Vibeke Horstmann, Andrew Kilpatrick, Frank Lambert, Ronald Newburgh, Maria Strömme, Philip Swigard, and William Thompson. The reader shouldn't assume that any of these people agree with what I have written in this book. Any misconceptions, deficiencies or errors are mine alone.

Thanks to JoAnna Cunningham who gave valuable editing advice.

Finally, I wish to thank my wife, Monica, who read every sentence with critical eyes. Whatever I have achieved in life I owe her. She is the wind beneath my wings. Monica, you are the best.

Peter Bevelin

– CONTENTS –

A man who has committed a mistake and
doesn't correct it, is committing another mistake.
- Confucius (Chinese thinker, 6th to 5th Century BC)

Why do we behave like we do? American writer Mark Twain once wrote: "The character of the human race never changes, it is permanent." Why is it so?

What do we want out of life? To be healthy, happy with our families, in our work, etc? What interferes with this? Isn't it often emotions like fear, anger, worry, disappointment, stress, and sadness? Caused by problems, mistakes, losses, or unreal expectations. Maybe we misjudged people, situations, the time or some investment. We chose the wrong occupation, spouse, investment, or place to live. Why?

This book is about searching for wisdom. It is in the spirit of Charles Munger, Vice Chairman of Berkshire Hathaway, Inc. who says, "All I want to know is where I'm going to die so I'll never go there." There are roads that lead to unhappiness. An understanding of how and why we can "die" should help us avoid them.

This book focuses on how our thoughts are influenced, why we make misjudgments and tools to improve our thinking. If we understand what influences us, we might avoid certain traps and understand why others act like they do. And if we learn and understand what works and doesn't work and find some framework for reasoning, we will make better judgments. We can't eliminate mistakes, but we can prevent the really dumb ones.

How do we achieve wisdom? It is hard to improve ourselves simply by looking at our own mistakes. The best way to learn what, how and why things work is to learn from others. Charles Munger says, "I believe in the discipline of mastering the best that other people have ever figured out. I don't believe in just sitting down and trying to dream it all up *yourself*. Nobody's that *smart*."

My quest for wisdom originates partly from making mistakes myself and observing those of others but also from the philosophy of Charles Munger. A man whose simplicity and clarity of thought is unequal to anything I have seen. What especially influenced me were his lectures on worldly wisdom, many of them reproduced in the newsletter *Outstanding Investor Digest*. In one speech, he said that the best way to achieve wisdom was to learn the big ideas that underlie reality. In another, he referred to Charles Darwin as one of the best thinkers who ever lived. Darwin's lesson is that even people who aren't geniuses can outthink the rest of mankind if they develop certain thinking habits.

To learn more about Darwin's habits, I started to read his autobiography and other writings about him. I found him to be a fascinating character and a wonderful lesson on objectivity. In his autobiography, Darwin said:

> I think that I am superior to the common run of men in noticing things which easily escape attention, and in observing them carefully. My industry has been nearly as great as it could have been in the observation and collection of facts. What is far more important, my love of natural science has been steady and ardent... From my early youth I have had the strongest desire to understand or explain whatever I observed, that is, to group all facts under some general laws. These causes combined have given me the patience to reflect or ponder for any number of years over any unexplained problem. As far as I can judge, I am not apt to follow blindly the lead of other men. I have steadily endeavoured to keep my mind free so as to give up any hypothesis, however much beloved (and I cannot resist forming one on every subject), as soon as facts are shown to be opposed to it.

Darwin reinforced my interest in understanding human behavior. To improve my own thinking, I read books in biology, psychology, neuroscience, physics, and mathematics. As the 17th Century French philosopher Rene Descartes said: "The reading of all good books is like conversation with the finest minds of past centuries."

I started to write down what I learned. The result is this book. The ideas in it are built largely from the works and thoughts of others. As the Roman poet Publius Terentius (c.190-159 BC) wrote: "Nothing has yet been said that's not been said before." I have condensed what others have written in a usable form and added my own conclusions.

In this book you find a broad-based collection of wisdom from outstanding scientists like Darwin, Albert Einstein, Richard Feynman, and two of the world's most successful businessmen and investors, Charles Munger and the Chairman of Berkshire Hathaway, Warren Buffett. Albert Einstein once said that there are only a few enlightened people with a lucid mind and good taste within a century. Warren Buffett and Charles Munger are such people. I owe a great debt to them whose messages have been instructional as well as encouraging. If I had listened to them earlier in my life – so many expensive mistakes would have been avoided. They are my heroes!

I advise all of you to read the annual reports of Berkshire Hathaway and Wesco Financial (Charles Munger is chairman). These reports are the best educational tools about how to think about investing and business. The lessons also show us how to behave in life.

This book has four parts. First, I explore what influences our thinking. This serves as a foundation. In the second part, I give examples of psychological reasons for misjudgments. The third part explores reasons for misjudgments caused both by our psychology and a lack of considering some basic ideas from physics and mathematics. In the final part I reveal tools for better thinking. The appendix contains a speech from Charles Munger and quotes from Munger and Warren Buffett. It also contains checklists. Checklists often eliminate biases and make it easier for us to be sure we've covered the important things.

Why spend time studying wisdom? Charles Munger gives a compelling reason: "I think it's a *huge* mistake not to absorb elementary worldly wisdom if you're capable of doing it because it makes you better able to serve others, it makes you better able to serve yourself and it makes life more fun…I'm passionate about *wisdom*. I'm passionate about *accuracy* and some kinds of *curiosity.*"

This book is for those who love the constant search for knowledge. I have focused on explaining timeless ideas. The number of pages I have devoted to each idea does not reflect on its importance. My goal is to lay the foundation.

16th Century Spanish writer Miguel de Cervantes said: "He that publishes a book runs a very great hazard, since nothing can be more impossible than to compose one that may secure the approbation of every reader." You may feel that much has been ignored and what is left has been exaggerated. Since I am writing this, I take full responsibility for the content. Any mistakes or inaccuracies are my responsibility. If you, the reader, are convinced that I am clearly wrong about anything in this book, please write me at the address given in the beginning of the book.

I have cited quotations from a wide range of sources. Some books and material have been especially useful. Obviously, books about Charles Darwin. Also speeches and reports from Charles Munger and Warren Buffett. Many of them found in the excellent newsletter, *Outstanding Investor Digest.* Robert Cialdini, Regents Professor of Psychology at Arizona State University, gives an excellent summary of findings in social psychology in his great book *Influence.* Psychology Professors Daniel Kahneman and the late Amos Tversky's work on decision-making has also been useful. Richard Feynman (1918-1988), perhaps the most brilliant and influential physicist of modern times, was also a spellbinding teacher. I love his books and autobiographies. Human Ecology Professor Garrett

Hardin is one of my favorites. His books are treasures and offer many ways for clear thinking. I have also been fortunate to visit the NeuroSciences Institute in California. Every time I'm there, I learn something new about how our brain works.

I sometimes write in terms of "we", and other times I address "you", the reader. Just remember, "you" includes me, the writer. Italian mathematician and philosopher Gian-Carlo Rota's said in *Indiscrete Thoughts:* "The advice we give others is the advice that we ourselves need."

Instead of writing he or she, I have used "he". To quote the British zoologist, Professor of public understanding of Science at Oxford, Richard Dawkins from *The Blind Watchmaker:* "I may refer to the 'reader' as 'he', but I no more think of my readers as specifically male than a French speaker thinks of a table as female."

Let's start the journey for wisdom. I hope it will be inspiring.

Peter Bevelin
April 2003

Part One

What influences our thinking?

And men should know that from nothing else but from the brain come joys, laughter and jests, and sorrows, griefs, despondency and lamentations. And by this ...we acquire wisdom and knowledge, and we see and hear and know what are foul and what are fair, what sweet and what unsavory... and by the same organ we become mad and delirious and fears and terrors assail us.

– Hippocrates (Greek physician 460-377 BC)

One

Our anatomy set the limits for our behavior

To understand the way we think and why we make misjudgments, we must first determine what influences our behavior.

Why can't we fly?
To do what we do today demands the proper anatomical foundation. To fly we need wings. To walk we need legs, to see we need eyes, and to think we need a brain. Our anatomy, physiology and biochemistry are the fundamental bases for our behavior.

If we change anatomy, we change behavior. Birds can't fly if their wings are located in an area where no bones are present to anchor them. Birds can't talk because they need speech organs and these must be positioned in a certain way. For example, a small change in how our speech organs are positioned could make speech impossible.

Another example on how a change in anatomy changes behavior comes from the NeuroSciences Institute in California. In one experiment, scientists took a small portion of developing brain tissue from a quail and put it into the same spot of a chicken embryo. When the chick hatched, it had both quail and chicken nerve cells. Depending on what cells were transplanted, the results were either a chicken that crowed like a quail or a chicken that bobbed its head like a quail.

Studies have also shown that damage to a part of the brain, the prefrontal cortex (lying behind the forehead and eyes), results in a tendency to show a high degree of disrespect for social norms, including violent behavior. A classic example is that of railway construction foreman Phineas Gage. In 1848, he was victim of an explosion that drove an iron rod through the frontal region of his brain, damaging his prefrontal cortex. Before the accident he was considered stable, dependable, industrious, and friendly. Phineas survived the accident, but his personality changed. He became a drifter who was unreliable, arrogant, impulsive and inconsiderate.

Other studies show that damage to the amygdala – a region of the brain, linked with emotional states and social behavior – reduces the tendency to feel and respond to fear. Stimulating the amygdala can elicit intense emotional reactions. In 1966, Charles Whitman killed 14 people and wounded 38 from the clock tower at the University of Texas, Austin. An autopsy revealed he had a tumor pressing against his amygdala.

It is our brain, its anatomy, physiology and biochemistry and how these parts function that set the limits for how we think. But since our brain's parts also interact with our body's anatomy, physiology and biochemistry, we must see brain and body together. They are part of the same system – us.

Let's consider the anatomy of our brains to get a better understanding of what influences our behavior.

What we feel and think depends on neural connections
A lot is known about the brain, but far from everything. There are many controversies and unanswered questions.

Dr. Gerald Edelman at the NeuroSciences Institute says:

> The brain is the most complicated material object in the known universe. If you attempted to count the number of connections, one per second, in the mantle of our brain (the cerebral cortex), you would finish counting 32 million years later. But that is not the whole story. The way the brain is connected – its neuroanatomical pattern – is enormously inrricate. Within this anatomy a remarkable set of dynamic events take place in hundredths of a second and the number of levels controlling these events, from molecules to behavior, is quite large.

Weighing only three pounds, the brain is composed of at least 100 billion nerve cells or neurons. It also contains tens of billions of other cells called glial cells supporting neurons. Neurons are connected to other neurons and interact. Each neuron has a cell body with tiny branches called dendrites that receive information from other neurons. Extending from the cell body is long fibers called axons that send information to other neurons.

Since it is the connections between neurons that cause our mental capacities, it is not the number of cells that is important but the number of potential connections between them.

How do neurons connect and communicate?
Every neuron can connect with other neurons at contact points, the space between one neuron and another, called synapses. When a neuron fire an electrical impulse down the axon, the impulse is released as a chemical substance

called a neurotransmitter. When this chemical reaches the dendrite of another neuron it triggers an electrical impulse. Thereafter a series of chemical reactions begins. Some stimulation must happen for the neuron to fire. The strength of this firing and what kind of neurotransmitter is released depends on the incoming stimuli.

How does the neurotransmitter cause the electrical impulse? On the surface of the receiving neuron are proteins called receptors and every receptor is tailor-made for a specific chemical. The chemical acts as a key, and the receptor, or the lock, only "lets in" the right chemical.

Why does it feel good when our loved ones give us a kiss or a compliment?
It is the neurotransmitter dopamine that is being released. Dopamine is involved in the brain's reward and motivation system, and in addiction. High levels of dopamine are believed to increase feelings of pleasure and relieve pain.

Another neurotransmitter is serotonin. Serotonin is linked with mood and emotion. Too much stress can lead to low levels of serotonin and low levels are associated with anxiety and depression. What happens when we take an antidepressant drug? The drug increases the amount of serotonin in our brain. The drug mimics the structure of serotonin. Antidepressants don't make us happy; they just treat the state of unhappiness. Observe that even if neurotransmitters and the drugs that affect them alter our mental functions, they are part of a complicated system of interactions between molecules, cells, synapses, and other systems, including life experiences and environmental factors.

So far we know that the brain is a chemical system, and that neurons communicate with each other through the release of neurotransmitters (chemicals that carry messages between neurons). What we think and feel depends on chemical reactions. And these chemical reactions are a function of how our neurons connect.

What determines how these neurons connect and their patterns? Our genes and life experiences, situational or environmental conditions, and a degree of randomness.

Genes control brain chemistry but are turned on and off by the environment
What is a gene? What does it do?
Genes are what makes an individual, for example, to be built with two blue eyes, two arms, one nose, and a brain with certain architecture.

Our body is made up of different types of interconnected cells functioning together. Each cell has 46 chromosomes or a chain of genes. 23 chromosomes come from each parent. Every chromosome is made up of the chemical DNA or deoxyribonucleic acid. DNA is our inheritance; half is from our father and half from our mother. Genes are segments of our DNA and the units of our inheritance. A gene consists of four chemical molecules: adenine, cytosine, guanine, thymine or A, C, G and T joined together in a chain. The short chemical name for a chain of any number of these molecules, in any order, is DNA. The order of these molecules provides coded instructions for everything a cell does.

The job of genes is to make proteins – the building blocks of life. Proteins are molecules that carry out most of our biological functions and are made up of amino acids. There are twenty kinds of amino acids that can be used to make our skin, hair, muscles, etc. Some proteins called enzymes cause certain chemical reactions. One example is neurotransmitters. Proteins are also hormones that act as messengers between our cells.

Every living thing uses the same genetic code – from cats to humans. This means we can transfer a single human gene into a cat and the cat can read it and follow its instructions. But no individual has the same DNA or the same versions of genes (except for identical twins). Not all things are "spelled" alike. That's why people differ in eye color, height, etc. The closer related one living thing is to another, the fewer spelling differences. But even if the differences are small, gene expression or genetic activity is the key. As an example take our closest relative – the chimpanzee. Genetic studies show that humans and chimpanzees share at least 98.5% of their DNA sequences. This means that less than 1.5% of our DNA is responsible for the traits that make us different from chimpanzees. What causes the large difference in behavior? Studies show that the human brain shows strikingly different patterns of gene expression compared to the chimpanzee's brain.

Since we inherit all of our genes from our parents, why don't we look like a mixture of them?

In most organisms, genes come in pairs. We inherit two versions of each gene for a particular trait (for example one version for blue eyes and one for green eyes) from each parent. When a father and mother's genes combine, the effect of one gene may dominate the effect of the other. Certain characteristics are dominant. This is why a child who has one parent with blue eyes and one with green doesn't have eyes that are a blend of blue and green. The child has blue eyes because the blue-eyed gene won the race. Green eyes are recessive. But since the child inherited the green-eyed gene, it could still be passed on to future generations.

Since the recombination of the versions happens by chance, they can always produce a new combination. On the other hand, if both the child's parents have blue eyes, the child has no choice but to be blue-eyed.

Some versions of genes are dominant, in some cases they blend, and sometimes we'll see an equal expression of both versions. Since several pairs of genes govern most traits, lots of combinations are possible.

Interaction and flexibility characterize our biological functions
Does each gene have its own specific part to play?
No, we can't isolate one gene as causing something or arrange them in order of importance. They are part of an interconnected system with many possible combinations. And most genes contribute to more than one characteristic. Interaction is a fundamental property in biology. There are interactions between genes, neurons, brain regions, cells, and among these individual systems. Each system does its own job but they are all coordinated to produce a functional and unique individual.

Dr. Ralph Greenspan at the NeuroSciences Institute says:

> Isaac Newton might have liked the neat view of biological systems made up of dedicated components, with causal roles that can be studied in isolation, and in which particular conditions give rise to uniquely predictable responses. Charles Darwin, by contrast, might have felt more at home with the idea of a complex, emergent system made up of many non-identical components, with non-exclusive roles, non-exclusive relationships, several ways of producing any given output, and a great deal of slop along the way.

The most striking result of our interactive network is flexibility. A flexibility to take on new roles as conditions changes and an ability to produce the same result in different ways. For example, studies show that different configurations between neurons can achieve the same result. The configuration depends on which alternatives that are available at a given moment in a given situation (since behavior depends on context or situation), an individual's life experiences and an element of chance. Having alternative ways of producing the same outcome gives us a great benefit. For example, we can compensate for injuries and readapt to new conditions.

Do our genes have a life of their own?
No, gene expression depends on environmental conditions. Genes control the chemistry in the brain but need to be activated by the environment. An

environmental event must switch them on before they can start making proteins that influence neural connections. Our genes determine if we inherit a particular characteristic but it is the environment that causes our genes to make proteins that produce certain "response tendencies." So our behavior emerges from the mutually dependent activity of genetic and environmental factors.

Neural connections are shaped by life experiences

The brain changes continually as a result of our experiences. Experiences produce physical changes in the brain either through new neural connections or through the generation of new neurons. This means that the anatomy of the brain varies from individual to individual. Even identical twins with identical genes don't have identical brains. They have had different life experiences.

Experiences are the reason that all individuals are unique. There are no individuals with exactly the same upbringing, nutrition, education, social stamping, physical, social and cultural setting. This creates different convictions, habits, values and character. People behave differently because differences in their environment cause different life experiences. This is why it is sometimes hard to understand other people's behavior. To do that, we must adapt to their environment and share their experiences. This is often impossible.

If we encounter a stressful situation, how we respond depends on what we were born with, what we have experienced, and the specific situation. Assume that a person "Sam" and you both have genes for "being fearful." You are standing in a Savannah in Africa and are approached by a lion. Do both of you show the same reaction when exposed to the same situation? You are afraid but not Sam. Sam either knows that this lion is tame or Sam is a lion tamer. Sam's reaction comes from his life experiences. Sam may also be genetically predisposed to react differently to certain dangers. But even if Sam has a low genetic vulnerability to fear, he can develop a fear of the lion. One horrifying experience with a lion may be enough.

Behavior is influenced by our state of mind

Our life is what our thoughts make it.
- Marcus Aurelius Antoninus (Roman emperor and philosopher, 121-180)

Our state of mind is a function of our life experiences and the specific situation. Assume (1) we are eating tasty chocolate, listening to wonderful music and feeling relaxed or (2) we suffer from a cold, feel stressed and just ate a bad meal. If we have to make a judgment, will it be the same in both cases? Probably not, since our state of mind is different in case 1 and 2.

Can our state of mind influence our biochemistry and immune system?
It's not just what happens to us that counts – it's what we think happens to us. We convert our expectations to a biochemical reality meaning that our mental state and physical well-being are connected.

A placebo is a positive medical effect that has nothing to do with the efficiency of a drug, only with a patient's expectation of the treatment. Whenever patients believe that a drug will have a particular physiological, behavioral, or psychological effect, they are susceptible to placebo effects.

For example, there is clinical evidence that placebos have physical effects on the brain, just as drugs do. Recent studies in Sweden show that a placebo activates the same brain circuits as painkilling drugs. Nine male students were asked to voluntary participate in a study of painkilling drugs. Researchers first tested for the degree of pain the subjects would experience when a 48-degree Celsius metal surface was pressed to the backs of their hands. The test was repeated after the subjects were given a painkilling drug.

Later the subjects were told to test two new painkilling drugs and that one of these drugs was similar to the one they earlier tested. Once more the 48-degree metal surface was pressed to the backs of their hands. A man in a white coat, carrying a badge that said "professor", then entered the room. The "professor" gave the subjects intravenous injections of either an opioid (a drug acting like a drug made from opium) painkiller or a placebo. During the experiment researchers scanned the subjects' brains and compared brain responses. Both the painkiller and the placebo produced the same effect. Both increased blood flow in areas of the brain known to be rich in opioid receptors. Eight of the nine subjects said that the placebo produced a clear relief from the pain.

Other studies show that people who take sugar pills as a treatment for depression and other ills can undergo striking, although temporary, changes in brain activity and neural chemistry as their condition improves. It has also been shown that placebo's can improve blood pressure, cholesterol level and heart rate. It's like a pharmacy inside the body that has evolved during million of years of evolutionary time.

What happens when a healthy person finds out he may die?
Studies show that if people expect something to go wrong with their health, it often does. Negative expectations can influence our bodies and cause symptoms that over time may cause our body harm. In one study, women who expected that they were inclined to heart attack were nearly four times as likely to die as women with similar risk factors but without these expectations. Another study found

that patients who were warned about the gastrointestinal side effects of taking aspirin were three times more likely to feel them. Other studies show that if people worry about drug side effects, they are more likely to get them. Beliefs have biological consequences – good and bad.

Our genes and life experiences determine how neurons connect thereby influencing and setting the limits for our behavior. We were born with the basics of life. We had neural connections that regulated our breathing, heartbeat, temperature, etc. How does our brain select those neural connections that produce useful behavior? Our brain is a product of evolution.

Two

EVOLUTION SELECTED THE CONNECTIONS THAT PRODUCE USEFUL BEHAVIOR FOR SURVIVAL AND REPRODUCTION

What do we mean by evolution?

Evolution is change – life changes gradually but perpetually over time through interaction with the environment. John Horner, Curator of Paleontology at the Museum of the Rockies in Montana, says in *Dinosaur Lives*: "When you flip through the pages of the family album you're witnessing evolution at work."

The theory behind evolution is that all individuals alive today have evolved from simpler, more primitive forms of life. Since every living thing uses the same genetic code, it is likely that life descended from a distant common ancestor that had that code. If a monkey and we and any other organism trace our ancestors back far enough, we eventually find a common ancestor.

What mechanisms are responsible for evolution and for how our brain evolved? Mutation and natural selection.

Mutations cause variations

Mutations are caused by a copying error in the sequence of A, C, G and T molecules when DNA is copied. This error in the genes "spelling" may cause a change in a protein leading to a modification in the individual that inherits the gene. For example, the new instruction could be "build Peter with a different eye-color." Since the change is random and unpredictable, no one can tell which gene(s) may be involved.

Natural selection

> *I have called this principle, by which each slight variation,*
> *if useful, is preserved, by the term Natural Selection.*
> - Charles Darwin (British naturalist, 1809-1882)

Charles Darwin and independently the British naturalist Alfred Russell Wallace, discovered the theory of evolution by natural selection. Darwin called his work *On the Origin of Species by Means of Natural Selection, or the Preservation of Favoured Races in the Struggle for Life.*

Darwin was inspired by the Reverend Thomas Malthus's *An Essay on the*

Principle of Population in which Malthus wrote: "Human population, grows exponentially, like compound interest in a bank account, but farm output rises at a slower, arithmetic rate; the result, human population will inevitably and repeatedly outstrip its food supply." Malthus noted that population can always outstrip resources but are held in check by diseases, war, predators, and by limited resources like food.

Darwin made the following three observations:

(1) Competition and environmental change. In most species (a species is a group of individuals capable of producing fertile offspring; like snakes, lion, humans) there are always more offspring born than can survive to adulthood and reproduce. Darwin saw two reasons for this: (1) Since there are a limited amount of resources (like food, space, mates) there is competition between individuals for these resources, and (2) Since the environment changes over time and from one region to another, there are threats (predators, change in climate, isolation, diseases, change in the physical environment) to the children's survival and their reproductive success.

(2) Individual variability. Within a species, there is an enormous amount of individual variation. No two individuals of the same specie are alike in their anatomical structure, physiology or behavior (we're not an exact copy of our parents). Individuals vary in their cell structure, fighting ability, and social skills. Variations make every individual unique and that variation must in some way be heritable otherwise children wouldn't resemble their parents more than they resemble other individuals.

(3) The world is not fixed but evolving. Species change, new ones arrive and others go extinct.

Darwin called his principle natural selection. Any slight variation in traits that gives an individual an advantage in competing with other individuals of the same or different species or in adapting to changes in their environment, increases the chance that the individual will survive, reproduce, and pass along its characteristics to the next generation. Maybe they have greater resistance to disease, or can run faster, survive climate changes better, etc.

Darwin used the word "selection," but nature doesn't care who gets selected for survival. Evolution has no goal. Another way to describe natural selection is as a process of elimination. Certain individuals survive because they have structural, physiological, behavioral or other characteristics that prevent them from being eliminated. Those that don't have these characteristics are eliminated. Heredity enhances the likelihood that the non-eliminated or "selected" variations are preserved. Darwin didn't know about genetics. Therefore he couldn't know that these characteristics were caused by mutations and that they could be passed on through the genes.

After a mutation changes an individual, the environment determines if the change gives the individual an advantage. If the new trait is helpful, the mutated individual is more likely to survive, reproduce and pass the new trait to his children.

Take a poisonous spider as an example. Assume that a population (a group of individuals belonging to one species that occupy the same geographic/ecological niche at the same time) of black widows differs in how toxic their venom is. If some spiders (mutants) are born with more toxins than others, two things could happen over time. If more toxins give an advantage in the spiders' environment, more toxins might be "selected" for and the "more-toxins" characteristic might be passed to children. If the more toxic black widow spiders survive and reproduce better than the less toxic ones, then black widow spiders, will, over time, evolve more toxic venom. The frequency of the "more-toxic" spiders in the population increases over time. If there is no advantage, the trait disappears and the population of less toxic spiders increases.

When organisms undergo selection, some characteristic may be carried along that wasn't selected. Even if some trait didn't provide an advantage it could still be carried along as long as it isn't harmful i.e. doesn't negatively influence survival and reproduction. But a situation may arise in the future when that trait can become useful.

What happens when the environment changes?
Since environments change over time and with geography, different variants are "selected" under different conditions. Characteristics that are successful in one environment may be unsuccessful in another. This is well expressed by the late American paleontologist Stephen Jay Gould in *Wonderful Life:*

> Even if fishes hone their adaptations to peaks of aquatic perfection, they will all die if the ponds dry up. But grubby old Buster the Lungfish, former laughing-stock of the piscine priesthood, may pull through – and not because a bunion on his great-grandfather's fin warned his ancestors about an impending comet. Buster and his kin may prevail because a feature evolved long ago for a different use has fortuitously permitted survival during a sudden and unpredictable change in rules.

Studies show that different organisms respond differently to environmental stress. But there seems to be one creature that survives and reproduces independent of changes and stresses in the environment – the cockroach. Writer Richard Schweid says in *The Cockroach Papers*, "If there is a God that made all life forms, a particularly rich blessing was bestowed on the roach, because it got the best design of all."

The cockroach is the oldest insect on our planet as evidenced by fossil records dating back 325 million years. It can eat almost anything, live 45 days without food, and has an effective reproductive system with female sperm storing capabilities lasting a lifetime and a great defense system. The cockroach is about the same organism it was millions of years ago because its characteristics were adaptive then and now.

Often a new trait or a change in an individual doesn't occur through a single step but through a gradual accumulation of small mutations being selected over a long period of time. By dating meteorites, most scientists say that the earth is about 4.6 billion years old. The oldest bacteria fossils go back 3.5 billion years. Given enough variation and time, even such a complicated thing as the eye has gradually developed.

Evolutionary changes can also act fast. Studies of fruit flies show that differences in wing size could take place in as little time as a decade. Studies also show that a change that involves few genes could come about faster (and cause large behavioral changes) than one that depends on small changes in many genes.

The evidence for evolution

There is fossil, anatomical and molecular evidence of evolution. The fossil record shows how morphology was modified. Similarities of organs in related organisms show common ancestry. There is also DNA fossils evidence where human relative relatedness can be measured by DNA sequencing.

Why aren't antibiotics as effective against dangerous bacteria as before?
Evolution is at work today. Evidence of evolution is seen in pesticide resistance among insects and the antibiotic resistance of bacteria.

There are a lot of bacteria around, and they can divide several times an hour. In any population of bacteria, there are some individuals that through mutations have developed genes causing them to escape elimination. The more non-resistant bacteria that are eliminated, the more opportunities for the resistant to reproduce and spread. Over time, the resistant bugs win the race, meaning the antibiotics become less and less effective. Until someone develops a new type of antibiotic and then the race starts all over again.

Bacteria are immensely adaptable. Expose them to antibiotics long enough, they adapt and find a way to survive. This also means that the more we use antibiotics, the faster resistance spreads. And any method we use to kill bugs will, unless it completely wipes out a species, cause a population of resistant bugs.

Just as we can't blame an animal for eating another animal to survive, we can't blame bacteria for giving us an infection. They have no intention of harming us. Bacteria do what comes natural to all of us – survive and reproduce.

Another example of evolution is industrial melanism. Before the Industrial Revolution in England, the color of the peppered moth was mainly light. When there was no industrial pollution, the darker moth cropped up by mutation. But since the darker moths were easier to spot against the tree bark, hungry birds snapped them up. Only when the environment changed, when soot from new factories covered the tree trunks, did darkness became an advantage. Selection began to favor the darker moth. Darker moths were better disguised on tree trunks covered by soot. The lighter moths were eaten and the darker ones increased in numbers. Around 1950 the environment started changing again. A decrease in the use of coal and better filtering equipment in the factories produced a cleaner environment and the peppered moth is in the process of returning to its lighter color.

Thus, evolution selected the behavior that made our ancestors survive and reproduce. What guidance system has evolution selected to help us make better decisions for survival and reproduction?

Guidance through values and life experiences
Human beings are pulled forward toward and by nature
seek pleasure, whereas they flee from and reject pain.
- Epicurus (Greek philosopher, 341-270 BC)

What drives us?
The 17th Century English philosopher John Locke said: "Good and evil, reward and punishment, are the only motives to a rational creature: these are the spur and reins whereby all mankind are set on work, and guided." We are driven by our need to avoid pain and a desire to gain pleasure. Evolution has made any behavior that helps us survive and reproduce feel pleasurable. Behavior that is bad for us feels painful. Feelings of pain and pleasure are a useful guide to what is good or bad for us. If we eat, we feel pleasure. If we starve ourselves, we feel pain.

Our brain is equipped to register pain more sensitively than any other emotion. Neurology Professor Antonio Damasio says in *Descartes' Error* that "it is the pain-related signal that steers us away from impending trouble." It makes evolutionary sense that we have the desire to avoid pain. Psychology Professor Randolph Nesse and biologist George Williams says in *Why We Get Sick:* "Pain is the signal that tissue is being damaged. It has to be aversive to motivate us to set aside other activities to do whatever is necessary to stop the damage."

That pain is the premier evaluator also explains why we have such aversion to loss. Richard Dawkins says in *The Blind Watchmaker:* "however many ways there may be of being alive, it is certain there are vastly more ways of being dead, or rather not alive." The fear of loss is much greater than the desire to gain. Research shows that we feel more pain from losing than we feel pleasure from gaining something of equal value and that we work harder to avoid losing than we do to win. As psychologist Timothy Ketelaar says in Steven Pinker's *How the Mind Works:*

> As things get better, increases in fitness show diminishing returns: more food is better, but only up to a point. But as things get worse, decreases in fitness can take you out of the game: not enough food and you're dead. There are many ways to become infinitely worse off (from an infection, starvation, getting eaten, a fall, ad infinitum) and not many ways to become vastly better off. That makes prospective losses more worthy of attention than gains.

How are certain connections strengthened?

If certain connections help us interact with our environment, we use them more often than connections that don't help us. Since we use them more often, they become strengthened.

Evolution has given us preferences that help us classify what is good or bad. When these values are satisfied (causing either pleasure or less pain) through the interaction with our environment, these neural connections are strengthened. These values are reinforced over time because they give humans advantages for survival and reproduction in dealing with their environment.

For example, light is preferred to darkness, eating certain food is better than not eating, etc. When we drank our mother's milk, our brains told us that "eating" was pleasurable. Our chance of survival increased. If we didn't eat after we were born, the feedback from our brain would be that "not eating" was painful. The chances are that we ate in the future. Since the feedback from eating was pleasurable, certain neural connections were strengthened. In the future, when we were exposed to the same stimuli, this group of neurons reacted stronger. Any behavior that we find rewarding, either pleasurable or less painful, are strengthened.

The connections in our brain are constantly strengthened and weakened, developing and changing. The more we are exposed to certain experiences, the more the specific connections are strengthened. We then use these stored representations of what works when we respond to people and situations. Essentially what we do today is a function of what worked in the past. We adapt to our environment by learning from the consequences of our actions. We do things that we associate with pleasure and avoid things that we associate with pain.

Now we reach a key question: What part of the value system is called "human nature?"

So far we've learned that connections between neurons determine how we think and behave. Our genes provide us with the framework for neural development and our life experiences and our environment shapes our brain.

Since the brain is formed by life experiences and since an individual doesn't keep doing what doesn't work (learns through trial and error), evolution has reinforced the behavior and values that help us survive and reproduce. This behavior must be the behavior that was adaptive in the environment in which humans spent most of their evolutionary history. The question then becomes: What was the operating environment in which the human brain evolved?

The hunter-gatherer environment has formed our basic nature
Human evolution started about 4 to 7 million years ago and today's "modern" human brain appeared on the scene some 150,000 to 200,000 years ago. For most of that time our ancestors lived in primitive hunter-gatherer societies. These societies existed until the end of the last Ice Age, around 13,000 years ago. Soon thereafter, some 10,000 years ago, agriculture was developed.

This means that humans have spent more than 99% of their evolutionary history in the hunter-gatherer environment. If we compress 4 million years in 24 hours, and if the history of humans began at midnight, agriculture made its appearance on the scene 23 hours and 55 minutes later.

If the conditions and challenges of the hunter-gatherer environment is the environment in which natural selection has selected the adaptive traits for survival and reproduction, we must find out what the environment looked like back then. What drove our ancestors evolution? What were the characteristics of the environment that has shaped today's brains? What were the environmental conditions in which the hunter-gatherers lived? What was the availability of resources like food and mates? How was the climate and the geography? Size of population? What enemies, predators, and dangers existed?

There is no observational evidence from the hunter-gatherer environment. It seems likely though, that the environment of our ancestors represented ecological, social and human conditions that are quite different from today. People were living in small villages where everyone knew everyone else and strangers didn't show up often. There were enemies, predators and diseases. Limited resources created competition for food and mates.

What different roles did men and women likely play? Men were responsible for hunting, and defending the group from predators and enemies. Women gathered and prepared food near the home, and cared for the children.

If this were the environment, what would be appropriate behavior to increase the likelihood for survival and reproduction? What behavior has been natural during 99% of our history?

THREE

ADAPTIVE BEHAVIOR FOR SURVIVAL AND REPRODUCTION

The individual comes first

*There's no such thing as society. There are individual
men and women, and there are families.*
 - Margaret Thatcher (Former British Prime Minister)

Do people do what they perceive is in their best interest?
Yes, one basic trait that all individuals share is self-interest. We are interested in
protecting our close family and ourselves. Why?

Since natural selection is about survival and reproduction, and individuals either
survive or die and reproduce or not, it makes sense that individuals are predisposed
to act in ways that enhance their own prospects for survival and reproduction. The
ancestral environment consisted of limited resources, including reproductive
resources, and fierce competition. Self-interest came naturally.

What if our ancestors were composed of altruists – individuals that helped
others at their own expense? Altruistic individuals are at a disadvantage. They are
always vulnerable to some mutants that take advantage of them. Altruistic
behavior cannot evolve by natural selection since natural selection favors
individuals that are best at promoting their own survival and reproductive
success. Only behavior that is selfish or for the mutual good is in an individual's
self-interest and therefore favored by natural selection. Some behavior may under
certain conditions look like altruism but can often be explained by self-benefit.
Social recognition, prestige, fear of social disapproval, shame, relief from distress,
avoidance of guilt, a better after-life or social expectations are some reasons
behind "altruistic" acts.

But how did our social and moral qualities develop? In chapter five of *The
Descent of Man,* Charles Darwin wrote:

But it may be asked, how within the limits of the same tribe did a large number of members
first become endowed with these social and moral qualities, and how was the standard of
excellence raised? It is extremely doubtful whether the offspring of the more sympathetic
and benevolent parents, or of those who were the most faithful to their comrades, would

be reared in greater numbers than the children of selfish and treacherous parents belonging to the same tribe. He who was ready to sacrifice his life, as many a savage has been, rather than betray his comrades, would often leave no offspring to inherit his noble nature. The bravest men, who were always willing to come to the front in war, and who freely risked their lives for others, would on an average perish in larger numbers than other men. Therefore, it hardly seems probable that the number of men gifted with such virtues, or that the standard of their excellence, could be increased through natural selection, that is, by the survival of the fittest; for we are not here speaking of one tribe being victorious over another.

He continues: "But another and much more powerful stimulus to the development of the social virtues, is afforded by the praise and the blame of our fellow-men." A high standard of morality would also benefit a tribe:

To the instinct of sympathy… it is primarily due, that we habitually bestow both praises and blame on others, whilst we love the former and dread the latter when applied to ourselves; and this instinct no doubt was originally acquired, like all the other social instincts, through natural selection…We may therefore conclude that primeval man, at a very remote period, was influenced by the praise and blame of his fellows. It is obvious, that the members of the same tribe would approve of conduct which appeared to them to be for the general good, and would reprobate that which appeared evil. To do good unto others – to do unto others as ye would they should do unto you – is the foundation-stone of morality. It is, therefore, hardly possible to exaggerate the importance during rude times of the love of praise and the dread of blame. A man who was not impelled by any deep, instinctive feeling, to sacrifice his life for the good of others, yet was roused to such actions by a sense of glory, would by his example excite the same wish for glory in other men, and would strengthen by exercise the noble feeling of admiration. He might thus do far more good to his tribe than by begetting offspring with a tendency to inherit his own high character…

It most not be forgotten that although a high standard of morality gives but a slight or no advantage to each individual man and his children over the other men of the same tribe, yet that an increase in the number of well-endowed men and an advancement in the standard of morality will certainly give an immense advantage to one tribe over another. A tribe including many members who, from possessing in a high degree the spirit of patriotism, fidelity, obedience, courage, and sympathy, were always ready to aid one another, and to sacrifice themselves for the common good, would be victorious over most other tribes; and this would be natural selection. At all times throughout the world tribes have supplanted other tribes; and as morality is one important element in their success, the standard of morality and the number of well-endowed men will thus everywhere tend to rise and increase.

Often cooperation is in our best interest
If people aren't altruistic by nature, are they cooperative?
Mutual aid has great survival value. But under what conditions are people cooperative? The game of the prisoner's dilemma may shed light on this: Suppose you and a partner commits burglary. The police catch you both and question you one by one. The interrogator gives you a choice to cooperate or not.

> *"If you both deny the crime, you both go to jail for 1 year."*
> *"If you both confess, you both go to jail for 3 years."*
> *"If you confess but your partner denies, you will be free and your partner will go to jail for 10 years."*
> *"If you deny but your partner confesses, you will go to jail for 10 years."*

What should you do? The consequences for you depend on what your partner does. From an outsider's perspective, it seems that both of you would be better off denying the crime (1 year). But from your point of view, it seems best to confess (freedom). The problem is that you don't know what your partner will do. If your partner betrays you, it is better that you also betray him and get 3 years in prison, instead of the 10 years you get if you deny but your partner ends up confessing. If on the other hand your partner denies, it is still better that you confess because this way you will be free, instead of the 1 year you get if you deny.

Since both you and your partner follow this "logic" and confess, you will both go to jail for 3 years. Doing what you believe is in your best interest leads to a worse outcome than if you cooperate and deny. But here is the dilemma. You don't know if you can trust your partner. Cooperation only works if you and your partner can trust each other.

Tests show that if people play the game over and over, they learn that it is more profitable to cooperate. Repetition tests trust. Trust is key and fragile. It can vanish in a moment. As the 19th Century American President Abraham Lincoln wrote: "If you once forfeit the confidence of your fellow citizens, you can never regain their respect and esteem."

Another way to create cooperation is to let the partners communicate during the game. Talking encourages cooperation. Since people are social animals, they may change their behavior to keep others goodwill. In the end, it's a matter of trust and giving individuals an incentive to cooperate.

In chapter four of *The Descent of Man,* Charles Darwin wrote:

At the moment of action, man will no doubt be apt to follow the stronger impulse; and though this may occasionally prompt him to the noblest deeds, it will more commonly lead him to gratify his own desires at the expense of other men. But after their gratification when past and weaker impressions are judged by the ever-enduring social instinct, and by his deep regard for the good opinion of his fellows, retribution will surely come. He will then feel remorse, repentance, regret, or shame; this latter feeling, however, relates almost exclusively to the judgment of others. He will consequently resolve more or less firmly to act differently for the future; and this is conscience; for conscience looks backwards, and serves as a guide for the future.

But we also have to recognize that communication may be deceptive. People may bluff.

The strategy that is effective in the long run is a modern version of "a tooth for a tooth" or TIT-FOR-TAT. It says that we should cooperate at the first meeting and then do whatever our "opponent" did the last time. When our opponent cooperates, we should cooperate. When our opponent doesn't cooperate, we should retaliate. Then forgive and go back to cooperating next round. This rewards past cooperation and punishes past defection. This assumes that the game is repeated time after time. In reality we never know if we meet our opponent again in the future. As long as neither our opponent nor we knows when the game ends, it pays to be nice.

There is one group that scientists say we treat better than others – our close genetic relatives. This is kin selection. We act altruistic to our kin because they share our genes. Studies show that in all social species, relatives are more likely to help each other. The greater degree of genetic relatedness between two individuals, the more likely it is that an individual treats the other individual better. If you sacrifice something for your children, it may harm you but since your children share your genes, the overall effect is positive. Scientists say that one test of kin selection is what we would do if a relative and a good friend were close to drowning. We can only save one of them. What if one of them was a distant cousin that you'd seen only twice in your life and the friend was a person you spent every day with? Who would you save?

What other behavior was appropriate for our ancestors?

A tendency for fear
Our fears are always more numerous than our dangers.
- Lucius Annaeus Seneca (Roman rhetorician, c.4 BC-65 AD)

The passengers boarded flight 651 to Chicago. Two hours after takeoff, the flight attendant heard suspicious noise from the lavatory. The passengers started to talk among themselves. Panic erupted.

We fear dramatic and threatening events. We fear the loss of our health, family, friends, security, money, social status, power, or jobs. We also fear violence, crime, punishment, rejection, failure, the unknown, the immediate, the unpredictable or the uncontrollable.

Fear is our most basic emotion. Fear has evolved to help us anticipate danger and avoid pain. As science writer Rush Dozier writes in *Fear Itself:* "Fear is fundamental because life is fundamental. If we die, everything else becomes irrelevant."

Humans have developed a strong emotion for fear. Our ancestors environment was fraught with dangers. Fear of physical danger, social disapproval, lack of food, no mate, predators, etc. Self-survival was a powerful incentive. Mistakes could be extremely costly. Assume two individuals heard a strange sound behind the bushes. One of them looked behind the bushes, was bit by a poisonous snake and died. The other one saw what happened, ran away and survived. To always assume there was a threat behind the bushes and run away could save an individual's life. The cost of being wrong and running when there was no snake was minimal. But the cost of staying around when there was a snake could be life threatening. Our ancestors learned through trial and error that in the long run, pain could be avoided if they were fearful. They survived the dangers because they learned how to respond.

If pain and pleasure are guides to the behavior that leads to survival and reproduction, fear is our biological warning signal for avoiding pain. Fear warns us of potential harm and keeps us from acting in self-destructive ways. It helps us avoid threats and makes us act to prevent further damage. Fear guides us to avoid what didn't work in the past. Fear causes worry and anxiety, a normal response to physical danger. It activates hormones like adrenaline and cortisol which keeps us attentive to harm since we need full attention to escape from a threat.

The degree of fear we feel depends on our interpretation of the threat and our perception of control. The more helpless and vulnerable we feel, the stronger our emotion for fear becomes.

Assume that you are walking alone late at night on a deserted street in New York City. Suddenly, you hear steps behind you. What happens? Immediately you fear the worst – robbery, assault, etc. Your automatic nervous system takes over and prepares you for fight or flight. Your response begins in your brain and activates a biochemical process. Your heart rate, breathing, blood pressure, pulse and blood sugar increase. Normal behavior when you are the victim of stress, either perceived or real. You reacted with fear on the deserted street because evolution equipped your brain to register pain more sensitively than any other emotion. You were using the "memory" of your ancestral past – your primitive fear system of fight or flight.

What we fear and the strength of our reaction depend on our genes, life experiences, and the specific situation. You may react instinctively at first, but if the situation is one that you've experienced before (since our brain is continuously being "rewired" with life experiences), the final reaction may be to calm down. You could turn around to find an old lady walking her dog. Or you may run away, because you avoid situations that in the past have been painful. The more we are exposed to a stimulus, even a terrifying one, the higher our threshold of fear becomes. If you for example had walked the same deserted street many times before but found out each time that the noise was the old lady walking her dog, you would be less careful. Until something terrifying happened.

Fast classifications

There is a story about a man who went to visit a professor at his home. Outside the house a dog was playing on the lawn. When the professor opened the door to let the man in, the dog ran into the house. Later the professor asked the man, "Do you always travel with your dog?" The man replied, "It's not my dog. I thought it was yours."

Our brain is wired to perceive before it thinks – to use emotions before reason. As a consequence of our tendency for fear, fast classifications come naturally. Limited time and knowledge in a dangerous and scarce environment made hasty conclusions vital for survival. Waiting and weighing evidence could mean death. Don't we often draw fast conclusions, act on impulse and use our emotions to form quick impressions and judgments?

Males and females have different priorities

"What is the brain for?" asked Cognitive Neuroscience Professor Michael Gazzaninga in *The Mind's Past*. "The smart-aleck answer to the question is sex. Put more completely, the brain exists to make better decisions about how to enhance reproductive success." Reproduction is the central act in the life of every living thing. Once an individual has survived past the age of reproduction, the individual is evolutionarily useless.

Most animals (including humans) do something to attract the opposite sex. Since natural selection is ultimately about reproduction in a world of limited mates, some individuals were better at getting mates than others. The individuals that had an advantage in attracting prospective mates were "selected." What characteristics gave them the advantage? What anatomical features or behavioral traits attract the opposite sex or intimidate rivals?

Darwin realized that many anatomical and behavioral characteristics didn't have any survival value but could play an important role in attracting mates. Strength and beauty were such signals. He called this mechanism sexual selection. It has for example been shown that colors spark sexual interest among butterflies. And peahens prefer peacocks with big, colorful tails.

In *Parental Investment and Sexual Selection,* biologist Robert Trivers says that the force behind sexual selection is parental investment, or "any investment by the parent in an individual offspring that increases the offspring's chance of surviving (and hence reproductive success) at the cost of the parent's ability to invest in other offspring."

Men need to attract women. But they also need to keep other men away from "their" woman. A woman must invest in each of her children. There is a nine month pregnancy and thereafter many years of child-caring. She invests time, energy and increases her chance of earlier death. There are limits to how many children she can produce during her lifetime. A man has less costs of reproduction. He can interact with many women and produce an enormous amount of children. He doesn't need to be around all the time. Many women can raise their children without help.

Since the goal of evolution is reproduction, a man should want to have sex with as many women as possible. This causes competition among men for women. How does a man eliminate this competition? He can either make himself more attractive to the woman or he can eliminate or reduce the competition.

The reproductive success of women doesn't depend on how many men she has sex with, but on her ability to get access to resources (like food, shelter, and protection) for herself and her children. Women are therefore more discriminating than men. She won't pick the first guy around. This causes women to compete with each other for access to resources. A man that is perceived as wealthy and having status has an advantage. So mating choices (showing up as unconscious preferences) are influenced by the fact that women have more at stake than men do.

In 1989, evolutionary psychologist David Buss published a study of thousands of men and women from 37 cultures around the world showing the ranking of qualities that are most important in choosing someone to date or marry. Women placed more emphasis on a potential mate's financial prospects. Women also preferred ambitious and industrious men. Women preferred older men. Men preferred younger women. Men ranked physical attractiveness higher than women did. The study also showed that a man felt most jealous when his woman was having sex with someone else. A woman felt most jealous when her man become emotionally attached to someone else.

Studies show other differences between the sexes. Women are less inclined to take risks. They are more influenced by the chance of loss. They are less competitive and status-conscious. Other studies show that men and women differ in their behavioral and cognitive capabilities. Some of this reflects varying hormonal influences on brain development. Like most things, this is context-dependent.

The Social Animal

> *We do not care about our reputation in towns where we are only passing through. But when we have to stay some time we do care. How much time does it take? A time proportionate to our vain and paltry existence.*
> - Blaise Pascal (French mathematician and philosopher, 1623-1662)

Isn't it likely that a good reputation, status, resources and being socially accepted helped our ancestors survive, get a mate, and reproduce?

In a small hunter-gatherer society, what was good for the group often paid off for the individual. Cooperation was critical in an environment with limited resources, individual weaknesses and many dangers. Isolation from a group or society could mean destruction. There was safety in numbers. The group protected the individual against predators, hunted together, exchanged information about where food was, cooperated to defend food from enemies, and was a key resource for mates and help with infants. Together the group stood a greater chance of survival.

If we help another member of the small society, he may help us when we need it. If he doesn't, we may never help him again. This behavior is called reciprocation - the idea of "I scratch your back and you scratch mine." A reputation for being reliable and trustworthy is important because how we acted in the past is the only guide to how we act in the future. If we fool someone, he tells his friends, destroying our future possibilities for cooperation with others. Isn't that why we trust our friends but are careful when we meet strangers whom we know nothing about?

Zoologist and Psychology Professor Frans De Waal says about the role of reputation:

Inasmuch as every act is indicative of future acts by the same person, it pays to watch others closely and learn what to expect from them. This scrutiny produces a definite preoccupation with the social mirror, to the point of causing constant worry about possible loss of face…imagine the situation of our ancestors, who undoubtedly belonged to the same small community for most of their lives: virtually everything there was to know about them must have been known by virtually everyone. In order to become a respected member of the community, we need to be almost blindly consistent.

What happens if we help someone but the next time we need help, this person conveniently disappears? What about people who don't return favors? True reciprocity only works if (1) we live in the same small society so we recognize each other, can keep track of "services" given and received, and have future opportunities to interact, and (2) the cost of the act is pretty much the same as the future favor the recipient receives. One-shot encounters encourage selfishness as told by Professor Lee Alan Dugatkin:

At a small dinner gathering…one of the dinner guests noted that when he looked for a mechanic, he always stayed away from garages on big highways and near "strips." Such mechanics, he said, knew that they were never going to see you again and were notorious shysters. Go to a neighborhood garage, where word of mouth serves as advertising, and they know you will be a long-term customer.

Traits like fear of failure, losing social status or reputation were important because they affected an individual's standing in the ancestral hunter-gatherer society. Access to food and sex depended on it. Survival and reproduction could be threatened. Social punishment was dangerous. It could lead to exile. According to Human Ecology Professor Garrett Hardin, it is the same today:

Fear of disapproval is the major force that keeps a society intact: fear of God, fear of the police, and fear of the judgment of neighbors. Religious authorities want the fear of God to be the predominant controller. Civil authorities want fear of police and court to dominate. But, says Locke [John], the opinion of one's neighbors trumps all others.

Providing resources is another behavior that increases chances of survival and getting a mate. The better our ability to provide, the higher our status would be in the community.

As we saw earlier there is competition among men for women. Women compete with each other for access to resources. Women wanted males who could take care of the children. Resources like food, lodging, and status attracted them. Striving for authority, dominance, esteem, position, and respect were advertisements for wealth. Charles Darwin said: "Man admires and often tries to exaggerate whatever characteristics nature may have given him."

What other evidence is there that humans are social animals? One study of a group of men whose wives suffered fatal cases of breast cancer showed that the widowers had lower immune system activity. Another study showed that men who were socially isolated were more likely to die from any cause than more socially integrated people were.

Pecking order also matters. Norwegian biologist Thorleif Schjelderup-Ebbe discovered that in the world of chickens there is a social hierarchy. Science writer Robert Wright says in *The Moral Animal:*

> Throw a bunch of hens together, and, after a time of turmoil, including much combat, things will settle down. Disputes…will now be brief and decisive, as one hen simply pecks the other, bringing quick deferral. The deferrals form a pattern. There is a simple, linear hierarchy, and every hen knows its place.

Status hierarchies aren't only valid for hens. Studies show that when we put a group of children together, they will shortly fall into separate grades. The ones at the top are best liked, most often imitated, and most obeyed.

We must be careful not to carry these evolutionary explanations about adaptive behavior too far. There are many causes for behavior. We can't extrapolate the conditions of the ancestral environment to explain every behavior. No one knows what the ancestral environment really was like. There is no neurological or genetic evidence for or against certain behavior. And evolutionary explanations about the brain can't be experimentally tested. A trait that is found everywhere isn't necessarily genetically specified. But much of the behavior described is consistent with evidence we have from other organisms and documented human history.

Let's go back one million years and assume you were living in a small community with 150 people where everybody knew each other, and where the mating opportunities were limited. The environment was fraught with danger and challenges. The key was to avoid danger, get food and attract a partner. What behavior was critical to survival and reproduction?

Isn't it rewarding to make fast judgments? – "If noise behind the bush, then run." It is a natural tendency to act on impulse – to use emotions before reason. The behavior that was critical for survival and reproduction in our evolutionary history still applies today. Wouldn't being fearful help you survive? Social failure be costly? Maintaining status, resources and social approval help you survive and get a mate?

Wouldn't a common threat or a common goal make people cooperate? Wouldn't following social norms make sense? Wouldn't you have a strong aversion to losses and only take big risks when you were threatened? Wouldn't you be concerned with the short-term interest of yourself and loved ones?

Much of our psychology is the result of cultural influences

Human society is not only shaped by the evolution of genes, but also by cultural evolution. Practices, methods, tools, myths, ethics, and social norms that are important in the evolution of our behavior. Customs that we learn from the experience of our parents and others – either by teaching or observation.

Cultural evolution is faster than genetic evolution since it allows much of what we learn to be passed on and combined with what others around us have learned. Unlike biological evolution, cultural evolution is not inherited. We don't inherit our parents habits.

In a sense genetic and cultural evolution interact. Biology influences our culture. Take language as an example. We come equipped with an anatomy, physiology and biochemistry that gives us the ability to learn a language. But we are not born with a language. The language we speak is a product of our culture.

Our culture also influences our biology by creating the environment in which natural selection is tested. If a certain behavior proves to be beneficial generation over generation, that behavior is favored by natural selection. Assume individuals over time make certain social behavior choices. These choices were transmitted through learning and culture. Over time, they will be favored by natural selection since they positively influence survival and reproduction.

Our basic nature

Men's natures are alike; it is their habits that carry them far apart.
  - Confucius

What is our basic nature?
Our nature is a product of our biological and cultural history. Evolution explains how we are shaped and biologically constrained. Like our bones, kidney, eyes, and legs, our brain has been shaped by natural selection. Natural selection equipped us with traits that increase our chances for survival and reproduction. It then follows that we consciously or unconsciously behave according to what we perceive is in our own best interest. This is our biological base nature. It is

strengthened or weakened depending on our life experiences. If we assume that people on average act out of self-interest we'll be less disappointed than if we assume that people on average act out of altruism. This does not mean that we can't make things better. But doing so demands that we first understand why we are the way we are. Richard Dawkins said in *The Selfish Gene:* "Be warned that if you wish, as I do, to build a society in which individuals cooperate generously and unselfishly towards a common good, you can expect little help from biological nature. Let us try to teach generosity and altruism, because we are born selfish."

Let's summarize the forces that influence and set the limits for our judgments. *Genes* – environmental stimuli cause response tendencies from our genes. Our genes have evolved and their functions are primarily based on what was beneficial in the hunter-gatherer environment – the environment where humans spent most of their time. To survive, we must avoid all perceived threats to our survival and reproduction. Evolution has developed a value system based on pain and pleasure that help us deal with the environment. Since the ancestral environment consisted of limited resources and danger, we developed a strong aversion for loss and a tendency for fear. We made fast evaluations and became social animals. We were predisposed to evaluate situations by being fearful. To not respond with fear could be more costly than responding with fear and being wrong. We also acted in ways where the reward was important and the cost was minimal.

Life experiences – upbringing, nutrition, education, social stamping, physical, social and cultural settings create certain convictions, habits, values, attitudes and character traits. This in turn creates our individual beliefs and assumptions. Our judgments are influenced by our state of mind.

Present environment – outside factors like the environment, the context or circumstances, or the specific situation.

Randomness – we are prepared to be open minded to new experiences since environments vary; handling new challenges is a means of adaptation.

The consequences of our actions reinforce certain behavior. If the consequences were rewarding, our behavior is likely to be repeated. What we consider rewarding is individual specific. Rewards can be anything from health, money, job, reputation, family, status, or power. In all of these activities, we do what works. This is how we adapt. The environment selects our future behavior.

But it's not just what happens to us that counts. It's what we think happens. When we face a situation, our brains create an expectation. We can act in ways contrary to our self-interest if we don't understand the consequences.

Our behavior creates feedback from our environment. If we do dumb things and suffer the consequences, we may still do dumb things in the future even if it causes pain. Either because we don't understand the cause of our mistake, or the pain is less painful than other behavior.

Our experiences are stored in the brain and influence us in the future. New connecting patterns between neurons are created.

Some decisions are not in our best interest

There must certainly be a vast fund of stupidity in human nature, else men would not be caught as they are, a thousand times over, by the same snare, and while they yet remember their past misfortunes, go on to court and encourage the causes to which they are owing, and which will again produce them.

- Marcus Porcius Cato (Roman statesman and writer, 234-149 BC)

If we often act out of self-interest, why do we make decisions that are clearly not in our best interests?

Astronomy Professor John Barrow writes in *Impossibility:* "We are a package of abilities for social interactions, finding safe habitats, finding food, avoiding getting too hot or too cold, attracting mates, keeping out of the way of hazards and predators, and having as many offspring as possible."

Genetic and cultural evolution equipped us with behavioral tendencies (like the tendency for fear, reciprocal cooperation, fast classifications, concern for social approval, etc.) that help us interact with our environment. These tendencies are on average more helpful than not (otherwise we wouldn't be here today). Sometimes they lead us astray and cause us to make misjudgments.

For example, we may be biased by our automatic tendency to trust the people we like. Liking is often based on first impressions. We are superbly equipped to read other people for signs of trustworthiness. We look at their emotional state – their voice and general expression – but we often get this completely wrong. It is sometimes hard to spot the difference between a good and bad actor. An individual may be secretive and hostile, or warm and open. What consequences would these different behaviors have on our perception of that individual? We forget to think about other factors that are important in evaluating a person or a situation. Appearances may be deceiving. The best con artists always act, as if they were not acting in their best interest.

In Part One we have learned about our nature and our limitations. With this background let us now look at how our psychological abilities affect our decision-making.

Warren Buffett gives us some introductory remarks on why even smart people get bad results:

It's ego. It's greed. It's envy. It's fear. It's mindless imitation of other people. I mean, there are a variety of factors that cause that horsepower of the mind to get diminished dramatically before the output turns out. And I would say if Charlie and I have any advantage it's not because we're so smart, it is because we're rational and we very seldom let extraneous factors interfere with our thoughts. We don't let other people's opinion interfere with it…we try to get fearful when others are greedy. We try to get greedy when others are fearful. We try to avoid any kind of imitation of other people's behavior. And those are the factors that cause smart people to get bad results.

I always look at IQ and talent as representing the horsepower of the motor, but then in terms of the output, the efficiency with which the motor works, depends on rationality. That's because a lot of people start out with 400-horsepower motors and get a hundred horsepower of output. It's way better to have a 200-horsepower motor and get it all into output. So why do smart people do things that interfere with getting the output they're entitled to? It gets into the habits, and character and temperament, and it really gets into behaving in a rational manner. Not getting in your own way.

In Part Two, Three, and Four we use two fictional characters named John and Mary. At 40, John is a senior executive of TransCorp; a US company engaged in widely varied businesses. John is married to Mary, a part-time schoolteacher.

Part Two

The psychology of misjudgments

Why oh why are human beings so
hard to teach, but so easy to deceive.
- Dio Chrysostom
(Greek philosopher and orator, 2nd Century)

– ONE –

Misjudgments explained by psychology

*I came to the psychology of human misjudgment almost against
my will; I rejected it until I realized that my attitude was costing
me a lot of money, and reduced my ability to help everything I loved.*
- Charles Munger

Part One gave us a background to our behavior, psychology and limitations. We learned how pain and pleasure guide our behavior, our strong aversion to loss, and how it is natural for people to behave in ways they perceive is in their best interest.

Charles Munger says, "If you want to avoid irrationality, it helps to understand the quirks in your own mental wiring and then you can take appropriate precautions." This part explores 39 reasons for misjudgments that can be explained by our psychological make-up. Many of the reasons are rooted in psychological tendencies and biases that often influence us subconsciously. The more emotional, confused, uncertain, insecure, excited, distracted, tired or stressed we are, the easier we make mistakes. Geniuses aren't excluded.

Below is a list of 39 reasons for misjudgments and mistakes. It can be used as a checklist to explain or predict behavior or as a pilot's checklist to avoid fooling ourselves. Each item on the list will be explained in the next chapter.

1. Bias from mere association – automatically connecting a stimulus with pain or pleasure; including liking or disliking something associated with something bad or good. Includes seeing situations as identical because they seem similar. Also bias from Persian Messenger Syndrome – not wanting to be the carrier of bad news.

2. Underestimating the power of reinforcement and incentives – people repeat actions that result in rewarding consequences and avoid actions that don't work.

3. Underestimating bias from self-interest and incentives – people do what they perceive is in their best interest.

4. Underestimating that people are more easily persuaded when we appeal to

their self-interest.

5. Self-deception and denial – distortion of reality to reduce pain or increase pleasure. Includes wishful thinking.

6. Bias from commitment and consistency tendency – being consistent with our prior commitments and conclusions even when acting against our best interest or in the face of disconfirming evidence. Includes underestimating the power of small, publicly expressed or effortful commitments or conclusions.

7. Confirmation bias – looking for evidence that confirms our actions and beliefs and ignoring disconfirming evidence.

8. Ideological bias – strong convictions for an idea, political, religious or philosophical principle.

9. Bias from deprival syndrome – strongly reacting (includes over-desiring and overvaluing) when something we have or almost have is (or threatens to be) taken away (losing). Includes over-desiring and overvaluing what we can't have or what is (or threatens to be) less available. Contributes to willingness to take risks or expend effort to avoid losses.

10. Status quo bias – keeping things the way they are to avoid the pain of feeling responsible for making the wrong decision.

11. Impatience – overweighing the near-term consequences over more favorable but delayed consequences.

12. Bias from envy and jealousy.

13. Distortion by contrast – judging and perceiving the absolute magnitude of something not by itself but based only on its difference to something else presented closely in time or space or to some earlier adaptation level. Also underestimating the consequences over time of gradual changes.

14. Bias from anchoring – over-weighing certain information as a reference point for future decisions.

15. Over-influence by vivid evidence – information or experience.

16. Over-influence by the most recent evidence – information or experience.

17. Over-influence by framing effects – how an issue, situation or choice is presented.

18. Bias from reciprocation tendency – repaying in kind what others have done for or to us like favors, concessions, information and attitudes.

19. Underestimating that expectations influence behavior.

20. Bias from over-influence by liking tendency – believing and agreeing with people we know and like. Includes factors that produce liking – people who like us, are similar to us, attractive, cooperative or give us compliments.

21. Bias from disliking – our tendency to avoid and disagree with people we don't like.
22. Bias from over-desire for social acceptance and for avoiding social disapproval.
23. Bias from over-influence by social proof – imitating the behavior of others. Includes crowd folly – when part of a group, losing the ability to reason.
24. Bias from over-influence by authority – trusting and obeying a perceived authority or expert.
25. Overconfidence of our abilities and prospects. Includes over-optimism. Also self-attribution bias – crediting successes to ability and blaming failures on external circumstances.
26. Hindsight bias – thinking events that have happened were more predictable than they were.
27. Attribution error – underestimating situational factors (including roles) when explaining reasons for behavior.
28. Misreading personalities – misreading the character of people we deal with. Includes stereotyping.
29. Not understanding the "why" and the "how." Includes underestimating the power in giving people reasons.
30. Complying with requests merely because we've been given a reason – independent of whether we understand the reason.
31. Memory limitations – remembering selectively and wrong. Includes influence by suggestions.
32. "Man with a hammer" tendency – solving problems using only the field we know best or our favored ideas and solutions independent of applicability and reliability.
33. Do-nothing syndrome – procrastination and lack of execution.
34. Do-something syndrome – acting without a sensible reason.
35. Mental confusion from say-something syndrome – feeling a need to say something when we have nothing to say.
36. Emotional arousal – acting out of emotions rather than reason.
37. Mental confusion from stress.
38. Mental confusion from physical or psychological pain, the influence of chemicals or diseases.
39. Bias from over-influence by the combined effect of many psychological tendencies operating together.

These psychological tendencies (that also interact) have been verified by a number of experiments. Some people are more vulnerable to them than others. But we can't study them independent of an individual's values and the situation. Behavior that seems irrational may be fully rational from the individual's point of view. There is always some background within which behavior makes sense. Behavior can't be seen as rational or irrational independent of context. We are created with a series of emotions that are appropriate depending on circumstances. If we change context or environment, we change behavior.

The next chapter describes the 39 psychological reasons why we make misjudgments and mistakes. But observe that there are many reasons for a given behavior. Many of the real-world illustrations can be explained by more than one tendency and also by non-psychological factors. Misjudgments are often caused by many factors working together.

Most of the explanations are based on work done by Charles Munger, Psychology Professor Robert Cialdini, Behavioral Finance Professor Richard Thaler and Psychology Professors Daniel Kahneman and the late Amos Tversky.

– TWO –

PSYCHOLOGICAL REASONS FOR MISTAKES

Man is, and always was, a block-head and dullard, much
readier to feel and digest than to think and consider.
- Thomas Carlyle (Scottish philosopher, 1795-1881)

1. MERE ASSOCIATION

Inside the jewelry boutique, surrounded by enchanting music and gorgeous women,
how could John resist not buying Mary the $5,000 necklace?

We automatically feel pleasure or pain when we connect a stimulus – a thing, situation or individual – with an experience we've had in the past or with values or preferences we are born with. As we've learned, we move towards stimuli we associate with pleasure and away from those we associate with pain. We most easily associate to the events whose consequences we have experienced most often and the ones we easily remember. The more vivid or dramatic an event is, the easier we remember it.

Every time Mary served bacon for breakfast, she sung a special melody. After awhile,
if John heard her singing the melody, he expected bacon.

The Russian scientist Ivan Pavlov studied the digestive system of dogs when he observed that a stimulus unrelated to food made the dogs salivate. In one experiment he rang a bell just before giving food to the dog. He repeated this several times until the dog salivated at the sound of the bell alone. No sight or smell of food was present. The sound of the bell produced the same response as the food. The dog learned to associate the bell with food.

Experiments have shown that we can learn to fear a harmless stimulus if it is paired with an unpleasant one. If for example rats consistently receive mild electrical shock after hearing a tone, the rats learn to develop a fear of the tone alone.

Association can influence the immune system. One experiment studied food aversion in mice. Mice got saccharin-flavored water (saccharin has incentive value due to its sweet taste) along with a nausea-producing drug. Would the mice show signs of nausea the next time they got saccharin water alone? Yes, but the mice also developed infections. It was known that the drug in addition to producing nausea, weakened the immune system, but why would saccharin alone have this effect? The mere pairing of the saccharin with the drug caused the mouse immune system to learn the association. Therefore, every time the mouse encountered the saccharin, its immune system weakened making the mouse vulnerable to infections.

John's supplier took him to the best steakhouse in town and picked up the check. The next time it was time to buy new supplies, John associated the supplier with pleasant feelings. People can influence us by associating a product, service, person, investment, or a situation with something we like. Many times we buy products, enter relationships, and invest our money merely because we associate them with positive things. No wonder advertisers or politicians connect what they want to sell with things we like and avoid associating themselves with negative events. Pair a sports car with something that produces a positive feeling – a beautiful and sexy model – and we automatically associate the car with pleasure.

John was afraid to deliver bad news to the CEO.
Whether we like someone is influenced by the events with which an individual is associated. Bad news isn't welcome. We tend to dislike people who tell us what we don't want to hear even when they didn't cause the bad news i.e., kill the messenger. This gives people an incentive to avoid giving bad news. To protect themselves, they tell the news in a way they believe we want to hear it. This tendency is called the Persian Messenger Syndrome and traces its origins back to ancient Greece. In *Antigone,* a messenger feared for his life since he knew the king would be unhappy with the news he brought.

Warren Buffett says on being informed of bad news: "We only give a couple of instructions to people when they go to work for us: One is to think like an owner. And the second is to tell us bad news immediately - because good news takes care of itself. We can take bad news, but we don't like it late."

Seeing the fish salad, John remembered the time when he'd eaten fish salad and gotten sick, and once more felt nauseous.
We see similar situations where they don't exist because a situation resembles an earlier experience. We therefore believe that the future mirrors the past and that history will repeat itself.

Keep in mind
• Evaluate things, situations and people on their own merits.

- Individuals are neither good nor bad merely because we associate them with something positive or negative.
- Encourage people to tell you bad news immediately.
- Merely because you associate some stimuli with earlier pain or pleasure doesn't mean the stimuli will cause the same pain or pleasure today. Past experiences are often context dependent.
- Create a negative emotion if you want to end a certain behavior. If you want someone to stop smoking, one way could be to show them what they stand to lose. Terrifying pictures may cause them to associate smoking with death.

2. Reinforcement and Incentives

The things that hurt, instruct.
- Benjamin Franklin (American politician and scientist, 1706-1790)

John's actions brought him praise and money, making him continue his behavior. Reinforcement is a form of associative learning through which we learn – right and wrong – from the consequences of our actions. Whatever causes us to repeat a certain behavior is reinforcing and whatever makes us stop is punishing. Behavior that is rewarding or feels pleasurable tends to be repeated. We don't continue doing what we're being punished for. Give people what they desire (or take away something undesirable) and their behavior will repeat. Give them something undesirable (or take away what they desire) and their behavior will stop. Rewarding (or punishing) people is most effective when it is administered without delay and each time the behavior is repeated.

We base what is rewarding or punishing on our associations to past experiences and their consequences or with values or preferences we are born with.

An action that is reinforced becomes stronger over time. This is how habits and addictions are created. Both are hard to change. As the great 18th Century English writer Samuel Johnson said: "The chains of habit are too weak to be felt until they are too strong to be broken."

What does all this mean? It means that people do what works. Like bees to honey, they go where there is a reward. To quote Charles Munger: "The iron rule of nature is: you get what you reward for. If you want ants to come, you put sugar on the floor." This also implies that if we reward what we don't want, we get it. As Garrett Hardin says in *The Ostrich Factor:* "If the laws of society reward for bank robbing, society will get more bank robbing. If our methods of winnowing candidates for high positions favor stupidity, we will get stupid politicians."

Studies in Sweden show that changes in the sickness insurance system affect sick leave behavior. Reforms implying more generous compensation for sick leave tend to be associated with permanent increases in total sick leave per person employed. Other studies from the U.S. regarding health services have shown that in cases where someone else picks up the costs, patients tend to over-consume the health services.

Why do people abuse the health care and welfare system? Isn't it natural that people use the system if they don't have to pay anything? And if people don't have to pay for a benefit, they often overuse it. The more people that benefit from misusing the system, the less likely it is that anyone will draw attention to what really happens. Individually they get a large benefit and it's a small loss for society. Until everyone starts thinking the same. The ancient Greek philosopher Aristotle said: "That which is common to the greatest number gets the least amount of care. Men pay most attention to what is their own; they care less for what is common."

Why do people steal?
Studies show that 23% of people say they would steal if they couldn't get caught. It is estimated that U.S. businesses lose $400 billion a year from fraud and about a third of that is from employees stealing from their employer. Why? Opportunity and reward. In Charles Munger's words: "The worst abuses come where people have the greatest temptations." If we make it easy for people to steal, they steal (and bad behavior will spread).

Why does a tennis player always wear his lucky shirt in the finals?
In one experiment, American psychologist B.F. Skinner fed pigeons small quantities of food at regular intervals. After some time the pigeons began to behave superstitiously. If a pigeon was bobbing its head when food appeared, it got the idea that bobbing its head must have made the food appear. The pigeons continued with the behavior that worked – every time they performed the behavior, food appeared. But food appeared independent of what the pigeons did. Skinner wrote in *"Superstition" in the pigeon:* "There are many analogies in human behavior…A few accidental connections between a ritual and favorable consequences suffice to set up and maintain the behavior in spite of many nonreinforced instances."

Are the right incentives important?
Incentives act as reinforcers. Charles Munger tells a story about the importance of getting the incentives right:

From all business, my favorite case on incentives is Federal Express. The heart and soul of their system - which creates the integrity of the product - is having all their airplanes come to one place in the middle of the night and shift all the packages from plane to plane. If there are delays, the whole operation can't deliver a product full of integrity to Federal Express customers. And it was always screwed up. They could never get it done on time. They tried everything - moral suasion, threats, you name it. And nothing worked. Finally, somebody got the idea to pay all these people not so much an *hour,* but so much a *shift* - and when it's all done, they can all go home. Well, their problems cleared up overnight.

John invested in a biotech start-up that went sour and he lost money.
After a success, we become overly optimistic risk-takers. After a failure, we become overly pessimistic and risk-averse – even in cases where success or failure was merely a result of chance. Good consequences don't necessarily mean we made a good decision, and bad consequences don't necessarily mean we made a bad decision.

The next time someone presents John an investment opportunity in a biotech start-up the chances are he will decline. He associates the new proposal to his earlier experience. And since people tend to believe that the future mirrors the past, he declines. But what happens if John's first investment made him a lot of money? Wouldn't John associate the new proposal to his old pleasurable experience? Isn't he therefore more likely to invest? This automatic association to what worked in the past causes people to under-react to new conditions and circumstances.

Mark Twain understood the dangers of blindly trusting past experience for dealing with the future. "We should be careful to get out of an experience only the wisdom in it, and stop there, lest we be like the cat that sits down on a hot stove-lid. She will not sit down on a hot stove-lid again – but also she will never sit down on a cold one anymore."

Mere association and reinforcement are both examples of conditioned reflexes.

Charles Munger gives an example how these forces can be used as he describes the invention of non-alcoholic drinks:

The food value and so forth of the beverage is the *reinforcer.* And the trade dress, trade name and look of the beverage is the *stimulant*…

Then, you go on to the second kind of conditioned reflex – and that's straight Pavlov… Well, how do you *get* Pavlovian mere-association effects? Obviously, you *associate* this beverage and its trademarks with every good thing that people like generally: exalting events, sex objects, happy times – you name it.

How can we lose a conditioned reflex that's working for us? Charles Munger continues:

> Well, the customer tries something else and discover that *it's* a big reinforcer. So he shifts brands. We know, in matrimony, that if you're always *available,* the spouse is less likely to shift brands. And people don't tend to organize marriage to include permanent long separations. Similarly, if you're selling a product and it's always available, people are less likely to shift to some other product and get reinforced by it.

Keep in mind
- Benjamin Franklin tells us that: "A spoonful of honey will catch more flies than a gallon of vinegar." Praise is more effective in changing behavior than punishment. It is better to encourage what is right than to criticize what is wrong.
- Don't over-learn from your own or others bad or good experience. The same action under other conditions may cause different consequences.
- Separate between skill and chance. Charles Munger says, "As you occupy some high-profit niche in a competitive order, you must know how much of your present prosperity is caused by talents and momentum assuring success in new activities, and how much merely reflects the good fortune of being in your present niche."
- American novelist Upton Sinclair said: "It is difficult to get a man to understand something when his salary depends upon him not understanding it." Since people do what works be sure to make the incentives right. Tie incentives to performance and to the factors that determine the result you want to achieve. Make people share both the upside and downside. And make them understand the link between their performance, their reward and what you finally want to accomplish. For example, tie a manager's compensation to gain in business value (of the unit under his control) minus a cost factor for capital that is used to produce this value. The auto insurer GEICO's plan exemplifies Berkshire Hathaways's incentive compensation principles. Warren Buffett says:

> Goals should be (1) tailored to the economics of the specific operating business; (2) simple in character so that the degree to which they are being realized can be easily measured; and (3) directly related to the daily activities of plan participants. As a corollary, we shun "lottery ticket" arrangements, such as options on Berkshire shares, whose ultimate value – which could range from zero to huge – is totally out of the control of the person whose behavior we would like to affect. In our view, a system that produces quixotic payoffs will not only be wasteful for owners but may actually discourage the focused behavior we value in managers.

- Reward individual performance and not effort or length in organization and reward people after and not before their performance.
- Don't let money be the only motivation. If we reward people for doing what they like to do anyway, we sometimes turn what they enjoy doing into work. The reward changes their perception. Instead of doing something because they enjoy doing it, they now do it because they are being paid. Psychology Professor David Myers says in *Social Psychology* that the key issue is what a reward implies: "Rewards and praise that *inform* people of their achievements (that make them feel, 'I'm very good at this') *boost* intrinsic motivation. Rewards that seek to *control* people and lead them to believe it was the reward that caused their effort ('I did it for the money') *diminish* the intrinsic appeal of an enjoyable task."
- Install systems and rules that encourage the behavior you want. Never let it pay someone to behave in a way you don't want. Have systems that make it hard for people to get away with undesirable behavior. Make undesirable behavior costly. The painful consequences of undesirable behavior must outweigh its pleasurable consequences. For example, the consequences of spending time in jail ought to be more painful than the pleasure of getting away with burglary.
- Systems can be hard to change as Warren Buffett observes, "It's very hard to change a system when the guy whose hand is on the switch benefits enormously and, perhaps, disproportionately *from* that system."
- Decision-makers should be held accountable for the consequences of their actions. In *The Case for Modern Man,* American philosopher Charles Frankel defines responsibility: "A decision is responsible when the man or group that makes it has to answer for it to those who are directly or indirectly affected by it." Charles Munger adds, "An example of a really responsible system is the system the Romans used when they built an arch. The guy who created the arch stood under it as the scaffolding was removed. It's like packing your own parachute."

3. SELF-INTEREST AND INCENTIVES

"Damn it all, we want to get at the truth" [said Lord
Peter Wimsey] "Do you" said Sir Impey dryly. "I don't.
I don't care two pence about the truth. I want a case."
- Dorothy Sayers (British writer, 1893-1957)

The organizers of a tennis tournament needed money. They approached the CEO of TransCorp and asked him to sponsor the tournament.

"How much?" asked the CEO.

"One million," said the organizer.

"That is too much money," said the CEO.

"Not if you consider the fact that you personally can play one match, sit at the honorary stand next to a member of the presidential family and be the one that hands over the prize," said the organizer.

"Where do I sign?" said the CEO.

People do what they perceive is in their best interest and are biased by incentives. For example, when the first Dead Sea rolls were discovered and the archeologists wanted more fragments of the rolls to be found, they offered a reward per fragment. The result: the fragments were split into smaller pieces before they were turned in.

The comedian Groucho Marx once interviewed a U.S. Senator about a miracle cure-all vitamin and mineral tonic that the Senator had invented. When Groucho asked him what it was good for, the Senator answered: "It was good for five and a half million for me last year."

Incentives for the decision-maker determine behavior. This means that we have to recognize self-interested behavior in others.

Are advisors always to be trusted?

There is an old saying: "Never ask the village barber if you need a haircut." We are biased by our incentives as are others including lawyers, accountants, doctors, consultants, salesmen, organizations, the media, etc. What is good for them may not be good for us. Advisors are paid salesmen and may trick us into buying what we don't need.

Warren Buffett tells us that one of Berkshire's compensation arrangements was worked out, "without the "help" of lawyers or compensation consultants. This arrangement embodies a few very simple ideas - not the kind of terms favored by consultants who cannot easily send a large bill unless they have established that you have a large problem (and one, of course, that requires an annual review)."

Charles Munger tells us about the common tendency of salesmen:

All commissioned salesmen have a tendency to serve the transaction instead of the truth. …I put consultants in the same category, sometimes even lawyers – sometimes especially lawyers.

Many years ago, a Pasadena friend of mine made fishing tackle. I looked at this fishing tackle – it was green and purple and blue – I don't think I'd ever seen anything like them. I asked him "God! Do fish bite these lures?" He said to me, "Charlie, I don't sell to fish."

Let's look at the brokerage and investment banking business. Brokers have a strong incentive to get us to trade. They advise us what to buy and sell. Volume creates commissions. Investment bankers encourage overpriced acquisitions to generate fees. Investment bankers have every incentive to get initial public offerings (IPO) deals done, regardless of the company's quality. Their compensation is tied to the revenues the deal brings in. Analysts are rewarded for helping sell the IPO. Brokers want to move the stock. What did Groucho Marx say? "I made a killing on Wall Street a few years ago…I shot my broker."

Similarly, in the medical field, some psychologists ensure themselves successive paydays by telling their patients that another visit is required. And they don't talk about the limits of their knowledge. Their careers are at stake. As American actor Walther Matthau said, "My doctor gave me six months to live. When I told him I couldn't pay the bill, he gave me six more months."

Why do bankers approve risky loans?
People who are rewarded for doing stupid things continue to do them. From their frame of reference, they acted logically based on how they were rewarded. The system paid them to do the wrong thing. So if market share rather than profits pay a banker, he will write as many loans as possible. He is being rewarded every year while the net consequences of the bad loans won't be realized for a long time.

Charles Munger gives an example of how Lloyd's Insurance rewarded their people:

> They were paid a percentage of the gross volume that went through. And paying everybody a percentage of the gross, when what you're really interested in is the net, is a system - given the natural bias of human beings toward doing what's in their own interest even though it has terrible consequences for other people - that really did Lloyd's in.

John knew that if he didn't show good figures, his project wouldn't be funded so he cooked the books.
Why do people give a biased picture of reality? Why do they make figures look better than they are or fake data to support something? Behavior that is not acceptable but understandable if we remember that people are driven to do what they perceive is in their best interest.

Charles Munger says that projections should be handled with care:

> Mark Twain used to say, "A mine is a hole in the ground with a liar on the top." And a projection prepared by anybody who stands to earn a commission or an executive trying

to justify a particular course of action will frequently be a lie - although it's not a *deliberate* lie in most cases. The man has come to believe it himself. And that's the worst kind. Projections should be handled with great care - particularly when they're being provided by someone who has an interest in misleading you."

Warren Buffett adds:

I have no use whatsoever for projections or forecasts. They create an illusion of apparent precision. The more meticulous they are, the more concerned you should be. We never look at projections, but we care very much about, and look very deeply at, track records. If a company has a lousy track record, but a very bright future, we will miss the opportunity.

I do not understand why any buyer of a business looks at a bunch of projections put together by a seller or his agent. You can almost say that it's *naive* to think that those projections have *any* utility whatsoever. We're just no interested.

If we don't have some idea ourselves of what the future is, to sit there and listen to some other guy who's trying to sell us the business or get a commission on it tell us what the future's going to be - like I say, it's very naive.

Buffett also gives us a test:

When they make these offerings, investment bankers display their humorous side: They dispense income and balance sheet projections extending five or more years into the future for companies they barely had heard of a few months earlier. If you are shown such schedules, I suggest that you join in the fun: Ask the investment banker for the *one-year* budgets that his own firm prepared as the last few years began and then compare these with what actually happened.

The consultant to TransCorp was hired and paid by the company to advise the CEO on how he should be paid. "If I tell the CEO what he wants to hear, he will pay me well, rehire me and recommend me to other CEOs. And if I make it sound complicated it will be easier to send a larger bill."
How do we act as an employee? If our boss wants a particular answer, do we give it? To quote the German proverb: "Whose bread I eat, his song I sing." Warren Buffett says:

I would say that the typical corporate organization is structured so that the CEOs opinions, biases and previous beliefs are reinforced in every possible way. Staffs won't give you any contrary recommendations – they'll just come back with whatever the CEO wants. And the Board of Directors won't act as a check, so the CEO pretty much gets what he wants.

Keep in mind
- Don't automatically trust people who have something at stake from your decision.
- Understand people's motivations. Money, status, love of work, reputation, position, power, envy? What are they rewarded or punished for? Are they benefiting or losing from the present system?

4. APPEAL TO SELF-INTEREST
> *Would you persuade, speak of interest not of reason.*
> - Benjamin Franklin

"I don't like to be embarrassed and have my name and reputation threatened with disgrace," said the CEO of TransCorp.
Since the risk of losing is more motivating than the chance of gaining, we stand a better chance changing people if we appeal to their fear of losing something they value – job, reputation, status, money, control, etc.

Keep in mind
- The ancient Greek philosopher Plato said: "Do not train boys to learning by force and harshness, but lead them by what amuses them, so that they may better discover the bent of their minds." Pressuring people or giving them orders often doesn't work. It is better to convince people by asking questions that illuminate consequences. This causes them to think for themselves and makes it more likely that they discover what's in their best interest.
- Use a combination of psychological tendencies to change behavior.
- It is often better to avoid situations where we need to change people. Changing people is hard as Warren Buffett says, "I'd say that the history that Charlie and I have had of persuading decent, intelligent people who we thought were doing unintelligent things to change their course of action has been *poor*…When people want to do something, they want to do something."
- Changing people affects their motivation, feelings of responsibility, and tendency to reciprocate. It is better when people act out of their own free will.

Warren Buffett illustrates:

> We want the manager of each subsidiary to run their business in the way they think is best for their operation. …we'll never tell a subsidiary manager which vendor to patronize or anything of that sort. Once we start making those decisions for our managers, *we* become responsible for the operation and *they're* no longer responsible for the operation. And they're responsible for their operations. That means that they get to make the call, that it's up to them to do what's best for their subsidiary and that it's up to any other company that wants to do business with their operation to prove to them *why* it's best…That's the Berkshire approach. I think, on balance, our managers *like* it that way - because they're not going to get second-guessed and nobody will go over their heads.

5. Self-deception and Denial

*Nothing is easier than self-deceit. For what
each man wishes, that he also believes to be true.*
- Demosthenes (Greek statesman, 384-322 BC)

John couldn't admit to others that he'd made a bad deal. "I lost money, but others lost more. It wasn't my fault. It was out of my control! You win some, you lose some."
We deny and distort reality to feel more comfortable, especially when reality threatens our self-interest. To quote the Austrian psychologist Sigmund Freud: "Illusions commend themselves to us because they save us pain and allow us to enjoy pleasure instead." We view things the way we want to see them. We hear what we want to hear and deny what is inconsistent with our deeply held beliefs. We deny unpleasant news and prefer comfort to truth. We choose the right people to ask.

"I hope the project succeeds in time and on budget."
Wishful thinking is rooted in denial, offering us a more pleasant reality. In business, this is one reason for project delays and cost overruns.

We believe something is true because it sounds believable or we want to believe it, especially with issues of love, health, religion, and death. This is one reason why people follow gurus. They encourage followers to trust their hearts and forget their heads. Philosopher and mathematician Bertrand Russell said in *Skeptical Essays:* "What is wanted is not the will to believe, but the will to find out, which is the exact opposite."

Keep in mind
• In his famous 1974 commencement address at Caltech, American physicist

Richard Feynman warned against self-deception: "The first principle is that you must not fool yourself - and you are the easiest person to fool."

- Austrian philosopher Ludwig Wittgenstein said in *Culture and Value:* "Nothing is so difficult as not deceiving oneself." We have to see the world as it is. Not for what it was or for what we want it to be. Refusing to look at unpleasant facts doesn't make them disappear. Bad news that is true is better than good news that is wrong.

- Denial must be weighed against social, financial, physical and emotional costs. When the cost of denial is worse than the benefit of facing reality, we must face reality.

6. COMMITMENT AND CONSISTENCY

The difficulty lies not in the new ideas, but in escaping
the old ones, which ramify, for those brought up as most
of us have been, into every corner of our minds.
- John Maynard Keynes (British economist, 1883-1946)

Once we've made a commitment – a promise, a choice, taken a stand, invested time, money or effort – we want to remain consistent. We want to feel that we've made the right decision. And the more we have invested in our behavior the harder it is to change.

Scottish philosopher and economist Adam Smith said in *The Theory of the Moral Sentiments:* "The opinion which we entertain of our own character depends entirely on our judgments concerning our past conduct. It is so disagreeable to think ill of ourselves, that we often purposely turn away our view from those circumstances which might render that judgment unfavorable."

Why do we keep a promise? How do we justify our actions? We are always trying to understand ourselves in light of our behavior. We judge both others and ourselves by observing behavior. When there is an inconsistency between our attitudes and our behavior, we experience an unpleasant inner conflict. To avoid this feeling we often change our attitudes by looking for evidence that our behavior is right.

How does the internal drive for consistency cause us to act?

"I can't behave in a way that is inconsistent with my self-image. I have a reputation to uphold."
We behave in ways that are consistent with how others see us. If people label us as talented, we try to appear talented whether or not it is true.

Why do we hang on to a bad idea, an unhappy relationship or a losing investment? Why do politicians continue fighting wars long after it is clear the war is a bad idea?

The more time, money, effort or pain we invest, the more we feel the need to continue, and the more highly we value something – whether or not it is right. We don't want to waste our efforts. This way we protect our reputation and avoid the pain of accepting a loss. If people challenge our decisions, we become even more committed we are right. And the more individual responsibility we feel for a commitment, the harder it is to give up.

In *Too Much Invested to Quit*, psychologist Allan Teger said about the Vietnam War: "The longer the war continued, the more difficult it was to justify the additional investments in terms of the value of possible victory. On the other hand, the longer the war continued, the more difficult it became to write off the tremendous losses without having anything to show for them."

"I don't want to sell this declining stock and face a loss. I put $100,000 into this. I must prove to others and myself I made the right choice."
After we buy a stock, we are more confident it was a good buy than before the investment. We want to feel we did the right thing and keep our beliefs consistent with what we've done. But nothing has changed. It is the same business before and after.

"I think it's foolish to abandon a project on which $10 million has been sunk," said the CEO of TransCorp.
Why do we do things merely because we've paid for them?

Assume John paid a $1,000 non-refundable fee for a conference, but he no longer wants to participate. He feels he can't afford to waste the already spent $1,000. Should he go to the conference because he already spent $1,000? Should he pay $1,000 to do something he doesn't want to do? The money is lost forever. Isn't it better to say that the already spent $1,000 is the cost of doing what he really wants to do? Isn't it better to pay to do what you want?

John and Mary sit through a lousy movie because they bought the tickets. They can't get the $8 back so it shouldn't make a difference whether they leave or not. The choice is between having a good time or a lousy time.

"We invested in a new machine based on the volume-increase set out in the strategic plan. Unfortunately, volume decreased."
We are most consistent when we have made a public, effortful or voluntary

commitment. The more public a decision is, the less likely it is that we will change it. Written commitments are strong since they require more effort than verbal commitments and can also be made public.

Isn't it better to do what makes sense than to stay consistent with a strategic plan that isn't working? Warren Buffett says, "we do have a few advantages, perhaps the greatest being that we *don't* have a strategic plan. Thus we feel no need to proceed in an ordained direction (a course leading almost invariably to silly purchase prices) but can instead simply decide what makes sense for our owners."

Charles Munger says on the value of long-term plans:

We have very much the philosophy of building our enterprise that Sir William Osler had when he built the John Hopkins Medical School from a very poor start into a model medical school for the whole world. And what Sir William Osler said - and he quoted this from Carlyle - was: "The task of man is not to see what lies dimly in the distance, but to do what lies clearly at hand."

We try to respond intelligently each day, each week, each month, each year to the information and challenges at hand – horrible assaults that have to be deflected, things that have to be scrambled out of, the unusual opportunities that come along – and just do the best job we can in responding to those challenges. Obviously, you look ahead as far as you can. But that's not very far. But if you respond intelligently and diligently to the challenges before you, we think you'll tend to end up with a pretty good institution.

In his *Scientific Autobiography and Other Papers,* German physicist Max Planck said: "A new scientific truth does not triumph by convincing its opponents and making them see the light, but rather because its opponents eventually die and a new generation grows up that is familiar with it."

Warren Buffett adds:

I think it was Keynes who said, "Most economists are *most* economical about *ideas* - they make the ones they learned in graduate school last a lifetime." What happens is that you spend years getting your Ph.D. in finance. And [in the process], you learn theories with a lot of mathematics that the average layman can't do. So you become sort of a high priest. And you wind up with an *enormous* amount of yourself in terms of your ego – and even professional security – invested in those ideas. Therefore, it gets very hard to back off after a given point.

"I have invested 15 years of my life in this, so I won't walk away now."
Let's say that a couple is in a bad marriage but have spent 15 years together.

Should they get a divorce or should they "stay in there" and remain unhappy because they have invested 15 years of their life?

What other traps may consistency cause us to fall into?

John and his family decided to buy a new car. They chose a dealership that agreed to sell the car $1,000 below the competition. Then the salesman changed the terms. He had discovered an error. In the end, the price ended up $200 above competition.

In the low-ball technique, the salesperson gets the customer an incentive to enter an agreement with the intention of changing the terms to the seller's advantage (either by removing the advantage or adding something undesirable). Once John made the decision and took the time and effort to buy a new car, he committed to the purchase. Otherwise he would appear inconsistent. Instead of backing out of the deal, he finds new reasons to justify buying the car.

"What a great deal for a refrigerator," Mary said, reading the advertisements.

When she gets to the store, the salesperson tells her that they ran out of the advertised specials. But they have a similar one in stock. And it is only $150 more. She buys the refrigerator. She is already committed to buying a refrigerator and the salesperson only forces her to be consistent.

"Will you take my kids to school today?" Mary's neighbor asked. One month later, Mary found herself still driving her neighbors' kids to school and even to the movies.

How do people seduce us financially, politically or sexually? They make us first agree to a small request, so small that no one would refuse. This way they create a commitment. Then they make a second and larger request (the one they wanted all along). We are then more likely to comply. This "foot-in-the-door technique" is based on the principle that if people ask us to make a small commitment, we are more likely to agree to a larger request because we want to appear consistent.

One study showed that 76% of a group of homeowners agreed to put a large billboard on their front lawn, saying "Drive Carefully." Two weeks earlier, the homeowners had been approached by other researchers, asking them to place a tiny sign saying "Be a Safe driver" on their car windows. They now saw themselves as concerned citizens and people who care enough about driver safety to take a stand. They also believed that was how other people saw them. When they were later approached, 76% agreed putting up the large sign just to be consistent. In contrast, only 17% of subjects who hadn't received the earlier visit agreed to put up the large sign.

When people get us to commit, we become responsible. One experiment staged a theft to find out if onlookers would risk personal harm to stop a crime. A researcher sat on a beach blanket and listened to his portable radio five feet from the blanket of a randomly chosen person. After awhile, the researcher left the blanket to stroll the beach. A few minutes later a second researcher, pretending to be a thief, grabbed the radio and ran away. Four people out of twenty put themselves in harm by challenging the thief. But when the procedure was tried somewhat differently, nineteen people became vigilantes, and tried to stop the thief. The difference? Before taking his stroll, the researcher asked the subject to "please watch my things" which they all agreed to do.

How do we get people to take inner responsibility for their actions? Make it voluntary. We take responsibility for our behavior in cases when we are internally motivated by satisfaction or interest, when we feel in control, and when we are free from incentives or outside pressure.

Keep in mind
- A decision must be active. When you get new facts or insights, change! British writer Jonathan Swift said: "A man should never be ashamed to own that he has been in the wrong, which is but saying, in other words, that he is wiser today than he was yesterday." J.M. Keynes said: "When somebody persuades me that I am wrong, I change my mind. What do you do?" Sometimes things don't go the way we believe they will. The solution is to face it and act. Charles Munger says: "We've done a *lot* of that – scrambled out of wrong decisions. I would argue that that's a big part of having a reasonable record in life. You can't *avoid* wrong decisions. But if you recognize them promptly and *do* something about them, you can frequently turn the lemon into lemonade."
- If we can get people committed in advance, they tend to live up to their commitment. For example, make people take a voluntary and public position on some issue.
- Don't force people to publicly make commitments that you don't later want the opportunity to change.
- When you are asked to perform a future action but are uncertain, ask yourself: Would I do this if I had to do it tomorrow?
- Warren Buffett says, "The most important thing to do when you find yourself in a hole is to stop digging." Merely because you've spent money or time on some project or investment doesn't mean you must continue to spend it in the future. Time, effort, and money spent are gone. Decisions should be based on where you want to be. Not where you've been. Base decisions on the present situation and future consequences. What happened in the past may be a guide

for estimating how likely something is to happen in the future. Ask: What do I want to achieve? What causes that? Considering what I know today and what is likely to happen in the future, how should I act to achieve my goal? Will new money and time invested achieve my goal? Assume I never invested in this and it was presented to me for the first time, would I invest in it today? If not, then stop and do something about it. As Charles Munger says:

Berkshire extracted a lot of capital out of it [the textile business] and put it elsewhere. And if Berkshire had tried to keep fighting the decline of that business with more and more money, it would have blown most of its capital. There's a time to fight and there's a time to run away. One of my favorite stories, relevant to this story, involves a town in the South. There was this huge grocery store owned by one of the great national chains. They're a formidable competitor and they had the dominant big grocery store in this town for many, many years doing big volume. Sam Walton of Wal-Mart announced that he was opening a much bigger, better grocery store with a lot of other wonderful products at incredibly low prices. And the existing very experienced and successful chain, did not wait for Sam Walton's store to open. They just closed their store right away.

7. Confirmation

What the human being is best of doing, is interpreting all
new information so that their prior conclusions remain intact.
- Warren Buffett

We look for evidence that confirms our ideas, beliefs, and actions. For example, when we've made an investment, entered a relationship or made other types of commitments, we tend to seek out evidence confirming that it was the right decision and ignore information that shows it was wrong.

John wanted to employ a new vice president. He told everyone that the guy was terrific but the new employee turned out to be a disaster. Instead of dealing with the mistake, John kept the guy, costing him much money and aggravation.
We tend to make hasty judgments. It is hard to change a first conclusion since a change implies we may be wrong. We associate being wrong with a threat to our self-interest.

Keep in mind
- "Facts do not cease to exist because they are ignored," said British novelist Aldous Huxley. If we only look to confirm our ideas, we will never discover if

we're wrong. Be self-critical and unlearn your best-loved ideas. Search for evidence that disconfirms ideas and assumptions. Consider alternative outcomes, viewpoints, and answers. Have someone tell you when your thinking is wrong. Warren Buffett says, "Charlie and I believe that when you find information that contradicts your existing beliefs, you've got a *special* obligation to look at it – and *quickly*."

- Follow the advice of the Italian artist and scientist Leonardo da Vinci: "We know well that mistakes are more easily detected in the works of others than in one's own. When you are painting you should take a flat mirror and often look at your work within it, and it will then be seen in reserve, and will appear to be by the hand of some other master, and you will be better able to judge of its faults than in any other way."

8. Ideology

Convictions are more dangerous enemies of truth than lies.
- Friedrich Wilhelm Nietzsche (German philosopher, 1844-1900)

People with various political, religious, and philosophical interests are motivated to seek the truths that confirm these interests. Strong convictions for political, religious or philosophical ideas can be dangerous. They can act as a device for justifying war and violence. As Blaise Pascal wrote: "Men never do evil so completely and cheerfully as when they do it from religious conviction."

Charles Munger tell us about the danger of ideology:

Heavy ideology is one of the most extreme distorters of human cognition. Look at these Islamic Fundamentalists who just gunned down a bunch of Greek tourists shouting, "God's work!"

Ideology does some strange things and distorts cognition *terribly*. If you get a lot of heavy ideology *young* – and, then, you start expressing it – you are really locking your brain into a very unfortunate pattern. And you are going to distort your general cognition.

There's a very interesting history if you take Warren Buffett as an example of worldly wisdom: Warren adored his father – who was a wonderful man. But he was a very heavy ideologue, (right wing, it happened to be), who hung around with other very heavy ideologues, (right wing, naturally). Warren observed this as a kid. And he decided that ideology was dangerous – and that he was going to stay a long way away from it. And he *has* throughout his whole life. That has *enormously* helped the accuracy of his cognition.

I learned the same lesson in a different way. My father hated ideology. Therefore, all I had to do was imitate my father and, thereby, stay in what I regard as the right path. People like Dornan on the right or Nader on the left have obviously gone a little daft. They're extreme examples of what ideology will do to you – particularly violently *expressed* ideology. Since it pounds ideas *in* better than it convinces *out,* it's a very dangerous thing to do.

Keep in mind
- Be objective.

9. DEPRIVAL SYNDROME
You don't change something people love.
- Faith Popcorn (American futurist marketing consultant)

When something we like is (or threatens to be) taken away, we often value it higher. For example, why do we get upset when we lose our freedom, status or reputation? We fear the loss of control we possess over our own life. When we perceive this control is threatened, we experience anxiety, anger and depression. For example, people are more likely to fight a restrictive law that takes away a benefit they have enjoyed for a long time, and that they feel entitled to. The more we like what is taken away or the larger the commitment we've made, the more upset we become.

How do people react when we try to lower their income?
Charles Munger illustrates the power of deprival when negotiating takeaways in labor negotiations:

> (A) You're facing deprival super-reaction syndrome - people just go *bananas.* And (B) the union representative has to bring his members the deprival message and endure the Pavlovian mere-association hatred that results. Therefore, *he* won't do it - largely for *that* reason. So you have *two* powerful psychological effects making it hell.
>
> All of those strikes in the late 1800s and the early 1900s where Pinkerton guards were shooting people were about takeaways. Arriving immigrants were willing to work cheap. And capitalist proprietors tried to reduce wages – sometimes because they felt they *had* to because their competitors were doing it and sometimes because they simply wanted to make more money. At any rate, all of that murder and mayhem was the result of deprival super-reaction syndrome plus the reality that nobody wanted to be the carrier of bad news.

Deprival also helps cause what Munger calls the Serpico syndrome. Frank Serpico became known after exposing corruption at the New York Police

Department in the 1970s. When Frank Serpico entered the New York Police force in 1960, payoffs and kickbacks were rampant in the department. When he refused to take money, his fellow officers saw him as a potential danger. Then he blew the whistle on them, and became their enemy.

John tells Mary: "I can't sell the stock now. I have to wait until it gets back up to what I paid for it. Anyway, I don't realize a loss unless I sell."

We hate to admit we've lost money. As we've seen in Part One we have an aversion to loss. We feel more pain from losing than we feel pleasure from gaining something of equal value. Our loss aversion contributes to status quo bias – we prefer to hang on to what we have. We even put a higher value on the things we already own than we are willing to pay for the same things if we didn't own them.

Charles Munger says, "The deprival super-reaction syndrome of man helps cause much ruin as people's cognition is distorted as a result of their suffering losses and seeing near misses." We hate to sell losing stocks. It is the same as admitting to others and ourselves that we've made a mistake. We therefore hold on to our losers too long and sell our winners too soon. A realized loss feels worse than suffering the same loss on paper. The pain of feeling responsible for making a bad decision also plays a role (regret). The stock may bounce back after we've sold. And the more money and effort we've put in, the harder it is to let it go.

We also feel that losing the opportunity to make money is less painful than losing the same amount of money. But a lost opportunity of making $100 has the same value as a real loss of $100.

John's friend Allan bought a house five years ago for $200,000.

Four years later, Allan's company moves to another city. The local real estate market is depressed. He is offered $170,000 but feels he can't afford a loss. So he waits another year and this time the offered price is $150,000.

Isn't it better for Allan to concentrate on what the house is worth rather than on what he paid?

John kept pouring dollars in the machine. "I got Cherry, Cherry, Bar. I'm close now."

We want and place higher value on something when we almost have it and lose it. Charles Munger says, "One reason why horse races, bingo and these things have always been so popular is because of all these near *misses.*"

Just as people take larger risks when threatened, after a loss, we want to catch up, so we end up taking more risks to get even. But as Warren Buffett and Charles Munger says:

Buffett: A very important principle in investing is that you *don't* have to make it back the way you lost it. In fact, it's usually a *mistake* to try to make it back the way you lost it.

Munger: That's the reason so many people are ruined by gambling - they get behind and then they feel like they have to get it back the way they lost it. It's a deep part of human nature. It's very smart just to *lick* it – by *will…*

Buffett: One of the important things in stocks is that the stock does not know that you own it. You have all these feelings about it: You remember what you paid. You remember who told you about it – all these little things. And it doesn't give a *damn*. It just sits there. If a stock's at $50, somebody's paid $100 and feels terrible; somebody else has paid $10 and feels wonderful – all these feelings. And it has no impact whatsoever…

John and Mary's daughter didn't want the toy they gave her, she wanted the toy they didn't give her.

We want what we can't have. Forbidden fruit tastes best. Mark Twain said, "It was not that Adam ate the apple for the apple's sake, but because it was forbidden. It would have been better for us – oh infinitely better for us – if the serpent had been forbidden." Forbid someone to do something and they find it more attractive than they did before it was forbidden.

"Since a real estate lot in this area is both rare and hard to obtain, I want it."

We want and value more what is scarce or unique. We want what is (or threatens to be) less available. The less available it is, the more we desire it. That's why we subscribe to newsletters containing exclusive and restricted information. And why we participate in initial public offerings and buy stocks on hot tips.

We value higher what has recently been less available than things that have been scarce all along. We fall for limited offers and deadlines like, *"The offer ends at midnight. We only have a few left. This is the last chance."* By making things less available, merchants make them seem more valuable.

"A lot of people are competing for this lot at the auction."

How do we create demand? Create competition. Make people perceive there is a huge competition for the item and limit the number of people that can participate in the bidding. If others want what's scarce, we want it even more.

When we can't get something, we lower our opinion of it. When we can get something that others don't want, we don't want it either.

Keep in mind
- Know your goals and options. Ask: Why do I want this? For emotional or rational reasons?
- What you paid for your house, stock, or car has no relevance to its value. If the value is below what you paid, you don't have to get even. If you bought a stock for $100 and it is now $50, you should sell it, if it is not worth more than $50. Ask: Suppose I hadn't made the investment, would I make this investment today at today's price?
- Remember that people respond to immediate crisis and threats. Anything that happens gradually, they tend to put off.
- Charles Munger shows how we can use the force of deprival to persuade (for a reputable reason):

In Captain Cook's day, he took these long voyages. At the time, scurvy was the dread of the long voyage. And in scurvy, your living gums putrefy in your mouth - after which the disease gets unpleasant and kills you. And being on a primitive sailing ship with a bunch of dying sailors is a *very* awkward business. So everybody was terribly interested in scurvy, but they didn't *know* about Vitamin C. Well, Captain Cook, being a smart man with a multiple-model kind of approach, noticed that Dutch ships had less scurvy than English ships on long voyages. So he said, "What are the Dutch doing that's different?"

And he noticed they had all these barrels of sauerkraut. So he thought: "I'm going on these long voyages. And it's very dangerous. Sauerkraut may help." So he laid in all this sauerkraut which, incidentally, happens to contain a trace of vitamin C. But English sailors were a tough, cranky and dangerous bunch in that day. They hated "krauts". And they were used to their standard food and booze. So how do you get such English sailors to eat sauerkraut?

Well, Cook didn't want to tell 'em that he was doing it in the hope it would prevent scurvy - because they might mutiny and take over the ship if they thought that he was taking them on a voyage so long that scurvy was likely.

So here's what he did: Officers ate one place where the men could observe them. And for a long time, he served sauerkraut to the officers, but not to the men. And then, finally, Captain Cook said, "Well, the men can have it *one* day a week."

In due course, he had the whole crew eating sauerkraut. I regard that as a very constructive use of elementary psychology. It may have saved God knows how many lives and caused God knows how much achievement.

10. STATUS QUO
When John and Mary bought their new car, they stuck to their usual brand.
We prefer to keep things the way they are. We resist change and prefer effort

minimization. We want to feel good about the choices we make so we can justify our actions for others and ourselves.

The more emotional a decision is or the more choices we have, the more we prefer the status quo. This is why we stick with our old jobs, brand of car, etc.

"I fear the social consequences if I make the wrong choice, so I decide to do nothing." We feel worse when we fail as a result of taking action than when we fail from doing nothing.

Keep in mind
- Deciding to do nothing is also a decision. And the cost of doing nothing could be greater than the cost of taking an action.
- Remember what you want to achieve.

11. Impatience
The CEO of TransCorp wants his bonus today and therefore he makes a decision that increases this years profit at the cost of a possibly larger profit in the future.
We seek pleasure today at a cost of what may be better in the future. We prefer an immediate reward to a delayed but maybe larger reward. We spend today what we should save for tomorrow. This means that we may pay a high price in the future for a small immediate reward.

We are impatient in the short run and patient in the long run. Studies show that we tend to become less patient when rewards are more immediate. Our discount rates (the values we assign to something) are higher in the short run than in the long run. For example, when a small reward is due tomorrow and a larger reward is due in one year, people often prefer the small immediate reward. But when the small reward is due in one year and the larger reward in two years, people tend to prefer the larger long-term reward. Studies show, for example, that most workers prefer a 15-minute break today to a 30-minute break tomorrow. But they also prefer a 30-minute break in 101 days to a 15-minute break in 100 days. The difference in the value of a break between today and tomorrow is much greater than the difference between waiting 100 days and waiting 101 days. Studies show that one explanation for this is that outcomes occurring in the future are perceived as less certain.

Keep in mind
- The 16th Century French essayist Michel de Montaigne said: "I conceive that pleasures are to be avoided if greater pains be the consequence, and pains to be

coveted that will terminate in greater pleasures." Consider both the short and long-term consequences of a decision. Weigh present good/bad against future good/bad. Short-term suffering may lead to long term pleasure.

12. Envy and Jealousy

Man will do many things to get himself loved;
he will do all things to get himself envied.
- Mark Twain

We evaluate our own situation by comparing what we have with what others have. As Aristotle said: "We envy those who are near us in time, place, age or reputation." It is people similar to us we envy most.

Keep in mind

- As long as you achieve your goals, it shouldn't matter if someone else does better.
- Aristotle said: "The best way to avoid envy is to deserve the success you get."

13. Contrast

Fill one bucket with cold water, another with hot water, and a third with water at room temperature. Put one hand in the bucket of cold water and the other hand in the bucket of hot water. Then put both your hands in the bucket of room temperature water. What happens? You will feel that your cold hand feels warmer and that your warm hand feels colder. Why? Because we perceive things differently when they are presented one after another.

There is a difference between what we think we see and what we really see. For example, we don't judge objects, people, feelings, or information by themselves but in contrast to other objects, people, feelings or information presented closely in time or space. For example, we evaluate things like temperature, loudness, brightness, health, status, or prices based on their contrast to a reference point and not absolute magnitudes. This reference point changes with new experiences and context.

The grossly overpriced $100 tie seemed reasonable after John bought the fairly priced $1,500 suit.
The order in which something is presented matters. Sales people often try to sell the more costly item first. We are out buying a computer and some diskettes. In comparison to $1,500 computer, diskettes at $10 seem like a bargain. After we buy the big ticket items, the add-ons seem cheap in comparison.

Experiments have shown that we go across town to save $10 on a clock radio but not to save $10 on a large-screen TV. The difference between $100 and $110 seems like a larger saving than the difference between $2850 and $2860. But it's the same $10 saving.

The same thing may appear attractive when compared to less attractive things and unattractive when compared to more attractive things. For example, studies show that a person of average attractiveness is seen as less attractive when compared to highly attractive others.

In one experiment, a group of people was asked to choose between $6 and an elegant pen. Most choose the cash. Another group of people was asked to choose between $6, the elegant pen, or an inferior pen. Most choose the elegant pen. By adding an inferior option, another option seemed more attractive.

Mary is looking at houses. The real estate broker knows that the house he is trying to sell Mary is in poor shape and a bad area. He starts by showing Mary bad properties in an ugly neighborhood. Afterwards, he takes her to the house he wanted to sell all along. Suddenly this house and the area seem great in comparison to the other houses she saw.

Keep in mind
- Evaluate people and objects by themselves and not by their contrast.
- Contrasts may blind us to change until it's too late. Often we see reality as constant, although it gradually changes. Sometimes it is the small, gradual, invisible changes that harm us the most.

14. Anchoring

The CEO informs John what he told the board members of TransCorp: "Our costs were one million over budget but I told them we were three million over. They were thrilled when I later told them it was only one million. I always set low targets to exceed expectations."

We are over-influenced by certain information as a reference point for future decisions. For example, when we estimate, we start with a figure that is familiar and don't adjust it to reality. We also evaluate choices and judge consequences based on changes from a reference point – often the status quo.

"I made a bad investment, paying $50 for something now worth $40," says John.

We don't price a thing according to its value but its relative price. If we for example bought a stock for $50 with a present price of $40, we judge how good our decision was in reference to our purchase price. Or if a stock we consider buying trades around $50 for some time and drops to $35, we tend to get anchored on the $50 and automatically assume that $35 is a bargain.

Investors loved Enron enough to value it at $63 billion in December 2000.
A friend called me before Christmas of 2001 and suggested I should buy stock in Enron. When I asked why, he said: "The stock falls from $80 to $10, and you ask me why? I mean how much lower can it go?" What if it had traded at $1 a year ago? Does it mean it's now grossly overpriced? The present price of a stock in relation to some past quote doesn't mean anything. The underlying business value is what matters.

John's friend said: "As a used car salesman, I anchor a potential buyer to a high price and then slowly reduce it. This way I get a good final price and the customer perceives he got a good deal."
A friend of John and Mary was selling his chain of ice cream stores. The buyer had discussed a price of $10 million. But the seller researched prices of similar businesses. He outlined his research for the buyer and told him his target price of $15 million. Then the seller started to negotiate on his methodology, not on the price. The $15 million got anchored with the buyer as the basis for further discussion. The seller finally sold his stores for $13 million.

Keep in mind
- Consider choices from a zero base level and remember what you want to achieve.
- Adjust information to reality.
- Consider what numbers really mean and what is realistic.

15. VIVID EVIDENCE

The attention which we lend to an experience is proportional to its vivid or interesting character; and it is a notorious fact that what interests us most vividly at the time is, other things equal, what we remember best.
- William James (American psychologist and philosopher, 1842-1910)

John invests in a company based on a beautifully written quarterly earnings report and an entertaining presentation.
The more dramatic, salient, entertaining, or emotional some information, event or experience is, the more influenced we are.

We are easily influenced when we are told stories because we relate to stories better than to logic or fact. We love to be entertained. Information we receive directly, through our eyes or ears has more impact than secondhand information that may have more evidential value. A vivid description from a friend or family member is more believable than true evidence. Statistical data is often overlooked. Studies show that jurors are influenced by vivid descriptions. Lawyers try to present dramatic and memorable testimony.

A Chinese proverb says: "Kill one, frighten ten thousand." We often overestimate events that are unlikely to happen merely because they receive attention in the news. Drama and danger sells. The media capitalizes on fear because there is money in it. Major accidents, such as airplane crashes or shark attacks, grab people's attention and make headlines regardless of their probability. This causes us to believe a problem is larger than it really is. The media ignores events that didn't result in a catastrophe.

Keep in mind
- The media have its weaknesses, bias and vulnerability to manipulation and deception. Consider what is relevant and what happens on average.
- Accurate information is better than dramatic information. Back up vivid stories with facts and numbers.

16. Recent Evidence
John sold every stock he owned since the media reported bad economic news.
We give too much weight to information we've seen, heard, read or experienced most recently. For example, when judging performance, we overweigh what happened most recently and ignore what on average happens.

We make predictions by extrapolating recent trends. The stock market falls into nose bleed territory and we assume the world is going under. After a bad event happens, we tend to overestimate the likelihood of it happening again.

Keep in mind
- Separate noise and chance events from what is important. Ask: Is it relevant? Does it make sense? Is it representative evidence? Was it a random event?
- Trends may be wrong. Ask: Is it a permanent or temporary effect?

17. Framing
> *How often misused words generate misleading thoughts.*
> - Herbert Spencer (British philosopher, 1820-1903)

When John makes presentations, he says whatever his listeners want to hear.
The less knowledgeable we are about an issue, the more influenced we are by how it

is framed. Consider how a statement, problem, consequence, or question is presented. How is it worded? What is its context? Are we considering certain features and ignoring others? Emotional, selective and appealing frames influence us.

"The more I didn't understand, the more I believed the expert."
Sometimes we are too impressed by how something is phrased. For example, some people buy into investments just because they don't understand them. They assume it must be something unique. As Warren Buffett says, "Techniques shrouded in mystery clearly have value to the purveyor of investment advice. After all, what witch doctor has ever achieved fame and fortune by simply advising 'Take two aspirins'?"

The doctor told Mary: "You may lose your life if you do not change your behavior."
How we frame a problem has an impact on the answers we receive. That's why we can get opposite answers to nearly identical questions.

Studies show that health-related messages involving uncertainty of diseases or cures are more effective when focusing on potential negative consequences. One study showed that women were more likely to engage in breast self-examination when they were presented with information emphasizing the negative consequences of not performing self-examination compared to information that focused on the benefits of doing it.

We are influenced by the order, first or last, in which a presentation happens. The key variable is the amount of time that separates the presentations, the time when we have to make a judgment, and which presentation is the most easily remembered.

Assume that two presidential candidates are speaking on an issue, one directly after the other. If some time passes before we have to make a judgment, we are likely to be more influenced by the first presentation. Assume now that some time passes between the first and last presentations, but we have to make a judgment immediately after the last presentation. Then we are more likely to be influenced by the last presentation.

"I put my paycheck in the bank at 4% interest, and borrowed money for a car loan at 10% interest."
We create our own frames by doing mental accounting. We treat assets of the same value differently depending on where they come from or their importance. We put different values on the same dollar, and are more willing to risk money we have won than money we have earned. A gain of $1,000 from playing roulette

has less value than $1,000 earned from hard work. *"I didn't gamble with my $1,000, I only gambled with the $1,000 I won on the casino."* But it is the same amount of money.

In one experiment psychologists found that people who lost a $10 theater ticket on the way to the theater were reluctant to buy a second ticket. Those who instead lost a $10 bill on the way to buy a $10 theater ticket saw the loss of the money and the purchase of the ticket as unrelated, so they would buy the ticket. But, in both cases, the loss was the same.

We prefer a sequence of experiences that improve over time. Losing $100 first and then gaining $50 seems less painful than gaining $50 and then losing $100. We want to get rid of the bad experiences first. Immediate losses are preferred over delayed ones.

Since our experiences seem longer when broken into segments, we like to have pleasurable experiences broken into segments but painful ones combined. It feels better to gain $50 twice than $100 once and it feels less painful to lose $100 once than $50 twice.

Keep in mind
- Make it clear what an issue is about, what is to be achieved, and its cause.
- View your assets in terms of their entirety. A dollar is a dollar independent of where it comes from. What counts is what you put in or take out of your pocket.

18. Reciprocation
There is no duty more indispensable than that of returning
a kindness. All men distrust one forgetful of a benefit.
- Marcus Tullius Cicero (Roman statesman and writer, 106-43 BC)

In return for his loyalty to the CEO, John received a promotion.
We tend to pay back in kind what others have done for us – good or bad.

Do you return Christmas cards? In one study a researcher sent out cards to strangers. Dozens of people sent back cards, even though they'd never heard of the person. Whenever someone does something for us we want to do something back. No wonder companies use free trials and send out free samples. A gift with our name on it is hard not to reciprocate.

"I praised him for a job well done, and I received a motivated employee."
"I told him about his mistake, and he became hostile towards me."
We respond the same way as we are treated. If we are unfair to others, people are unfair back. If people trust us, we tend to trust them. If people criticize us, we

criticize them back. If people we don't like do us a favor or an uninvited favor, we reciprocate anyway.

Warren Buffett tell us how Berkshire treats management:

Three quarters of our managers are independently wealthy. They don't need to get up and go to work at all. Most of them have tens and tens of million of dollars. So I've got to create or I've got to maintain an environment where the thing they want to do most in the world is to go to work that day and the next day. And, I say to myself, "What would make me feel that way?" One way is to feel you are running your own show. If I had people second-guessing me all day, I would get sick of it. I would say, "What the hell do I need this for?" And, that's exactly the way our managers would feel if I went around second-guessing them or telling them how to run their business.

John is negotiating to buy a small business. The seller asks a higher price than John is prepared to pay and he declines. The seller then makes a concession and reduces the price. We make a concession to people who have first made a concession to us. Since John views the lower price as a concession, he feels a need to reciprocate and accepts the lower price. This price was what the seller wanted all the time.

Keep in mind
- People don't want to feel indebted. We are disliked if we don't allow people to give back what we've given them.
- A favor or gift is most effective when it is personal, significant, and unexpected.
- Before you make concessions, think about what you want to achieve.
- The American car manufacturer Henry Ford said: "If there is any one secret of success, it lies in the ability to get the other person's point of view and see things from his angle as well as from your own."
- Follow Confucius: "What you don't want yourself, don't do to others. Reward hostility with justice, and good deeds with good deeds." Give people what you want in return from them. Ask: Assuming others are like me, how would I like to be treated if the roles were reversed?
- Set the correct example. In Confucius words: "Example is better than law. For where the laws govern, the people are shameless in evading punishment. But where example governs, the people have a sense of shame and improve."

19. EXPECTATIONS
What we observe is not nature itself but nature exposed to our method of questioning.
- Werner Heisenberg (German physicist, 1901-1976)

"Why is John tense when people watch his golf swing?"
The fact of the observation changes the observed. People may change their behavior merely because they are being observed.

"I expect you to understand what I'm saying. I know you can do this."
Our behavior can be influenced by the expectations of others – teachers, coaches, bosses, etc. For example, to please the observer, a research subject may read in a desired result. A patient may wish to respond to a treatment in what they see as the correct way. We live up to what is expected of us.

We often see what we want or expect to see. A doctor may see an effect in a patient because he expects to see it. We often don't see what we don't expect to see.

Do we treat people according to our expectations?
Assume Mary is on her way to meet someone for the first time. Does it matter if this person has been described as friendly or emotionally cold? Yes, it produces a change in Mary's expectations of that individual and a change in her behavior. Mary will expect friendliness or hostility and behave according to her expectations. The person may react to Mary in a way that confirms her expectations. We treat people like we expect them to be. If we expect people to be bad, we treat them in a certain way, which may cause them to behave badly.

Assume that a new teacher is told that half of the class has high IQs and half has low IQs. The teacher is given the names of the supposed intelligent kids and the supposed not so intelligent ones. In reality, someone has randomly selected the two groups. By the end of the year, the experimental premise will become a self-fulfilling prophecy. The kids the teacher thought had high IQs will be doing better than the kids with supposedly low IQs. This has been demonstrated in studies of elementary school students. Teachers taught much better when they expected a lot from their students.

Keep in mind
- "Things are not always what they seem," said the 1st Century Roman philosopher Phaedrus.
- The answers you get depend on the questions you ask.

20. LIKING

Personal beauty is a greater recommendation than any letter of introduction.
- Aristotle

"John likes his colleague, Ted, because they share the same values and prefer the same type of suits."

We believe, trust and agree with people we know and like. We do things for people we like. We like the people who like us (because we like to be liked.) And if we feel that a person likes us, we tend to like them back.

What can people do to make us like them? We like people who are similar to us in background, opinion, lifestyle, interest, attitude, looks, values, and belief. Also, those who are physically attractive, prestigious, wealthy, successful, popular, familiar, cooperative, or people we have positive associations with.

Studies show that we believe that physically attractive people have a more desirable personality than average-looking or unattractive people. Experiments show that attractive criminals are seen as less aggressive and get a milder punishment than ugly criminals. But like the 6th Century Greek writer Aesop wrote, "Appearances often are deceiving."

"I am a sucker for flattery."

We like people who compliment us – true or not – and make us feel special. To quote the British Prime Minister and novelist Benjamin Disraeli: "Talk to a man about himself and he will listen for hours." We also like the people who give us what we are missing in life.

"To get them to do business with me, I associate myself with powerful friends and disassociate myself from losers. I also try to get introduced by someone of established credibility."

People believe we have the same personality as those we associate with. Credibility leads to trust.

"We have a common enemy. By cooperating we both gain."

We like people who cooperate with us. How do we get people to cooperate? Create an external common threat or an opportunity for mutual gain.

"I believe she likes me, so I like her to."

We reciprocate the way others see us. If we perceive others dislike us, we tend to dislike them.

Keep in mind
• Concentrate on the issue and what you want to achieve.

21. DISLIKING

Our enemies' opinion of us comes closer to the truth than our own.
- Francois Duc de la Rochefoucauld (French writer, 1613-1680)

"I don't like him because he is egoistic, defensive, always complains and has a bad temper."
We don't learn from people we don't like and we don't want to be associated with them. The people we don't like are the ones we perceive as dissimilar to us, people we are in competition with or people that are self-absorbed, complaining, greedy, etc.

Keep in mind
• Benjamin Franklin wrote: "Love your enemies, for they tell you your faults."

22. SOCIAL APPROVAL

The deepest principle in human nature is the craving to be appreciated.
- William James

We want to be socially accepted and not disliked or rejected. This contributes to conformity.

William James says: "A man's Social Self is the recognition which he gets from his mates…No more fiendish punishment could be devised…than that one should be turned loose in society and remain absolutely unnoticed by all the members thereof."

"Since I want to be accepted, I always focus on the way I appear to others."
We adapt what we say and do to suit our audience and create a desired impression. We behave like others do and don't speak the truth or openly question people for fear of the consequences. We don't want to be the person who stands out. This is one reason why people who are overly concerned about what others think about them prefer to be around like-minded people. It's more comfortable than standing out and risking social disapproval.

Why are we terrified to speak in public?
It's not like we're going to die. Science writer Rush Dozier says in *Fear Itself:* "The primitive fear system may interpret speaking before a group as standing alone in the midst of a group of strangers. The fear of public speaking may also be related to a fear of losing status in the social group, a form of humiliation that would

have had real consequences among early humans, jeopardizing access to food, shelter, and reproductive opportunities."

Keep in mind

- Don't depend on the encouragement or criticism of others. Marcus Aurelius Antoninus said: "How much time he gains who does not look to see what his neighbor says or does or thinks."
- Don't automatically mistake people's appearance for reality. It may be a social mask.
- Social approval is an effective way to make people behave correctly. Why do people avoid certain actions? Because they are afraid of the social punishment these actions may cause.

23. SOCIAL PROOF

If 40 million people say a foolish thing, it does not become a wise one.
- Somerset Maugham (British novelist, 1874-1965)

Do you rely on others for advice and actions? Most people do. In *True Believer,* American philosopher Eric Hoffer wrote, "When people are free to do as they please, they usually imitate each other." We are social animals, influenced by what we see other people doing and believing. We believe that others know more than we do.

We want what others want. Since everybody else wants it, we assume there has to be a reason. We avoid what others avoid. We imitate without thinking. Especially when many people do it, people we like are doing it, when we are uncertain, in an unfamiliar environment, in a crowd, lack knowledge, or suffer from stress or low self-esteem.

Sellers of fashion, books, movies, etc., know that if enough people like something, others will eventually follow. We trust testimonials from people that we see as similar to us.

Warren Buffett tells an instructive story:

This friend, who ran a property-casualty insurer, was explaining to his directors why he wanted to acquire a certain life insurance company. After droning rather unpersuasively through the economics and strategic rationale for the acquisition, he abruptly abandoned the script. With an impish look, he simply said: "Aw, fellas, all the other kids have one."

John's stockbroker recommends the same stock as other brokers. When John asked him why, he replied "I'd rather be wrong in a group than right by myself."

We feel more comfortable as part of a majority. It acts as a protection from criticism. If we are wrong and everybody else is too, we get less blame. To quote J.M. Keynes: "Worldly wisdom teaches that it is better for reputation to fail conventionally than to succeed unconventionally." Warren Buffett adds:

> Most managers have very little incentive to make the intelligent-but-with-some-chance-of-looking-like-an-idiot decision. Their personal gain/loss ratio is all too obvious: if an unconventional decision works out well, they get a pat on the back and, if it works out poorly, they get a pink slip. (Failing conventionally is the route to go; as a group, lemmings may have a rotten image, but no individual lemming has ever received bad press.)

John invested in an exclusive oil project since a group of sophisticated, wealthy investors were involved. They promised that he would quadruple his money in one year. A year later, he'd lost it all.

Former chairman of the U.S. Securities and Exchange Commission, Arthur Levitt, Jr. says, "If you are dumb enough to invest based on a lavatory wall, you deserve to lose money."

In the early 1900s, Italian immigrant Charles Ponzi, took investors for $10 million by promising 40% returns on International Postal Reply Coupons. What he didn't tell investors was that their money was being used to pay off earlier investors. In the end, the house of cards collapsed.

In the Foundation for New Era Philanthropy, some of the U.S.'s leading charities and donors believed they could double their money in six months. New Era used contributions from one group to pay off another – until there was no money left. New Era was a $350 million Ponzi Scheme. Charles Munger says, "Grown-up people actually believed that there was a tooth fairy out there that would double their money in six months provided they agreed to give it to charity."

Blindly following the lead of others can have dangerous consequences.

"Oh my God, he stabbed me. Please help me!"

We have a tendency to not act in situations where we are uncertain if there is danger and when we don't feel individual responsibility. Also when we want to avoid embarrassment and when we're among strangers. The more people, the more reduced we see our own responsibility.

Just after 3 a.m., March 13, 1964 in New York City, Catherine Genovese, a 28-year old woman, was stabbed to death as she returned from her job. 38 people witnessed at least one of her killer's three attacks from the safety of their apartment windows for 25 minutes without calling the police..

Why didn't the neighbors help? Were they indifferent? Frightened? Why should they be afraid of calling the police from the safety of their own homes? A pair of psychology professors found the answer. No one had helped *just* because thirty-eight witnesses were present. A bystander to an emergency is unlikely to help when there are other people around. Why? They saw two reasons for this.

First, we must interpret an event as an emergency. When we are uncertain, we have a tendency to look at people around us to see how they react. If others don't react, we interpret that as evidence that it is not an emergency, and we therefore don't react. We don't want to be the ones that stand out in a crowd and risk embarrassment for acting in a non-emergency situation. But here comes the problem. If each person reasons the same way, everyone draws the same conclusion. *"Since nobody is concerned, nothing is wrong. It can't be an emergency."* This is called pluralistic ignorance.

The second reason is called diffusion of responsibility. The more people there are, the less personal responsibility we feel. We often rationalize by saying, *"Someone else probably called the police."* If we all think that way, no one will help.

The more people we see around us, the less likely we are to help. We can't force people to help. If we punish people for not helping in an emergency, we will only create an incentive for people to avoid the punishment by not getting involved. This will cause them to interpret a situation as a non-emergency. .

So, how should we act if we are involved in an accident in a public place and need help? We should be specific. "You there, in the blue shirt. This is an emergency. Please help me!"

The board members of TransCorp were asked if they had any questions. They looked around at the other members. All appeared confident. "Am I the only one confused?" wondered John and kept quiet.
"Since no one disagrees, my idea seems to have everyone's support," the CEO said.
If we believe that we are the only one who doesn't understand, we may keep quiet. Speaking up may lead to embarrassment. Group pressure may contribute to our silence.

John attended a meeting where an investment proposal promising a 200% return was presented. All 30 people present at the meeting invested and all lost money.
How could 30 smart individuals be fooled? Some basic math would have told

them that the project was doomed to fail. Each individual automatically assumed that the other 29 individuals present at the meeting had evaluated the proposal. If there was something bad, someone else would have said so. "And since they invest, I invest." It turned out that no one had taken the time to read through the proposal.

"I flattered them and made them feel special. I gave them purpose and hope, and they ate out of my hand."

In a group we are easily seduced because of our need for social acceptance. The French social psychologist Gustave Le Bon said in *The Crowd,* "The masses have never thirsted after truth. They turn aside from evidence that is not to their taste, preferring to deify error, if error seduce them. Whoever can supply them with illusions is easily their master; whoever attempts to destroy their illusions is always their victim."

German philosopher Friedrich Nietzsche said: "Madness is a rare thing in individuals – but in groups, parties, peoples, and ages it is the rule." In a group, we feel anonymous, which reduces our feelings of responsibility. We can't be blamed. This can lead to overconfident, risky behavior. We may also become impulsive and destructive. Especially in situations of severe stress. Benjamin Franklin said: "A mob has heads enough but no brains."

Imitation, obedience to authority, and the fear of being different are forces that drive crowds. Groups don't encourage differences of opinion. If a member of the group disagrees, he may be seen as disloyal. Unanimity is better than independent thought. Individuals in the group reinforce each other into believing that they collectively are right. They focus on favorable consequences and ignore the downside.

Is the tendency for imitating the group so strong it can make people commit collective suicide?

In 1978, 913 followers of the cult leader Jim Jones and his People's Temple organization died during a mass suicide and murder in a place called Jonestown in Guyana, South America. Among the dead: more than 270 children. Why?

The People's Temple started in San Francisco and moved to Guyana in 1977. Armed guards surrounded the settlement in Jonestown, food was scarce, and the members of the cult were forced to work long hours and follow strict codes of behavior. Cult leader Jim Jones committed his followers one step at a time. He controlled the information, the rewards, and the punishment. In 1978, an American congressman and three others went on a fact-finding mission to Jonestown and were murdered. Jim Jones thought that he would be implicated in the killings and that the isolation of Jonestown would result in the end of the cult. So he gathered the community to participate in an act of mass suicide by drinking a fruit drink mixed with poison.

American social psychologist Robert Cialdini writes:

> His [Jones] masterstroke was the decision to move the People's Temple community from its roots in urban San Francisco to the remoteness of equatorial South America, where the conditions of uncertainty and exclusive similarity would make the principle of social proof operate for him as perhaps nowhere else.

Cialdini continues: "In a country like Guyana, there were no similar others for a Jonestown resident but the people of Jonestown itself."

Keep in mind

- The 19th Century American poet Ralph Waldo Emerson said: "It is easy in the world to live after the world's opinion; it is easy in solitude to live after our own; but the great man is he who in the midst of the crowd keeps with perfect sweetness the independence of solitude." What is popular is not always right. If you don't like what other people are doing, don't do it. Warren Buffett says: "We derive no comfort because important people, vocal people, or great numbers of people agree with us. Nor do we derive comfort if they don't."
- Disregard what others are doing and think for yourself. Ask: Does this make sense? Remember the advice from Benjamin Graham, the dean of financial analysis:

> Have the courage of your knowledge and experience. If you have formed a conclusion from the facts and if you know your judgment is sound, act on it – even though others may hesitate or differ. (You are neither right nor wrong because the crowd disagrees with you. You are right because your data and reasoning are right.)

- A lot of our children's personality traits and habits are shaped outside the home. Children learn from their friends what is acceptable or not so make sure the right "peer group" surrounds them.
- When part of a group, remember that the participants may have different goals, information and interpretations. Appoint someone in the group to question things and point out the risks and pitfalls.
- Make people responsible for their actions. Remember though, when all are accountable, no one is accountable.

24. AUTHORITY

In questions of science, the authority of a thousand is
not worth the humble reasoning of a single individual.
- Galileo Galilei (Italian astronomer and physicist, 1564-1642)

After the break-in at John's office, he said: "Of course, I believed he was a security
guard, since he had a uniform."
We tend to obey an authority, especially when we are uncertain, supervised, or
when people around us are doing the same.

"I read it in the New England Journal of Medicine, so it must be correct."
Names and reputation influence us. And symbols of power or status like titles,
rank, uniforms, or a nice suit and tie. For example, in one study 22 hospital
nurses got a telephone call from an unknown physician and were ordered to
administer an obvious overdose of an unauthorized drug. All but one nurse
obeyed.

Another example is when advertisers use famous people to endorse their
products. But being famous doesn't give people special expertise.

"I believed he was making a mistake, but I didn't dare tell him. After all, he is the
expert."
A study involving airline pilots cited conflict avoidance as a contributing factor
to crashes. Officers are reluctant to disagree with the authority of pilots. For
example, in a crash of a DC-8 in 1978, the flight engineer told the captain that
they were running out of fuel. The captain dismissed the warning and the plane
crashed.

In 1997, a female police officer in Scotland was assigned to a murder
investigation. Forensic investigators later found her thumbprint in the house
where the murder victim was found. But the woman insisted, under oath, she
had never been inside the house. Four experts from the Scottish Criminal Record
Office said that the print was hers. She was suspended and accused of perjury.
Subsequent events showed that the fingerprint was neither hers nor from a
thumb, but from a forefinger. Thus, experts make mistakes.

Authority is so powerful that we may cause pain to other people to comply.
The British novelist and scientist Charles Percy Snow said in *The Two Cultures*
and the Scientific Revolution: "When you think of the long and gloomy history of
man, you will find more hideous crimes have been committed in the name of
obedience than have ever been committed in the name of rebellion."

In one experiment at Yale University, Psychology Professor Stanley Milgram tricked people by posing as an authority and caused normal people to impose what they had every reason to believe was intense pain to other people. The participants in the experiment were instructed to shock another person if they answered a question wrong. No real pain was delivered during the experiment. But it showed that when we are given orders from what we believe to be a legitimate authority, we obey even if the result is that we end up hurting others. Milgram said in *Obedience to Authority:* "It is psychologically easy to ignore responsibility when one is only an immediate link in a chain of evil action."

Keep in mind
- Evaluate the truth of a statement on the basis of its underlying facts, without regard to the authority's personal qualities or social status.
- Anyone can call themselves an expert. Separate between real and false experts.
- An authority may have an interest in persuading you to believe something that is in their interest. Always consider reliability, credibility, sensibility and bias.

25. Overconfidence

Man suffers much because he seeks too much, is foolishly
ambitious and grotesquely overestimates his capacities.
- Isaiah Berlin (British philosopher, 1909-1997)

After making a huge mistake, John said: "I was arrogant. My past success caused me to believe I could do anything."
We tend to over-estimate our abilities and future prospects when we are knowledgeable on a subject, feel in control, or after we've been successful. As financial writer Roger Lowenstein writes in *When Genius Failed: The Rise and Fall of Long-Term Capital Management:* "There is nothing like success to blind one of the possibility of failure."

Most of us believe we are better performers, more honest and intelligent, have a happier marriage than the average person, etc. But we can't all be better than average.

We tend to overestimate our ability to predict the future. People tend to put a higher probability on desired events than on undesired events. Optimism is good but when it comes to important decisions, realism is better.

Experiments show that when we are successful (independent if by chance or not), we credit our own character or ability. Warren Buffett says:

Any investor can chalk up large returns when stocks soar, as they did in 1997. In a bull market, one must avoid the error of the preening duck that quacks boastfully after a torrential rainstorm, thinking that its paddling skills have caused it to rise in the world. A right-thinking duck would instead compare its position after the downpour to that of the other ducks on the pond.

When we fail, we blame external circumstances or bad luck. When others are successful, we tend to credit their success to luck and blame their failures on foolishness. When our investments turn into losers, we had bad luck. When they turn into winners, we are geniuses. This way we draw the wrong conclusions and don't learn from our mistakes.

When using advisers and if something turns out well, we take the credit, assigning the outcome to our skill. But if something turns out bad, we blame the advisor.

Keep in mind
- German missionary Dr. Albert Schweitzer said: "An optimist is a person who sees a green light everywhere, while the pessimist sees only the red stoplight. The truly wise person is colorblind."
- Overconfidence can cause unreal expectations and make us more vulnerable to disappointment.
- Recognize your limits. How well do you know what you don't know? Don't let your ego determine what you should do. Charles Munger says, "It is remarkable how much long-term advantage people like us have gotten by trying to be consistently not stupid, instead of trying to be very intelligent. There must be some wisdom in the folk saying: 'It's the strong swimmers who drown."
- Warren Buffett provides an example on the importance on staying within our circle of competence:

We won't do anything that we don't think we understand ourselves. Now we may be wrong. But we will never go into something because we had Arthur D. Little or Booz Allen or McKinsey come and tell us what a wonderful business it is or analyze it for us. Because if we don't know enough to make the decision ourselves, we don't want to be involved at all. Period.

- Focus on what can go wrong and the consequences. Build in some margin of safety in decisions. Know how you will handle things if they go wrong.

- When comparing records or performances, remember that successes draw far more attention than failures.

26. Hindsight
"I-knew-it-all-along."
We overestimate events that have happened as more predictable than they were. "Every problem becomes very childish when once it is explained to you," said Sherlock Holmes in Arthur Conan Doyle's *The Adventure of The Dancing Men.*

Keep in mind
- Hindsight bias causes us to simplify events and forget that there are many contributing factors. In hindsight, everything seems obvious. In reality, the future is uncertain.

27. Attribution
We tend to overestimate personal characteristics and motives when we explain behavior. We underestimate situational factors like social pressure, roles or things over which there are no control. An example is, blaming an individual rather than a poorly designed system for failure.

The Romanian dramatist Eugene Ionesco said in Claude Bonnefoy's *Conversations with Eugene Ionesco:* "The unpleasant thing about society today is nowadays is that there's a confusion between people and their function; or rather people are tempted to identify with the function they perform."

Put good people in a bad situation and their normal behavior changes. The Zimbardo prison experiment at Stanford studied the roles people play in prison situations. Students were randomly assigned to the roles of prisoners and guards for a two-week period. Tests showed that all students were normal people and physically and mentally healthy. A simulated prison environment was created to mimic real-life prison conditions, where they lived for several days. Students playing guards behaved aggressively and students playing prisoners behaved helplessly. Guards rapidly began to treat the prisoners as if they were non-humans. The prisoners began acting depressed and showed extreme stress. The more the prisoners acted like non-humans, the more the guards mistreated them. The experiment ended after six days.

In a statement prepared for the U.S. House of Representatives Committee on the Judiciary, the originator of the experiment, Philip Zimbardo, said: "We were horrified because we saw some boys treat other boys as if they were despicable animals, taking pleasure in cruelty, while other boys became servile, dehumanized robots who thought only of escape, of their own individual survival, and of their mounting hatred of the guards."

Often when we are in a role, we tend to act as others expect. Zimbardo said: "Even when they thought they didn't have to meet anyone's expectations, the role of prison guard determined their actions."

Keep in mind
- When explaining behavior consider personality, organizational, and situational factors.
- The American novelist Kurt Vonnegut said in *Mother Night:* "We are what we pretend to be: and so we must be careful what we pretend to be."

28. Misreading personalities

Character is destiny.
- Heraclitus (Greek philosopher, 535-475 BC)

Sherlock Holmes says in Arthur Conan Doyle's *The Sign of Four* that: "It is of the first importance not to allow your judgment to be biased by personal qualities. I assure you that the most winning woman I ever knew was hanged for poisoning three little children for their insurance-money, and the most repellent man of my acquaintance is a philanthropist who has spent nearly a quarter of a million upon the London poor."

We often allow one trait to color all other characteristics and therefore judge people as better or worse than they really are. Preconceived ideas about certain people, races, religions, or occupations cause us to automatically assume that an individual from a particular group has special characteristics.

Physics Professor Roger Newton observes in *The Truth of Science:* "Scientists are human...they sometimes succumb to weaknesses such as jealousy, vanity, and, on very rare instances, even dishonesty." Italian Mathematician Gian-Carlo Rota says in *Indiscrete Thoughts:* "A good mathematician is not necessarily a nice guy."

"I hired her as my assistant since she was good-looking, articulate and had a university degree. She gave a great first impression."
"When I interview someone I have already formed an impression from reading the job applications. Then I just try to find confirming evidence at the interviews."
Interviews are often of limited use to predict a potential employee's future behavior. As Carnegie-Mellon Psychology Professor Robyn Dawes notes in *Rational Choice in an Uncertain World:* "What can an interviewer learn in a half-hour to an hour that is not present in the applicant's record?"

An articulate person may be more persuasive than a reserved person, but the latter may know what he is talking about.

We sometimes use unreliable tests for evaluating people. Take the Rorschach inkblot test as an example. Can we evaluate personality by studying how an individual perceives a series of inkblots? Interviewers can read into it whatever they wish to see. This test is still used today although research has shown that it allows for countless interpretations and has no predictive value.

Why do some people seem to have an intuition for evaluating people? Maybe their life experiences gives them the ability (by asking questions and observing behavior) to look for clues to an individual's character. Experiences help, as told by Nobel Laureate Herbert A. Simon:

> If one could open the lid, so to speak, and see what was in the head of the experienced decision maker, one would find that he had…at his disposal repertoires of possible actions; that he had…checklists of things to think about before he acted; and that he had mechanisms in his mind to evoke these, and bring these to his conscious attention when the situations for decision arose.

Keep in mind

- Consider people's actual accomplishments and past behavior over a long period of time rather than first impressions. Since people leave track records in life, an individual's paper record is often predictive of future performance and behavior.
- Charles Munger says, "Good character is very efficient. If you can trust people, your systems can be way simpler. There's *enormous* efficiency in good character and dis-efficiency in bad character."
- Warren Buffett says, "I'm not saying that you can take 100 people and take a look at 'em and analyze their personalities or anything of the sort. But I think when you see the *extreme* cases – the ones that are going to cause you nothing but *trouble* and the ones that are going to bring you nothing but *joy* – well, I think you can identify those pretty well." Charles Munger adds, "Actually, I think it's pretty simple: There's integrity, intelligence, experience, and dedication. That's what human enterprises need to run well."

29. Not Understanding

We are generally the better persuaded by the reasons we discover ourselves than by those given to us by others.

- Blaise Pascal

"I'm confused. I don't understand this. Please explain."

To remember and use something, we must ask and understand "why" and "how." What is the cause? What is the purpose? What is good about this?

Carl Braun, the creator of CF Braun Engineering Company, understood the importance of telling people "why." Charles Munger tell us the story:

> His rule for all the Braun Company's communications was called the five W's - you had to tell *who* was going to do *what, where, when* and *why.* And if you wrote a letter or directive in the Braun Company telling somebody to do something, and you didn't tell him why, you could get fired. In fact, you would get fired if you did it twice.
>
> You might ask why that is so important? Well, again that's a rule of psychology. Just as you think better if you array knowledge on a bunch of models that are basically answers to the question, *why, why, why,* if you always tell people why, they'll understand it better, they'll consider it more important, and they'll be more likely to comply. Even if they don't understand your reason, they'll be more likely to comply.
>
> So there's an iron rule that just as you want to start getting worldly wisdom by asking why, why, why in communicating with other people about everything, you want to include why, why, why.

Keep in mind

- People can't be persuaded by what they don't understand. We underestimate the importance of giving people a reason. It is often easier to get people to change with a well-explained reason backed by solid evidence. Tell them so they understand why a specific action is needed, what the expected objective is, and why you think the action is right.
- Of course, this doesn't work in every case. Sometimes you don't change people's opinions by showering them with logic. In Jonathan Swift's words: "You cannot reason a person out of a position he did not reason himself into in the first place." Aristotle adds: "For argument based on knowledge implies instruction, and there are people whom one cannot instruct." Sometimes it is better to appeal to emotions than to reason since people are moved by what they feel than by what they understand.

30. COMPLIANCE

"Please would you tell me," said Alice, a little timidly, *"why your cat grins like that?"*

"It's a Cheshire Cat," said the Duchess, *"and that's why."*

- Lewis Carroll (British writer, 1832-1898, from *Through the Looking Glass*)

When people ask us for a favor we are more likely to comply if they give us a reason – even if we don't understand the reason or it is wrong. Often it isn't the reason itself that is important, but the way the reason is phrased. Sometimes the word "because," without a sensible reason, is all that matters. In one experiment a social psychologist asked people standing in line to use a copying machine if she could go in front of them, *"Excuse me, I have 5 pages. May I use the Xerox machine because I have to make some copies?"* Nearly all agreed.

31. MEMORY LIMITATIONS

Everyone complains of his memory, and no one complains of his judgment.
- Francois Duc de la Rochefoucauld

Our memory is selective. We remember certain things and distort or forget others. Every time we recall an event, we reconstruct our memories. We only remember fragments of our real past experiences. Fragments influenced by what we have learned, our experiences, beliefs, mood, expectations, stress, and biases.

Certain experiences create strong feelings and are therefore more memorable than others. Dramatic or fearful experiences or events stick in our memories. Emotional events are better remembered than unemotional ones. That is why we learn better if information is tied to a vivid story. Learning is also tied to mood. We learn better in a positive mood. That is why teaching should be performed in a way that creates powerful positive emotions among students.

Harvard Psychology Department Chairman Daniel Schacter, proposes in *The Seven Sins of Memory* that our memory's malfunctions can be divided into seven "sins."

(1) Our memory weakens and we lose memory over time. (2) We are preoccupied with distracting issues and don't focus attention on what we need to remember. (3) We search for information that we may be desperately trying to retrieve – something we know that we know – but are blocked. (4) We assign memory to the wrong source. (5) Memories are implanted as a result of leading questions, comments, or suggestions when we try to call up a past experience. (6) Our present knowledge influences how we remember our pasts. We often edit or entirely rewrite our previous experiences. (7) We recall disturbing events that we would prefer to eliminate from our minds altogether: remembering what we cannot forget, even though we wish that we could.

Individuals remember the same things differently. We remember events that never happened or assign what happened to the wrong place, time or person. Studies show that memories of emotional experiences are often different from what actually happened. We misinterpret what we saw. That is why there are variations in eyewitness accounts. Many cases show that eyewitness identification evidence has been a significant cause of wrongful convictions. Especially the accuracy of eyewitness identification of strangers.

One of the most well known English cases involved Adolph Beck, who was identified as a swindler by several eyewitnesses and was convicted in 1895, served six years and then was released. The swindles continued and Beck was once more arrested. He was awaiting sentencing when the real criminal was apprehended.

Studies show that we remember a face but wrongly remember the time and place we saw it. Leading and suggestive questions can cause misidentification, and influence by information obtained after the event. Studies show that it is easy get a witness to believe they saw something when they didn't. Merely let some time pass between their observation and the questioning. Then give them false or emotional information about the event. Social Ecology Professor Elisabeth Loftus' work has shown that people can be led to remember rather familiar and common experiences, even when they had not happened. For example, her studies show that people can believe that a childhood experience had happened when it never happened.

Studies show that jurors believe witnesses even when they are later shown to have made an incorrect identification. Eyewitnesses can be highly inaccurate but appear confident. The more confident people are when they appear as witnesses, the more believable the jurors will find them. The more detailed their memory of a situation is, the more the jurors trust them. Testimonial evidence is vivid and therefore more believable.

Is a child witness always to be trusted in a courtroom?
Can a psychologist who interviews a troubled child falsely implant the idea that a bad event happened to them?

Childhood memories are unreliable and influenced by fantasies and suggestions. Experiments have shown how normal children behave in response to suggestions. Implanted false stories can have a huge impact. Children can actually believe an event that never happened or produce false narratives for the event. Over time, their stories may become elaborate and filled with vivid details, making them more believable.

Keep in mind
• Keep records of important events.

32. "Man With a Hammer" Tendency

*If the only tool you have is a hammer, you tend
to approach every problem as if it were a nail.*
- Mark Twain

We solve problems using the field we know best. The more we know, or think we know, about a subject, the less willing we are to use other ideas. And the more useful a given idea is – whether or not it's appropriate to the problem at hand – the more overconfident we are about its usefulness.

Charles Munger says:

What happens is that people are trained in economics or engineering or marketing or investment management or something else. So they learn a few models and then they run around trying to solve all their problems with a limited number of models. And they don't really understand how their models intermix with other people's models.

Experts love their favorite tools. They extrapolate their ideas from one field to all other fields. They define problems in ways that fit their tools rather than ways that agree with the underlying problem. For example, a surgeon may use surgery to handle a health problem that could be cured by a less invasive procedure. Give someone a tool and they'll want to use it, and even overuse it, whether it's warranted or not.

Keep in mind
- Since problems don't follow territorial boundaries, you must compensate for the bias of one idea by using important ideas from other disciplines.
- "Better to be roughly right than precisely wrong," said J.M. Keynes.
- Ask people to explain why they are right.

33. Do-nothing Syndrome

Nothing will ever be attempted if all possible objections must first be overcome.
- Samuel Johnson

Sometimes we don't act when we know we should. We ignore Warren Buffett's Noah principle: "Predicting rain doesn't count; building arks does."

Keep in mind
- Once we know what to do, we should do it. The 19th Century British biologist

Thomas Henry Huxley said: "Perhaps the most valuable result of all education is the ability to make yourself do the thing you have to do when it ought to be done whether you like it or not. It is the first lesson that ought to be learned and however early a person's training begins, it is probably the last lesson a person learns thoroughly."

34. Do-something Syndrome

I have often said that the sole cause of man's unhappiness is
that he does not know how to sit quietly in his room.
- Blaise Pascal

When John asked why the company continued making acquisitions when so many of them turned sour, the CEO replied: "All my colleagues do deals like this. Plus how can I keep my job and all my perks if I don't keep busy?"

Blaise Pascal said: "Man finds nothing so intolerable as to be in a state of complete rest, without passions, without occupation, without diversion, without effort." We sometimes act because we can't sit still. We feel bored, impatient, threatened or pressured or we simply desire excitement and stimulation. We act without a sensible reason.

Warren Buffett tells why CEOs like acquisitions:

The sad fact is that most major acquisitions display an egregious imbalance: They are a bonanza for the shareholders of the acquiree; they increase the income and status of the acquirer's management; and they are a honey pot for the investment bankers and other professionals on both sides…often the CEO asks a strategic planning staff, consultants or investment bankers whether an acquisition or two might make sense. That's like asking your interior decorator whether you need a $50,000 rug.

The acquisition problem is often compounded by a biological bias: Many CEO's attain their positions in part because they possess an abundance of animal spirits and ego. If an executive is heavily endowed with these qualities - which, it should be acknowledged, sometimes have their advantages - they won't disappear when he reaches the top. When such a CEO is encouraged by his advisors to make deals, he responds much as would a teenage boy who is encouraged by his father to have a normal sex life. It's not a push he needs.

Warren Buffett also provides an example from the insurance world on why it is more important to do what is right than to simply do something:

We hear a great many insurance managers talk about being willing to reduce volume in order to underwrite profitably, but we find that very few actually do so. Phil Liesche [manager National Indemnity Company's insurance operation] is an exception: if business makes sense, he writes it; if it doesn't, he rejects it. It is our policy not to lay off people because of the large fluctuations in work load produced by such voluntary volume changes. We would rather have some slack in the organization from time to time than keep everyone terribly busy writing business on which we are going to lose money.

Continuous reorganization may be dangerous. The Roman satirist Petronius Arbiter said in the 1st Century: "We trained hard, but it seemed that every time we were beginning to form into teams we would be reorganized. I was to learn later in life that we tend to meet any new situation by reorganizing, and what a wonderful method it can be for creating the illusion of progress while producing confusion, inefficiency, and demoralization."

Keep in mind
- The 19th Century American writer Henry David Thoreau said: "It is not enough to be busy; so are the ants. The question is: What are we busy about?" Don't confuse activity with results. There is no reason to do a good job with something you shouldn't do in the first place.
- Charles Munger says, "We've got great flexibility and a certain discipline in terms of not doing some foolish thing just to be active – discipline in avoiding just doing any damn thing just because you can't stand inactivity."
- What do you want to accomplish? As Warren Buffett says, "There's no use running if you're on the wrong road."

35. Say-something Syndrome
Wise men talk because they have something to
say; fools, because they have to say something.
- Plato

People tend to speak even if they have nothing to contribute. Mark Twain wrote: "If you have nothing to say, say nothing."

Why do we always need to give an answer? Isn't it better to say, "I don't know?" Greek philosopher Socrates said that awareness of ignorance is the beginning of wisdom.

Keep in mind
- Wisdom is a two-headed beast. Roman dramatist Publilius Syrus wrote in 1st Century BC: "I have often regretted my speech, never my silence."
- The less we speak, the more we hear.
- Benjamin Franklin said: "He that would live in peace and at ease, must not speak all he knows, nor judge all he sees."

36. Emotions

The heart has its reasons of which reason itself knows nothing.
- Blaise Pascal

Emotions come before reason. Often when we make a decision our emotions take over. We hear bad news first. The more emotionally aroused we are, the more likely we will make hasty judgments.

Keep in mind
- Understand your emotions and their influence on your behavior. Ask: Is there a rational reason behind my action?
- Remember the proverb: "A wise man controls his temper. He knows that anger causes mistakes."

37. Stress

You can't change the cards life has dealt you,
but you can determine the way you'll play them.
- Ty Boyd (American motivational speaker)

Too much information, lack of predictability or control, too many choices, social isolation, job status, crisis, catastrophes, fear, etc. cause stress. The less control we perceive we have over our lives, the easier we fall victim to stress. The more stress we experience, the more we tend to make decisions that are short-term.

Everything our brain interprets as a threat influences our biology. Our ancestors didn't suffer less stress than we did. But their stress was different. They met dangers that demanded fast physical reactions. Our stress is more social and psychological in nature.

The fear of losing both her job and social position caused Mary to suffer constant headaches.
Stress affects concentration and causes short-term memory loss. Long-term stress

exposure upsets the brain's chemical balance. Stress may cause high blood pressure, heart disease, diabetes, back and stomach problems, headache, and depression. Studies show that when we feel stress the concentration of cortisol rises in the bloodstream. One effect of cortisol is to suppress the workings of our immune system. This makes us more vulnerable to diseases. Stress also counteracts the production of insulin (the hormone that processes blood sugar), causing the process of repair to slow down. Studies show that emotional stress creates longer recovery times in our bodies and may be more harmful to our health than non-emotional stress events like physical exercise.

"I have lost control over the situation."
The more we believe we are in control, the less vulnerable we are to the negative effects of stress. Studies show that people who perceive themselves to be in control over a stressful situation experience less stress on their hearts and circulatory system.

The status of our job matters. The Whitehall study involving 17,000 civil servants showed that people with low perceived control over the work environment or people low in the organizational structure have an increased risk of cardiovascular disease. Our cortisol levels rise in response to the degree other people order us about. As we climb the social hierarchy health status improves. In *Genome*, science writer Dr. Matt Ridley comments on the Whitehall study:

> The status of a person's job was more able to predict their likelihood of a heart attack than obesity, smoking or high blood pressure. Somebody in a low-grade job, such as a janitor, was nearly four times as likely to have a heart attack as a permanent secretary at the top of the heap…The monkeys hold the clue. The lower they are in the pecking order, the less control they have over their lives.

In another study researchers tried to find out the differences between business executives who became sick from exposure to high stress and those who didn't. They found that executives who stayed healthy had a sense of commitment to work and families, felt in control, and had a positive attitude toward challenges. They saw challenges as part of life and an opportunity for growth rather than as a threat.

Warren Buffett says, "I have no stress whatsoever – zero. I get to do what I love to do very day. I'm surrounded by people that are terrific." He continues, "All the businesses I run don't take 5% of my time. We don't have regular staff meetings and the like. If you've got good businesses and the right managers, you don't need that sort of thing – and if you don't, they don't help."

Keep in mind

- Stress is neither good nor bad in itself. It depends on the situation and our interpretation. Stress can be controlled by our attitudes. The Austrian physician Dr. Hans Selye says in *Stress without Distress* that it is not stress that harms us but distress. We need challenges. He continues, "Without stress, there would be no life…Complete freedom from stress is death."
- The 1st Century philosopher Epictetus said: "Happiness and freedom begin with a clear understanding of one principle: Some things are within our control, and some things are not. It is only after you have faced up to this fundamental rule and learned to distinguish between what you can and can't control that inner tranquility and outer effectiveness become possible."
- If a problem can be solved, there is no need to worry. The thing to do is to correct it. If a situation can't be solved, we shouldn't worry about that either. We can't do anything about it. Mark Twain says: "I've suffered a great many catastrophes in my life. Most of them never happened." Sometimes keeping ourselves busy with something else may cause us to stop worrying.

38. Pain, Chemicals and Diseases

Pain upsets and destroys the nature of the person who feels it.
- Aristotle

"I can't think clearly because I am drunk. I don't care about the consequences if I act violent."

We become confused when we are in pain, under the influence of chemicals or have a disease. Physical and mental pain may cause fear, anger and stress. Chemical changes magnify the pain and can cause depression.

Drugs, stimulants (like nicotine, alcohol or coffee), and depressants distort our senses.

39. Multiple Tendencies

When you get two or three of these psychological principles operating together, then you really get irrationality on a tremendous scale.
- Charles Munger

Charles Munger gives an illuminating example on the issue of stealing:

A very significant fraction of the people in the world will steal if (A) it's very easy to do and, (B) there's practically no chance of being caught. And once they *start* stealing, the *consistency* principle will soon combine with operant conditioning to make stealing *habitual.* So if you run a business where it's easy to steal because of your methods, you're working a great moral injury on the people who work for you…

It's *very, very* important to create human systems that are hard to cheat. Otherwise you're ruining your civilization because these big incentives will create incentive-caused bias and people will rationalize that bad behavior is OK.

Then, if somebody else does it, now you've got at least *two* psychological principles: incentive-caused bias plus social proof. Not only that, but you get *Serpico* effects: If *enough* people are profiting in a general social climate of doing wrong, then they'll turn on you and become dangerous *enemies* if you try and blow the whistle.

John's acquisition experience caused him stress and cost TransCorp money.
John said, "I was dissatisfied having done so little for TransCorp last year. All of the other guys made acquisitions. If I could find a good acquisition, maybe I could move up the ranks. I needed a promotion.

I found a good-looking business, and saw the possibility of making TransCorp a lot of money. The CEO of the business was a nice guy and we always met in their relaxing conference room. The asking price was low in relation to past profits. I had experts telling me what a great company it was. I was presented entertaining information on new products. The investment banker did me a favor by bringing the deal and I wanted to reciprocate.

The banker told me that other people I admire would jump at the opportunity. I made a commitment to the financiers and told TransCorp's CEO about the deal. I committed myself publicly and felt a need to follow-through. I concentrated my search on evidence that confirmed the greatness of the deal. I denied reality and thought nothing could happen. I didn't say what I thought for fear of social disapproval. The CEO of the company I wanted to acquire continuously gave me good reasons to pursue the deal. The more effort I put into the deal, the more I felt I had to do it. I finally signed the papers. When reality kicked in and the deal turned sour, I was in deep trouble. And so was TransCorp."

Keep in mind
- Follow these three pieces of advice from Charles Munger:

(1) I don't want you to think we have any way of learning or behaving so you won't make a lot of mistakes. I'm just saying that you can learn to make *fewer* mistakes than other people – and how to fix your mistakes *faster* when you *do* make them. But there's no *way* that you can live an adequate life without [making] many

mistakes. In fact, one trick in life is to get so you can *handle* mistakes. Failure to handle psychological denial is a common way for people to go broke: You've made an enormous commitment to something. You've poured effort and money in. And the more you put in, the more that the whole consistency principle makes you think, "Now it *has* to work. If I put in just a *little* more, *then* it'll work."

And deprival super-reaction syndrome also comes in: You're going to lose the whole thing if you don't put in a little more. People go *broke* that way - because they can't stop, rethink and say, "I can afford to write this one off and live to fight again. I don't have to pursue this thing as an obsession - in a way that will break me." Part of what you must learn is how to handle mistakes and new facts that change the odds. Life, in part, is like a poker game, wherein you have to learn to quit sometimes when holding a much-loved hand.

(2) I've gotten so that I now use a kind of two-track analysis. First, what are the factors that really govern the *interests* involved, rationally considered? And second, what are the subconscious influences where the brain at a *subconscious* level is automatically doing these things - which by and large are useful, but which often misfunction. One approach is rationality - the way you'd work out a bridge problem: by evaluating the real interests, the real probabilities and so forth. And the other is to evaluate the psychological factors that cause subconscious conclusions - many of which are wrong.

(3) Take all the main models from psychology and use them as a *checklist* in reviewing outcomes in complex systems. No pilot takes off without going through his checklist: A, B, C, D… And no bridge player who needs two extra tricks plays a hand without going down his checklist and figuring out how to do it…And, to repeat for emphasis, you have to pay special attention to combinatorial effects that create lollapalooza consequences.

Don't our feelings, instincts or our intuition help us avoid misjudgments?
Natural selection equipped us with traits adapted for the environment in which humans spent most of their time. Feelings like love, compassion, anger, fear, jealousy, and embarrassment can be explained biologically. They exist for a reason – to help us survive and reproduce. Somerset Maugham said: "Love is only a dirty trick played on us to achieve a continuation of the species." Why does sex feel good? Because it makes us reproduce. If sex felt painful, we wouldn't be here today. Our emotions are also part of the human whole. Our "good" emotions wouldn't be good without our "bad" emotions.

Feelings and instincts helped our ancestors navigate in the world. The ancestral environment rewarded actions before thought, emotion before reason. Fast intuitions and quick reactions are vital responses for organisms. Spending time pondering may be dangerous.

The problem is that feelings can be twisted. Intuition is inconsistent and feelings can sometimes get out of control. Especially when we feel uncertain, distracted or stressed.

Remember Chinese philosopher Lao-Tsu (604-531 BC): "He who knows men is clever; He who knows himself has insight; He who conquers men has force; He who conquers himself is truly strong."

In Part Three we will study other reasons why we make misjudgments. These are partly rooted in our psychological make-up; our tendency to use crude rules of thumb, and make hasty judgments and other psychological tendencies discussed in Part Two. They also have their roots in a lack of considering some basic ideas from physics and mathematics.

Charles Munger gives us some introductory remarks on the value of knowing the methods of physics:

> One of the things that influenced me greatly was studying physics…If I were running the world, people who are qualified to do physics would not be allowed to elect out of taking it. I think that even people who aren't [expecting to] go *near* physics and engineering [in their planned profession] learn a thinking system in physics that is not learned so well anywhere else. Physics was a total eye-opener.
>
> The tradition of always looking for the answer in the most fundamental way available – that is a great tradition and it saves a lot of time in this world. And, of course, the problems are *hard* enough that you have to learn to have what some people call *assiduity*. Well, I've always liked that word – because to me it means that you sit down on your ass until you've done it.

PART THREE

THE PHYSICS AND MATHEMATICS OF MISJUDGMENTS

There will come a time when mathematical ignorance, like public smoking, will become socially unacceptable.
- Jerry King (Professor of Mathematics, from *The Art of Mathematics*)

This part illustrates reasons for misjudgments and mistakes that can be reduced by considering some basic ideas and principles from physics and mathematics. The big ideas are explained using examples from business, investing, law, medicine, etc. As in Part Two, we begin with a list of the causes of misjudgments and mistakes. Each item on the list will be explained over the next chapters.

1. Systems thinking
- Failing to consider that actions have both intended and unintended consequences. Also underestimating consequences and overweighing motives.
- Failing to consider the whole system in which actions and reactions take place, the important factors that make up the system, their relationships and effects of changes on system outcome.
- Failing to consider the likely reactions of others – what is best to do may depend on what others do.
- Failing to consider the implications of winning a bid – overestimating value and paying too much.
- Overestimating predictive ability or using unknowable factors in making predictions.

2. Scale and limits
- Failing to consider that changes in size or time influence function and behavior.
- Failing to consider breakpoints, critical points or limits.
- Failing to consider constraints – that a systems performance is constrained by its weakest link.

3. Causes
- Not understanding what causes desired results.
- Believing cause resembles its effect – that a big effect must have a big or complicated cause.
- Underestimating the influence of randomness in bad or good outcomes.
- Mistaking an effect for its cause. Includes failing to consider that many effects may originate from one common cause.
- Attributing outcome to a single cause when there are multiple causes.
- Mistaking correlation or association for cause.
- Identifying the wrong cause because it seems the obvious one based on a single observed effect. Includes failing to consider information or evidence that is missing.
- Failing to consider that an outcome may be consistent with alternative explanations.

- Not comparing the difference in conditions, behavior and factors between negative and positive outcomes in similar situations when explaining an outcome.

4. Numbers and their meaning
- Looking at isolated numbers – failing to consider relationships and magnitudes. Includes not using basic math to count and quantify. Also not differentiating between relative and absolute risk.
- Underestimating the effect of exponential growth.
- Underestimating the time value of money.

5. Probabilities and number of possible outcomes
- Underestimating risk exposure in situations where relative frequency (or comparable data) and/or magnitude of consequences is unknown or changing over time.
- Underestimating the number of possible outcomes for unwanted events. Includes underestimating the probability and severity of rare or extreme events. Also risk distortion by distant catastrophic scenarios.
- Overestimating the probability of low frequency events. Especially when consequences seem vividly favorable or frightening.
- Failing to consider both probabilities and consequences (expected value).
- Underestimating risk by using the laws of probability for short sequences.
- Believing events where chance plays a role are self-correcting – that previous outcomes of independent events have predictive value in determining future outcomes.
- Believing one can control the outcome of events where chance is involved.
- Judging financial decisions by evaluating gains and losses instead of final state of wealth and utility.
- Failing to consider the consequences of being wrong.

6. Scenarios
- Overestimating the probability of scenarios where all of a series of steps must be achieved for a wanted outcome. Also underestimating opportunities for failure and what normally happens in similar situations.
- Underestimating the probability of systems failure – scenarios composed of many parts where system failure can happen one way or another. Includes failing to consider that time horizon changes probabilities.
- Not adding a factor of safety for known and unknown risks. Size of factor

depends on the consequences of failure, how well the risks are understood, systems characteristics and degree of control.

7. Coincidences and miracles
- Underestimating that surprises and improbable events happen, somewhere, sometime, to someone, if they have enough opportunities (or time) to happen.
- Looking for meaning, searching for causes and making up patterns for chance events, especially events that have emotional implications.
- Failing to consider cases involving the absence of a cause or effect.

8. Reliability of case evidence
- Overweighing individual case evidence and under-weighing the prior probability (that a proposition is true before the new evidence is considered) considering for example, base rates or evidence from many similar cases. Includes failing to consider the probability of a random match, and the probability of a false positive and false negative. Also failing to consider a relevant comparison population that bears the characteristic we are seeking.

9. Misrepresentative evidence
- Failing to consider changes in context or conditions when using past evidence to predict likely future outcomes. Includes not searching for explanations to why past outcome happened, what is required to make past record continue, and what forces can change it.
- Overestimating evidence from a single case or small or unrepresentative samples.
- Underestimating the influence of chance in performance (success and failure).
- Only seeing positive outcomes – paying little or no attention to negative outcomes and prior probabilities.
- Failing to consider variability of outcomes.
- Failing to consider regression – in any series of events where chance is involved unique outcomes tends to regress back to the average outcome.

One

Systems thinking

Wanted and unwanted consequences

Everything is connected to everything else and we can never do merely one thing.
- Garrett Hardin (from *The Ostrich Factor*)

In one of Aesop's fables the following story is told:

A poor widow living alone in the country kept a faithful hen. Each morning the hen laid a big, brown egg for the woman's breakfast. One day the widow thought to herself: "Now if I were to double my hen's allowance of barley, she would lay me two eggs a day instead of one." So she started feeding her biddy a double measure of grain, and soon the hen began to grow fat and sleek and lazy. It wasn't long before she stopped laying altogether.

Every action has consequences. Both intended and unintended. Often we fail to consider what other things are likely to happen as a result of some action. Politics, medicine, welfare programs, technology, military actions and laws generate unexpected consequences. Whatever we do, there are consequences. They might not be what we expect. In one study, traffic engineers found that adding new routes (for example, adding a third, more direct road) could make traffic go slower. During merging, cars drive closer to each other and therefore slow down.

By solving one problem, we generate another one and sometimes create an even worse one.

There was a problem with mice on campus. The solution for exterminating the mice was to pay students $1 for every dead mouse they delivered. It worked! Until the students began breeding the mice in order to make more money.
Actions have consequences and consequences have further effects. Charles Munger gives an example regarding Medicare:

They had all these actuarial studies that showed the cost would be X. And the cost turned out to be more than 10X…They didn't factor in the fact that effects have effects…they didn't think through the *incentive* effects of the way they were changing the rules. They created a system wherein they were reimbursing both doctors and hospitals, in effect, on a cost plus percentage of cost basis. The minute they did that, the hospitals and doctors found wonderful ways to talk the patients into buying all kinds of care that got reimbursed…good for the hospital and good for the doctor, but bad for the patient and bad for the taxpayers.

Should good intentions eliminate bad consequences? No, intentions by definition apply only to intended consequences. But as Samuel Johnson said: "The road to hell is paved with good intentions." Isn't it more important to find out if the consequences are good rather than if the reasons are good? Garrett Hardin says in *Living Within Limits,* "Assertions made by others do not help because how can I know someone is telling the truth? Determinations of consequences don't have this shortcoming since consequences lie outside the brain of the actor."

Ask: What are we trying to improve? What can reasonably be expected to happen? Are the net effects positive or negative?

Good thinking is better than good intentions. In the 18th Century, Pierre S. du Pont, a deputy to the French National Assembly said: "Bad logicians have committed more involuntary crimes than bad men have done intentionally."

But even good thinking can have undesired consequences. Charles Munger gives an example:

An excess of what seems like professionalism will often wind up hurting you horribly precisely because those careful procedures themselves often lead to overconfidence in their outcome… Long Term Capital Management, the well-known hedge fund recently collapsed as a result of its principals' overconfidence in their highly leveraged methods. And it collapsed despite those principals having IQ's that must have averaged 160 or more…Smart, hard-working people aren't exempt from professional disasters resulting from overconfidence. Often they just go aground in the more difficult voyages on which they choose to embark based on self appraisals in which they conclude that they have superior talents and methods. It is, of course, irritating that extra care in thinking isn't all good – that it also introduces extra error. But *most* good things have undesired "side effects." And thinking is no exception.

One way to reduce unintended consequences is to stop focusing on isolated factors and instead consider how our actions affect the whole system.

The whole system

Sales volume dropped and John suggested: "Why don't we reduce price? It's a sure-fire way to win back customers and boost sales. We make up on volume what we lose on price and as a result we increase our market share. Profits will surely rise."

"Where did we go wrong? We lost market share. Profits and stock price declined."

Why didn't TransCorp's profit increase? They forgot to think about all the factors that influenced the outcome. They didn't anticipate the consequences of cutting prices. They didn't consider other factors and conditions that influenced the value of the business. Some were changed as a consequence of TransCorp's decision to reduce prices in anticipation of higher volumes. Volume increases affect costs and behavior and need for investments in operating assets. There may also have been production problems due to technical constraints or the price decrease wasn't enough to make customers switch from the competition.

How a system behaves is a function of all the factors (human and non-human) that make up and influence the system.

A system is a collection of parts that work together to function as a whole. Take a business as an example. It is a collection of parts but works as a complete system. There are variables like suppliers, employees, customers, demand, competition, etc. There are activities like purchasing, manufacturing, warehousing, logistics, and distribution. There are technological systems and equipment needed to conduct the business. All these parts work together.

TransCorp fired 200 people to cut costs.
We optimize one component at a time instead of optimizing the whole (what we finally want to accomplish). TransCorp forgot to consider how a change influences the whole system. Cost cutting doesn't automatically translate into higher value. TransCorp's decision to fire people caused manufacturing and delivery problems, which in turn caused delays in customer production. This created a loss of customers and reputation. The end result was lower profits.

Why reduce prices? What is the purpose? What does TransCorp ultimately want to achieve?

Systems adjust in response to feedback. Take the stock market as an example of a positive feedback. The stock market falls causing a sell-off. This creates a ripple effect of further sell-off and price declines. The opposite occurs in a stock market bubble.

Try to optimize the whole and not a system's individual parts. Think through what other variables may change when we alter a factor in a system. Trace out the short and long-term consequences in numbers and effects of a proposed action to see if the net result agrees with our ultimate goal.

Ask: What key factors influence the system and how do these factors interact to produce the outcome? What other things may change as a consequence of some action? What likely consequences (wanted and unwanted) will the proposed action have on the system, considering all the relevant factors that influence or are part of the system? Will the net result be what we want? A manager can for example ask: How is the value of the business likely to change considering important factors that influence business value?

Considering the whole includes anticipating the reactions of others.

The reaction of others

Game theory is a study of conflict between thoughtful
and potential deceitful opponents.
- William Poundstone (from *Prisoner's Dilemma*)

TransCorp cut the price and lost volume.
What happened? TransCorp's competitors matched the price cut. Competitors can match price cuts or even go below it to regain, keep or increase market share.

When thinking through consequences, consider what other people are likely to do. Since our interests may conflict with others, the final outcome of our decision often depends on what others will do. What other people do may depend on what they think we will do, their available choices, interests, and how they are thinking – including their misjudgments. As we have learned, humans don't always act rationally.

Game theory deals with how individuals or groups of people interact with one another to achieve their goals. We saw an example of game theory in Part One (prisoner's dilemma). It also applies to negotiations. Factors that decide the final outcome of a negotiation are: 1) the number of participants, 2) if we meet the participants again in the future, 3) the time lapse in between, 4) the degree of anonymity and communication, and 5) our relative position of strength which includes our other options, back-up alternatives and need to reach an agreement.

The winner's curse

I sent the club a wire stating, "Please accept my resignation.
I don't care to belong to any club that will have me as a member."
- Groucho Marx

Several mining firms including MineCorp, one of TransCorps subsidiaries, are bidding on the right to mine silver.

No firm knows for certain how much silver there is and hence what the true value is. They each hire an expert to make an educated guess. By definition, these expert guesses will range from too low to too high. Some firm's expert will probably be close. But they won't win. The winning firm was MineCorp since their expert had the most optimistic estimate of the value (the seller accepts the highest bid). But there was less silver in the mine than their expert guessed and less value than what MineCorp paid for the rights. This means that the winning bidder was cursed since the bid was higher than the value. Later it was shown that MineCorp also underestimated its costs of production.

Three Atlantic Richfield engineers, Capen, Clapp and Campbell, introduced the idea behind the Winner's Curse when they did a study of companies bidding for oil fields. Their basic idea was (*Journal of Petroleum Technology,* June 1971), that "a lease winner tends to be the bidder who most overestimates reserve potential."

Winning is an informative event, telling us whose estimate was most optimistic. When we place a bid on a house, company, project, or negotiate to buy something, we don't realize what is implied by an acceptance of our offer. That we may have overestimated its value and therefore paid too much.

Research shows that the more bidders there are competing for a limited object, each having the same information, and the more uncertain its value is, the more likely we are to overpay. Instead, if our objective is to create value, the more bidders there are, the more conservative our bidding should be. This also implies that the less information we have compared to other bidders or the more uncertain we are about the underlying value, the lower we should bid. If we participate in auctions, we must ascertain the true value of what's being sold or its value to us.

When we negotiate with one party and want an acceptance for an offer, the other party may have an informational advantage. The other party is most likely to accept our offer when it is least favorable to us, especially if it is a one-time relationship or if the other party is anonymous.

Consider the seller's perspective. Ask: Why are they selling? How would I reason if I think it through from the viewpoint of the other person? Why would I make a better decision than someone who has all the information?

Predictions

Do not, therefore, expect any prophecy from me: had I known what one will discover tomorrow, I would have published it long ago, to secure priority.
- Henri Poincaré (French mathematician and scientist, 1854-1912)

When asked about corporate responsibility for social problems, Charles Munger answered:

> I'm all for fixing social problems. I'm all for being generous to the less fortunate. And I'm all for doing things where, based on a slight preponderance of the evidence, you *guess* that it's likely to do more good than harm…
>
> What I'm *against* is being very confident and feeling that you know, for sure, that your particular intervention will do more good than harm given that you're dealing with highly complex systems wherein everything is interacting with everything *else*.

Heraclitus wrote: "Nothing endures but change." The world is too complicated to predict all the effects of some action. Maybe a business can predict scenarios like reduction in demand and intensified competition, but some events, their timing, magnitude or consequence, are impossible to anticipate.

Mark Twain said: "The art of prophecy is very difficult, especially with respect to the future." Unintended consequences occur when we don't (or can't) foresee or understand how a system works, what key variables are involved, their attributes, how they influence one another and their impact. Even if we know the key variables, they may be impossible to estimate. It may also be impossible to understand how parts interact to produce the whole. This makes it hard to make predictions.

The more parts involved and the more they interact, the more complicated the system is (the more can happen), and the harder it is to determine consequences of individual actions.

According to Dr. Gerald Edelman, the brain is an example of a complex system:

> A complex system is one in which smaller parts form a heterogeneous set of components which are more or less independent. But as these parts connect with each other in larger and larger aggregates, their functions tend to become integrated, yielding new functions that depend on such high order integration. This is, in fact, just what happens in the brain.

As the number of variables grow, the number of possible interactions grow even faster. Assume that two subsystems, A and B, cause the behavior of a system. Each subsystem consists of 5 parts. If we only consider two-way interactions among parts, there are 10 interactions between A parts, 10 between B parts, and 25 interactions between A and B parts. This means that the behavior of the system is composed of 55 determinants (5A parts + 5B parts + 10 interactions between A parts + 10 interactions between B parts + 25 interactions between A and B parts).

107

18% (10 of 55) of all determinants derive from individual effects of parts in A and B while about 82% (45 of 55) derive from interactions. Now imagine a system where A and B each consists of 100 parts. There are now 20,100 determinants (100+100+4,950+4,950+10,000) and 19,900 interactions meaning that 99% (19,900 of 20,100) of system determinants derive from interactions.

We often take too little notice of how variables interact. Take the economy as an example. There are many factors to consider. They include interest rates, currency exchange rates, balance of trade figures, unemployment rates, consumer confidence, political factors, the stock market, business cycles, biases, etc. These factors are interconnected, and it is hard to tell which is most important. For example, there are many factors that influence interest rates alone. Sometimes we can predict a range of future interest rates or under which conditions interest rates will go up or down in the short term.

Charles Munger says: "We try and predict what individual investments will swim well in relation to the tide. And then we tend to accept the effects of the tide as those effects fall."

"If someone could forecast the stock market, why are they selling advice through $100 newsletters?"
Fidelity's former manager Peter Lynch said in *One Up on Wall Street:* "There are 60,000 economists in the U.S., many of them employed full-time trying to forecast recessions and interest rates, and if they could do it successfully twice in a row, they'd all be millionaires by now… As far as I know, most of them are still gainfully employed, which ought to tell us something."

Don't believe people that say they can forecast unforeseeable variables. Nobody can forecast interest or currency rates, the GDP, the stock market, etc. And massive amounts of information, advanced computers or fancy mathematical formulas don't help. Warren Buffett says that we tend to put too much comfort in computer models and the precision they project: "We believe the precision they project is a chimera. In fact, such models can lull decision-makers into a false sense of security and thereby increase their chances of making a really huge mistake."

Financial writer Roger Lowenstein writes in *When Genius Failed:* "The next time a Merton [Robert Merton, 1997 Nobel laureate for developing mathematical risk-management formulas] proposes an elegant model to manage risks and foretell odds, the next time a computer with a perfect memory of the past is said to quantify risks in the future, investors should run – and quickly – the other way."

Just because an event has never happened before, doesn't mean it can't happen in the future. Take catastrophic events as an example. Who could have predicted the September 11, 2001 terrorist attack on the World Trade Center?

Cambridge Historian Professor Richard Evans wrote in *In Defence of History:* "Time and again, history has proved a very bad predictor of future events. This is because history never repeats itself; nothing in human society…ever happens twice under exactly the same conditions or in exactly the same way."

Sometimes we can guess that certain things are bound to happen, but we can't predict when they will happen.

Will it rain two weeks from now?
Some things are possible to predict long-term but impossible to predict short-term. Others are possible to predict short-term but impossible to predict long-term. Small changes make a big difference over time. Long-term weather forecasts are an example. There are many factors that determine the weather. Factors that can't be reliably measured ahead of time. Small changes in the temperature and pressure over the ocean can lead to large variations in the future development of storm systems. The weather predictions become more inexact as time goes on. The difficulty lies in the fact that one single event may make a big difference over time. So even if we know all the principles behind the weather and what governs the atmosphere, we still can't predict if it is going to rain beyond a week or so.

Two

SCALE AND LIMITS

Scale of size and time

Changes in size or time influence function and behavior. If something of a certain size is made bigger or smaller, it may not work the same way. For example, how does weight, strength and surface area change when we change size?

If we double the length of a similarly shaped object, surface area increases 4 times and volume 8 times. Surface area increases at the square of length and volume at the cube of length (to get areas we multiply two lengths together, and to get volumes we multiply three lengths).

Volume always grows faster than surface area as we increase size, independent of an object's shape. This places limitations on the size of things.

Does it make any difference in melting time if we use one ice cube (volume 8) or 8 smaller ones (total volume 8)?

If we increase size, volume grows faster than surface area. What does this mean? The relationship between surface area and volume decreases when we increase the size. It also means that the relationship increases when we decrease the size. Take ice cubes as an example. Let's assume the larger one has a side length of 2 and the smaller ones a side length of 1.

	Large ice cube	Side length
Small ice cube	1	2
Cross-section surface area (side length)^2	1	4
Total surface area (6 sides)	6	24
Volume (side length)^3	1	8 (weight)
Ratio of total surface area to volume	6	3

As we can see, the large ice cube has less surface area per unit volume than 8 small ice cubes. Total surface area is the total area of all 6 surfaces of the ice cube. This means that 8 ice cubes have a surface area of 48 (8 x 6) versus 24 for the larger ice cube. This also means that 8 small ice cubes melt faster than one large ice cube, since the amount of heat an ice cube can absorb depend on its surface area (the melting process occurs at the surface). Whenever we make objects smaller, we get more surface area per unit volume. For example, since iron rusts when exposed to air and rusting occur at the surface, a steel knife rusts more slowly than steel wool.

Why did the dinosaurs have such small heads in relation to their bodies?
Volume defines load and area load-bearing ability. The strength of a muscle or a bone is a function of cross-section area. Strength does not increase at the same rate as weight and volume. When we increase size, weight increase faster than strength. Scale up an organism and sooner or later it will be too weak to support its own weight. Double the size of a small dinosaur – twice as long, wide and high – and it weighs 8 times as much as before. We now need a neck that is 8 times stronger than before since it must hold 8 times the weight. But since the strength of the neck is proportional to its cross-section area, the neck is only 4 times stronger. There comes a point where the neck breaks.

What about the giants we see in the movies?
Assume we make a human 10 times larger than normal. This means he is now 10 times longer, 10 times wider, and 10 times higher. He now weighs 1,000 times more but he is only 100 times stronger (as muscular strength is proportional to the cross section area of a muscle). Since the load-bearing capacity of bones scales in the same manner his bones would be subject to ten times more stress than normal. He needs thicker bones to support more weight. Otherwise his legs will crush. This is why elephants have such thick stumpy legs to support their weight. The giant has 1,000 times more meat on the body but only 100 times the skin to hold it together meaning twice the pressure on its skin (since pressure is proportional to area). This also means that his skin surface area is too small to remove the heat emitted from his huge body. He would suffer from overheating since the amount of heat his body produces is proportional to the cube of his length (1,000), while the amount of heat he dissipates through the skin is proportional to the square of his length (100).

The British biologist Sir D'Arcy Wentworth Thompson said in 1917 *On Growth and Form:* "Everywhere nature works true to scale, and everything has its proper size accordingly. Men and trees, birds and fishes, stars and star-systems, have their appropriate dimensions, and their more or less narrow range of absolute magnitudes."

The concept of scale applies not only to ice cubes and dinosaurs, but to most things. Because of its size, a company may have advantages of scale in experience, purchasing, marketing, manufacturing, administration, research, logistics, distribution, etc. For example, expenses can be spread out over larger amounts of volume, lowering average costs.

Scale matters, says Warren Buffett discussing the private jet company NetJets®:

> Both we and our customers derive significant operational benefits from our being the runaway leader in the fractional ownership business. We have more than 300 planes constantly on the go in the U.S. and can therefore be wherever a customer needs us on very short notice. The ubiquity of our fleet also reduces our "positioning" costs below those incurred by operators with smaller fleets. These advantages of scale, and others we have, give NetJets a significant economic edge over competition.

"We increased production volume but employee focus, service, and motivation went down."
At some point the disadvantages of business size may eat into the advantages. For example, increased costs and investments, per-unit cost increases, systems become too complicated, bureaucracy and inefficiency, etc.

People's behavior may change when we change the scale of a group. What works well in a group of one size may not work at all in a group of another size. Garrett Hardin illustrates this as he examines the religious Hutterite communities in the northwestern U.S.:

> As a colony grows in size, the propensity of the individual to claim a share of production "according to his needs" increases, while his eagerness to work "according to his ability" diminishes. The effectiveness of the overseers (preachers or bosses) also diminishes. Then, as shrinking increases, those less inclined to "goof off" begin to envy the brotherhood of drones, whom they presently join.

The Hutterites learned that scale or the number of people in each decision unit is important. Up to 150 people per colony, the system can be managed by the force of shame. Above this size an appeal to conscience loses its effectiveness and individuals begin to need more than they contribute.

The concept of scale also applies to time – how things change over time or when something is repeated. Small, slow changes operating over long periods can have great consequences. For example, we have seen how small genetic changes can have major anatomical effects over time.

Breakpoints and limits

At a certain scale, a system reaches a critical mass or a limit where the behavior of the system may change dramatically.

Small interactions over time slowly accumulate into a critical state – where the degree of instability increases. A small event may then trigger a dramatic change like an earthquake. A web of cracks over time may increase vibrations that cause an accident. The underlying process may be simple and easy to understand but still remain unpredictable.

Another example is from chemistry. When a system of chemicals reaches a certain level of interaction, the system undergoes a dramatic change. A small change in a variable may have an unnoticeable effect but a further change may cause a system to reach a critical point making the system work better or worse.

Consider technological, human, biological and mathematical limits. We can't send signals faster than the speed of light. There are limits to how small or large something can be. Gordon Moore, one of the founders of Intel, predicted in 1965 that the number of transistors that could be economically produced and placed on a silicon chip would double every 18 months. In 1995 he updated his prediction to once every two years. Eventually though, physical, engineering or economic limits may stop this from happening.

Constraints

"Increase production!"

Optimization of one variable may cause the whole system to work less efficiently. Why? The performance of most systems is constrained by the performance of its weakest link. A variable that limits the system from achieving its optimum performance. An increase in production may for example be physically constrained by the production capacity on one of the machines. If one machine in a production line of two machines can produce 100 items and the second 90, the output is constrained (physically) by the second machine.

When trying to improve the performance of a system, first find out what limits the system and what causes this limitation. Then try to "strengthen" the weakest link and watch out for other effects – wanted or unwanted – that pop up as a consequence. Always consider the effects on the whole system.

Three

Causes

"We measure and reward performance by the quantity of steel produced."
What do we want to accomplish? It's hard to achieve a result if we don't understand what causes the result to happen. In order to solve problems or achieve goals, we must first understand what causes the result we want to accomplish. Start with examining what factors make up the system and how they connect. Then, define the key factors that determine outcome.

If a business measures performance by the amount of steel produced, they will get a lot of steel produced. But the amount of produced kilo steel is only one part of the equation. It's better to ask: What is the equation that achieves what we want to accomplish? What factors cause what we want to achieve? Under what circumstances? What causes business value? Do we have the factors needed? What must be changed in the equation to achieve what we want? Have we thought through what other effects our actions may have?

Large effects
A bird flies into the engine of an aircraft and disaster strikes.
We believe that cause resembles its effect – for example, that large or important effects must have large causes or that complicated outcomes have complicated underlying reasons. But the size of an effect may not be proportional to its cause. Small things may break a large system. In 1988, 35 people died and 113 were injured when a London-bound commuter train crashed into the back of a stationary train. The accident was caused by faulty wiring work. A mechanic worked more than 12 hours with only a 5-minute break and forgot to remove a small wire from an old switch when installing a new rail signaling system.

On September 23, 1999, the Mars Climate Orbiter spacecraft disappeared.
What happened? The core cause was the failed conversion of English units (pounds) to metric units (newton). The manufacturer measured the force of small control thrusters in pounds but the space officials expected newtons. A misunderstanding that sent the spacecraft about 56 miles too close to Mars, making it disappear into the Martian atmosphere. A simple mistake that caused the loss of a $125 million spacecraft.

Washing hands save lives.

Records at the Center for Disease Control and Prevention (CDC) show that every year close to 2 million people (out of 35 million admissions annually) in the U.S. pick up an infection in the hospital. Of those people, about 90,000 die as a result of their infection. And the major reason is bad hygiene like unsanitary conditions, germ-laden instruments and unwashed hands. CDC and the U.S. Department and Health and Human Services estimate that strict adherence to clean-hand policies alone could save the lives of 20,000 patients.

That washing hands saved lives was discovered in 1847 by the Hungarian gynecologist Ignaz Philipp Semmelweis. When working at the Maternity Department of the Vienna Hospital, he observed that women delivered by medical students had high mortality rates while those delivered by midwife trainees had low rates of childbed fever. The difference? The medical students had made pathological dissections, or had come into contact with dead bodies before the examination of the women. Semmelweis introduced the practice of washing hands in a solution of chlorinated lime before every examination and mortality rates plummeted.

Random events

When bad things happen, we try to find causal explanations or something to blame. The more unexpected or negative we find an event the more likely we are to look for explanations. We underestimate the influence of randomness.

What do we mean with a random event?

Isn't there always a reason for something to happen? Wouldn't a truly random event lack a cause? Is rolling dice a random event? Can't the outcome be determined by a number of factors that can be explained by physics? Yes, it is a matter of mechanics. Physical laws determine any particular throw, but there is so much uncertainty, we can't determine the outcome in advance. We can't measure all variables. We don't have enough information to predict the outcome. We don't have all data that we need to make a calculation. We can't write an equation. What we do know is that the statistical outcome is predictable for an infinite number of rolls under essentially the same conditions. Even though the outcome each time is unpredictable, over time each number will come up the same number of times.

"A fire in our supplier's factory caused delivery problems of components. We lost market share to competition, which resulted in huge losses. This outcome was unforeseeable since we couldn't have predicted the fire in advance."

Here we define a random event as an event that can't be predicted (regardless of past knowledge), including an event whose cause we don't and can't know or understand, without any identifiable intention or reason. It also includes an event that can take on one or more outcomes. Even a close physical investigation can't resolve the uncertainty.

Acting on symptoms

Take away the cause, and the effect ceases.
- Miguel De Cervantes (from *Don Quixote*)

Sometimes we mistake an effect for its cause. There is a story about a man that was walking by a river when suddenly a screaming girl floated by. The man jumped in the river and saved her. After five minutes another screaming girl floated by. He jumped in again and saved the girl. The same thing happened over and over again. The problem was a little further up the river. There was a man throwing girls from a bridge. Our hero solved the symptoms but not the cause of the problem.

"We have tons of problems. We are losing customers, we can't deliver on time, our inventory system doesn't work."
What is the core cause of these problems? Many times when we have a lot of problems, there may be one common reason for them all. When dealing with problems we must focus on what we want to achieve and make sure that we address the underlying cause and not act on symptoms that may look like causes. Maybe the symptoms were due to wrong policies or measuring instruments or goals, etc.

Multiple causes

We attribute an outcome to a single cause when there are multiple causes. We assume that A causes B but A may not be the only thing that causes B. There may be many causes for a given effect.

For example, behavior is determined by a multitude of psychological and non-psychological factors, individual characteristics and the given situation. Sometimes these factors interact and reinforce each other. When explaining behavior, think in terms of multiple causes. For example, Charles Munger says on the Milgram experiment discussed in Part Two (where a group of research subjects delivered electric shocks simply because they were told to do so by an authoritative figure):

For years it was in the psychology books as a demonstration of *authority* – how authority could be used to persuade people to do awful things. Of course, that's mere first-conclusion bias. That's not the complete and correct explanation. Authority is part of it. However, there was also quite a few other psychological principles [commitment, contrast, explaining why], all operating in the same direction, which achieved that lollapalooza effect precisely because they acted in combination toward the same end.

Mistaking correlation and association for cause

We tend to assume that when two things happen together, that one causes the other. But correlation doesn't mean causation. That a change in one variable is strongly correlated or followed by a change in another doesn't automatically mean that one causes the other. Some third factor may cause them both. Assume we detect a high correlation between money and happiness. But that doesn't tell us if money causes happiness, if happiness causes money, or if some third factor causes them both.

The same goes for associations. Two things, A and B, are only related if the probability of one event changes when the other event happens. If it has the same likelihood regardless of whether the other event happened, there is no association between the two things.

An example of statistical misuse is from 1992 when it was reported that 28 teenagers who frequently played the game of "Dungeons and Dragons" (D&D) committed suicide. What conclusion should be drawn? Is there a link between teenage suicide and the game?

The American mathematician John Allen Paulos tells us in *Innumeracy* to put this statement into the right perspective by considering two more facts. The game sold millions of copies and about 3 million teenagers played it. In that age group the annual suicide rate is about 12 people per 100,000. This means that we can expect 360 D&D playing teenagers (12/100,000 x 3 million players) to commit suicide.

Obvious causes

> *There is nothing more deceptive than an obvious fact.*
> - Sherlock Holmes (Arthur Conan Doyle, *The Boscombe Valley Mystery*)

We identify the wrong cause because it seems the obvious one based on a single observed effect. As Bertrand Russell says: "Obviousness is always the enemy to correctness."

We tend to ignore important comparative information. Often we only consider information or evidence that is available and don't consider information that is missing.

"The drug obviously worked since I used it and got better."
But the same outcome could have happened without taking the drug. Ask: How often does a specific action not produce the expected effect? How often does the specific effect happen when we don't take the specific action?

For example, when studying the effectiveness of a new treatment people often ignore the outcome of a non-treatment and only focus on a large number of successful treatments. In one study people were asked to judge the effectiveness of a treatment based on the following data from an experiment:

	Improvement	No improvement
Treatment	200 people	75
No treatment	50	15

Most subjects believed the treatment was effective. But it is rather ineffective. Why? We need to compare the outcome for the no treatment group with the outcome for the treatment group. 50 of 65 people (50+15) or about 77%, improved without any treatment versus 200 of 275 (200+75) people or about 73% who improved with the treatment.

Alternative explanations
"Mary has a fever and therefore she has a cold."
There may be many explanations for a given outcome. But we often jump to conclusions and fail to consider alternative explanations. A given effect may be consistent with a range of causes and don't help us find the core cause of a problem.

That Mary has a fever tells us that she is not well but it doesn't tell us why she is ill. Fever can occur from a range of diseases. Ask: What else can explain this outcome?

Comparisons
What caused customer complaints at TransCorp?
We look for obvious causes and look at the conditions and behavior that were present in the particular situation after we know what happened. But we should observe what is normally happening. Most outcomes are context-dependent.

Instead of concentrating on conditions and behavior preceding the customer complaint, TransCorp should examine both sales without complaints and with complaints and ask: What were the underlying conditions and behavior when customers didn't complain?

For similar situations, ask: Compared with what? What were the underlying conditions and behavior where something bad happened compared to the conditions and behavior when things worked? What differentiates the situations? Don't draw conclusions from what may have been a unique or random event.

FOUR

NUMBERS AND THEIR MEANING

Use basic math to count, quantify, and understand relationships

John bought all the stock he could since it was priced at only $1.

Something is only cheap or expensive in relation to something else. If an investor refers to a stock as "cheap," what is it cheap in relation to? 100,000 shares of stock priced at $1 have the same market valuation as 1,000 shares priced at $100. The relevant question is: What is the company worth in relation to its price?

TransCorp made a "huge" $1 billion in profits.

Words like "big" or "small" have no meaning in themselves. A number has only a size in relation to another number. $1 billion says nothing about economic performance unless we compare it with how much capital was needed to generate it. What if TransCorp needed $100 billion in equity and debt to run the business? That's only a 1% return.

"Research show that the new drug reduces the risk of getting the disease by 25%."

What benefits can be expected by taking the new drug? Assume statistics show the following: Without the drug 20 people in 1,000 get the disease. By taking the drug, the figure drops to 15 people in 1,000. How efficient is the drug if we look at the absolute number of people saved from the disease? The reduction in absolute risk is 5 people in 1,000 (20-15) or 0.5%. The reduction in relative risk or the relative number of people saved from the disease is 25% (5/20). A 25% reduction only means something if many people are saved.

How many people need to take the drug in order to save one individual from the disease? Since 5 people in 1,000 (or 1 in 200) are saved from the disease by taking the drug, only one person out of 200 that take the drug will be saved. For the other 199 people the drug does not have any positive effect.

What does it mean that our sun is 93 million miles away?

Often we need to translate a number to something more understandable. Light travels at an average speed of 186,281 miles per second. This means that it takes sunbeams about 8 minutes to reach the earth. The star Alpha Centauri is 4.35

light-years away. A light-year is the distance light travels in one year. Even if light-year measures distance, it implies time. If we were to ride on a beam of light, it would take us 4.35 years to reach our closest star. When we look up in the sky we see the past – the star as it appeared 4.35 years ago.

Always look at what numbers mean. For example, ask: Does the magnitude make sense? In relation to what? Also, think about what counts – not how it is counted. There was a sign hanging in the physicist Albert Einstein's office at Princeton that said: "Not everything that counts can be counted, and not everything that can be counted counts."

The effect of exponential growth

John's son David made a proposal, "I take out the garbage every day for a month, and you only have to pay me a penny today and then every day afterward I want double as much as I got the day before."

The sequence of numbers 2, 4, 8, 16 grows exponentially. Day 2 his son would have 2 cents, day 3, 4 cents. After 27 days, he would have $1.3 million dollars. The individual growth is constant – 100% a day – but the sum gets higher faster and faster. This is the power of doubling.

As we have seen there are limits to prolonged growth. Take bacteria as an example. Assume that a certain strain of bacteria divide in one minute. We put the bacteria in a bottle at 11 am and the bottle is full at noon. When was the bottle half full? – 11:59 am.

Even a small number of steady growth leads eventually to doubling and redoubling. For example, a country whose population grows by 2% a year, double in size in 35 years and redoubles in 70 years. A simple formula for doubling time is found by dividing 70 by the percent growth per year. If we assume the world's population is 6 billion, and it is growing at a rate of 1.3% per year, then it takes the world population about 53 years to double. The earth's resources are finite. When does the earth's capacity to support us reach its limits?

Compounding refers to "interest on interest." If we invest $1,000 with a return of 6% a year, we receive $60 in the first year. If we reinvest that $60, next year we get another $60 from our original $1,000 investment, plus $3.6 from the $60 we reinvested. If we reinvest all our returns, the total value of our original $1,000 investment after 5 years is: $1,000 x 1.06 x 1.06 x 1.06 x 1.06 x 1.06 = $1,338.

Time is the key to compound interest. Over short periods, compounding produces a little extra return. Over long periods, it has an enormous effect. Invest $2,500 each year for 40 years at 10% return and you will be a millionaire.

The time value of money

A bird in the hand is worth two in the bush.

- Aesop

Why must we reduce the value of money we receive in the future?

Money paid in the future is worth less than money paid today. A dollar received today is worth more than a dollar received tomorrow. If we have a dollar today, we can invest it and earn interest making that dollar worth more than a dollar in the future. This means that money has a price and that price is interest.

How much should we pay today for the right of receiving $1,000 a year from now? Or, how much do we need to invest today in order to have $1,000 a year from now? It's the same question. The answer depends on the interest rate. If the rate is 6%, then the answer is $943. If we invest $943 today at 6%, we have $1,000 one year from now. $943 is the present value of $1,000 a year from now. We have discounted or reduced $1,000 to its value today. The further out in time we receive the $1,000 or the higher the interest rate is, the less the present value is.

Let's enter the world of probability. An area of mathematics, with many real life applications.

FIVE

PROBABILITIES AND NUMBER OF POSSIBLE OUTCOMES

Probability is the very guide of life.
- Marcus Tullius Cicero

"One woman out of eight in the U.S. develops breast cancer during her lifetime."
Does this mean that the probability of Mary's getting breast cancer is 12.5%? No, probabilities don't say what may happen to a specific individual. Instead it means that past experience tells us that the proportion of women (with the same medical condition) that develop breast cancer is about 12,500 out of 100,000. Assuming no changes in the causes of these cancers, we can expect the same relative frequency (12,500 in 100,000) of breast cancer in the future.

How likely do we believe it is that an event will occur? The British 19th Century mathematician George Boole said in *An Investigation of The Laws of Thought:* "Probability is expectation founded upon partial knowledge. A perfect acquaintance with all the circumstances affecting the occurrence of an event would change expectation into certainty, and leave neither room nor demand for a theory of probabilities."

Probabilities are like guesses. But as Richard Feynman said in his *Caltech Lectures on Physics:* "There are good guesses and there are bad guesses. The theory of probability is a system for making better guesses."

We can either estimate the probability based on its relative frequency (proportion of times an event happens) over a large number of trials or we can make an educated guess using past experiences or whatever important and relevant information and evidence that is available.

We can also count possible outcomes. The only time we can calculate the exact probability of an event in advance (over a large number of trials) is in cases where we know all possible outcomes and where all outcomes are equally likely. This is applicable for games of chance such as tossing a coin or rolling a die. However we use the notion of probability, we need to follow its basic rules.

How likely is it that a hurricane strikes Texas?
According to the National Hurricane Center, there have been 36 hurricane

strikes in Texas from 1900 to 1996. Based on past experience and barring no change in conditions, we can estimate that there is about a 37% (36/97) chance that a hurricane will strike Texas in any given year. This figure – 36/97 – is also called the base rate frequency of outcomes (hurricanes in Texas).

We must make sure that the conditions that produced the relative frequency can be expected to be pretty much the same before we can use it as a guide for the future.

We must also look at variations of outcome and severity (how much damage an event may cause). Take tornadoes as an example. According to the National Climatic Data Center, between 1950 to 1999 there has been an average of 810 tornadoes yearly in the U.S. But in 1950 there was 201 tornadoes (causing 70 deaths), in 1975, 919 (causing 60 deaths), and in 1999, 1,342 tornadoes (causing 94 deaths).

A doctor says, "This is the first time I've seen this disease. I estimate there is a 50-50 chance that the patient will survive."
This statement has only two possible outcomes. Either the patient dies or not. Does it really make any sense to say "a 50-50 chance" if there are no past data or other evidence to base the probability on? Does it really tell us something? If there are no historical, comparable or representative data or other evidence to base an estimate on, the probability figure only measures the doctor's belief in the outcome of the event.

Another doctor says, "According to medical records of similar cases, under the same conditions, 50% of the patients survived five years or longer."
The more representative background data or evidence we have the better our estimate of the probability.

To narrow down the probability figure even more, we need a relevant comparison group. In the hurricane example, we defined the probability for a specific comparison group, referring to the relative frequency with which hurricanes have occurred (37 times in Texas during the 97 years for which we have data).

Events may happen with great frequency or rarely. Some events are not repeatable and some events have never happened before. For certain events, past experience may not be representative. Others are characterized by low past frequency and high severity. Unforeseen events occur where our actual exposure (measures vulnerability and potential cost or loss) is unknown. The more uncertainty there is, the harder it is to find a meaningful probability number. Instead our estimate must be constrained to a range of possible outcomes and their probabilities.

Uncertainty increases the difficulty for insurers to appropriately price catastrophes, such as hurricanes or earthquakes. Warren Buffett says:

Catastrophe insurers can't simply extrapolate past experience. If there is truly "global warming," for example, the odds would shift, since tiny changes in atmospheric conditions can produce momentous changes in weather patterns. Furthermore, in recent years there has been a mushrooming of population and insured values in U.S. coastal areas that are particularly vulnerable to hurricanes, the number one creator of super-cats. A hurricane that caused x dollars of damage 20 years ago could easily cost 10x now.

Occasionally, also, the unthinkable happens. Who would have guessed for example, that a major earthquake could occur in Charleston, S.C.? (It struck in 1886, registered an estimated 6.6 on the Richter scale, and caused 60 deaths.)

But it may still be possible to price sensibly. Warren Buffett says:

Even if perfection in assessing risks is unattainable, insurers can underwrite sensibly. After all, you need not know a man's precise age to know that he is old enough to vote nor know his exact weight to recognize his need to diet.

Warren Buffett also consider a worst case scenario:

Given the risks we accept, Ajit [Ajit Jain; manager of Berkshire's reinsurance operations] and I constantly focus on our "worst case," knowing, of course, that it is difficult to judge what this is, since you could conceivably have a Long Island hurricane, a California earthquake, and Super Cat X all in the same year. Additionally, insurance losses could be accompanied by non-insurance troubles. For example, were we to have super-cat losses from a large Southern California earthquake, they might well be accompanied by a major drop in the value of our holdings in See's, Wells Fargo and Freddie Mac.

We do, though, monitor our aggregate exposure in order to keep our "worst case" at a level that leaves us comfortable.

After the September 11, 2001, catastrophe, Warren Buffett wrote on the importance on focusing on actual exposure and how using past experience sometimes may be dangerous:

In setting prices and also in evaluating aggregation risk, we had either overlooked or dismissed the possibility of large-scale terrorism losses...In pricing property coverages, for example, we had looked to the past and taken into account only costs we might expect to incur from windstorm, fire, explosion and earthquake. But what will be the largest insured property loss in history (after adding related business interruption claims) originated from none of these forces. In short, all of us in the industry made a fundamental underwriting mistake by focusing on experience, rather than exposure, thereby assuming a huge terrorism risk for which we received no premium.

Experience, of course, is a highly useful starting point in underwriting most coverages. For example, it's important for insurers writing California earthquake policies to know how many quakes in the state during the past century have registered 6.0 or greater on the Richter scale. This information will not tell you the exact probability of a big quake next year, or where in the state it might happen. But the statistic has utility, particularly if you are writing a huge statewide policy…

At certain times, however, using experience as a guide to pricing is not only useless, but actually dangerous. Late in a bull market, for example, large losses from directors and officers liability insurance ("D&O") are likely to be relatively rare. When stocks are rising, there are a scarcity of targets to sue, and both questionable accounting and management chicanery often go undetected. At that juncture, experience on high-limit D&O may look great.

But that's just when *exposure* is likely to be exploding, by way of ridiculous public offerings, earnings manipulation, chain-letter-like stock promotions and a potpourri of other unsavory activities. When stocks fall, these sins surface, hammering investors with losses that can run into the hundreds of billions. Juries deciding whether those losses should be borne by small investors or big insurance companies can be expected to hit insurers with verdicts that bear little relation to those delivered in bull-market days. Even one jumbo judgment, moreover, can cause settlement costs in later cases to mushroom. Consequently, the correct rate for D&O "excess" (meaning the insurer or reinsurer will pay losses above a high threshold) might well, if based on *exposure,* be five or more times the premium dictated by *experience.*

Even if we for some events can't estimate their probability, there may be some evidence telling us if their probabilities are increasing or decreasing. Ask: Do I understand the forces that can cause the event? What are the key factors? Are there more opportunities for the event to happen?

Warren Buffett says on terrorism:

No one knows the probability of a nuclear detonation in a major metropolis area this year…Nor can anyone, with assurance, assess the probability in this year, or another, of deadly biological or chemical agents being introduced simultaneously…into multiple office buildings and manufacturing plants…

Here's what we *do* know: a. The probability of such mind-boggling disasters, though likely very low at present, is not zero. b. The probabilities are increasing, in an irregular and immeasurable manner, as knowledge and materials become available to those who wish us ill.

The more opportunities (possible wanted or unwanted outcomes) an event has to happen in relation to what can happen (all possible outcomes), the more likely it is to occur.

Number of possible outcomes

Toss a coin once. What can happen? There are 2 possible outcomes. Roll a die once. There are 6 possible outcomes. All equally likely. Roll a die twice. What can happen? There are 6 possible outcomes on each roll and therefore 36 possible combinations or outcomes when rolling a die twice. Roll a die 3 times. There are 216 possible outcomes.

This is a simplified way of saying that the more outcomes an event has, the less likely a specific outcome is (for example only one outcome satisfies the wanted event: "roll a die once and observe a six") and the more likely some outcome is (there are 6 possible outcomes to choose from).

The more possible outcomes a specific event has, and the more they are unwanted, and the more independent events that are needed to achieve a scenario, the less likely it is that the wanted scenario happens.

Treat rolling a die 3 times as 3 separate events where each event is "observe a six". What we see from the above is that the more events that must happen to achieve some scenario or wanted outcome ("3 sixes in a row"), the less likely the scenario is to happen. Observing "anything but 3 sixes in a row" is an unwanted event. There are 215 outcomes or ways for this to happen out of 216. This means that it is very likely that the unwanted event happens.

We talk about what is likely to happen in the long run. We might be lucky and roll 3 sixes in a row. We must also consider the consequences of an unwanted outcome.

What does this mean? If there are more ways of reaching a bad outcome, than a good outcome, the probability of a bad outcome is higher. It is easier to destroy a system than to create one merely because there are more opportunities for destruction than creation.

It means that surprises, coincidences, rare events and accidents happen, somewhere, sometime, and to someone if they have opportunities to happen.

It also means that eliminating risk is preferable to finding out where the risk lies (since there are so many opportunities for an unwanted outcome). For example, we can reduce risk by increasing the number of wanted possible outcomes, reducing the number of unwanted possible outcomes, reducing the magnitude of consequences or avoiding certain situations.

Ask some relevant questions:

Event: Type of event? Frequent? Unique?

Causes: What can initiate and cause the event? What factors contribute? What conditions and circumstances must be present? Have the causes changed over time?

Exposure: Known? Measurable? Possible consequences? Magnitude of consequences/loss? What's the worst that can happen?

Probability: Distribution of possible outcomes over time? Stable? Relative frequency or relevant past experience? Number of observations? Relative likelihood of different size of losses? How is average frequency produced? Variability in outcome and severity? Dependence on human factors?

Representative: Past data representative or change in conditions? Evidence of changes in causes or frequency of event? Temporary or permanent change? Small sample or too short observation time? Changing exposure as time proceeds?

Backups: Backup failure rate?

Let's observe some effects of what we've described in this chapter. More focus is put on the underlying ideas than the math. The theory of probability and its definitions, rules and calculations are found in Appendix Three.

Low frequency events

The chance of gain is by every man more or less overvalued,
and the chance of loss is by most men undervalued.
- Adam Smith (Scottish philosopher and economist, 1723-1790)

Supreme Court Justice Oliver Wendell Holmes, Jr. said: "Most people think dramatically, not quantitatively." We overestimate the frequency of deaths from publicized events like tornadoes, floods and homicides and underestimate the frequency of deaths from less publicized ones like diabetes, stroke and stomach cancer. Why? As we learned in Part Two, we tend to overestimate how often rare but recent, vivid or highly publicized events happen. The media has an interest in translating the improbable to the believable. There is a difference between the real risk and the risk that sells papers. A catastrophe like a plane crash makes a compelling news story. Highly emotional events make headlines but are not an indicator of frequency. Consider instead all the times that nothing happens. Most flights are accident-free.

John is boarding the day flight from Los Angeles to Washington and wonders, "How likely am I to die on this trip?"

What is the risk of a disaster? First we need to know the available record of previous flights that can be compared to John's. Assume, we find that in 1 out of 10,000 flights there was an accident. The record also shows that when an accident happens, on average 8 out of 10 are killed, 1 injured and one safe. This means that the chance that a passenger will be involved in an accident is 1 in 10,000; being killed, 1 in 12,500 (10,000/0.8); and being injured, 1 in 100,000 (10.000/0.1)

According to the Federal Aviation Administration, Dr. Arnold Barnett of Massachusetts Institute of Technology (MIT), a widely recognized expert on air traffic safety, measured a passenger's odds of surviving the next flight. It related the probability of not being in a fatal air carrier accident and the probability of not surviving if a fatal accident happens. In the year 2000 the odds were 5.8 million to 1. We could fly once a day for 22,000 years and not lose our lives in a commercial aviation accident.

According to the National Transportation Safety Board the number of passengers killed in air accidents in the U.S. during 1992 through 2001 was 433 (including the 232 aboard the four hijacked flights). For reference, in 2001, the annual number of lives lost in road traffic accidents in the U.S. was 42,119.

That people feel safer driving than flying makes sense since we are oriented towards survival. As Antonio Damasio says in *Descartes' Error,* "Planes do crash now and then, and fewer people survive plane crashes than survive car crashes." Studies also show that we fear harm from what's unfamiliar much more than mundane hazards and by things we feel we control. We don't feel in control when we fly.

Why do we lose money gambling? Why do we invest in exotic long shot ventures?

We often overestimate the chance of low probability but high-payoff bets. For example, how likely is it that anyone guesses a number between 1 and 14 million? What is Mary's chance of winning Lotto 6/49 if there are 14 million outcomes? What must happen? She must pick 6 numbers out of 49 and if they all match she wins. What can happen? How many numbers can she choose from? The possible number of ways she can choose 6 numbers out of 49 are 13,983,816. The probability that someone chooses the winning combination is therefore one in about 14 million. Merely slightly better than throwing heads on 24 successive tosses of a coin.

Imagine the time it takes to put together 14 million combinations. If we assume every combination on average takes 1 minute to put down on paper, and

Mary pick numbers for 24 hours a day, it will take her 27 years to write them all down.

Even if Mary invests $14 million to buy 14 million tickets in the hopes of winning a $20 million jackpot, she may have to share the jackpot with others that picked the winning number. If just one other person picked the winning combination, she would lose $4 million (20/2 – 14).

Why do people play a game when the likelihood of losing is so high? Even if we exclude the amusement factor and the reinforcement from an occasional pay-off, it is understandable since they perceive the benefit of being right as huge and the cost of being wrong as low – merely the cost of the ticket or a dollar. Remember the advice of Benjamin Franklin: "He that waits upon fortune, is never sure of a dinner."

Mathematical expectation

A lottery has 100 tickets. Each ticket costs $10. The cash price is $500. Is it worthwhile for Mary to buy a lottery ticket?

The expected value of this game is the probability of winning (1 in 100) multiplied with the price ($500) less the probability of losing (99 out of 100) multiplied with the cost of playing ($10). For each outcome we take the probability and multiply the consequence (a reward or a cost). This means that Mary's expected value of buying a lottery ticket is a loss of about $5 (0.01 x $500 – 0.99 x $10).

We need to separate between few games and many games. Expected value tells Mary that she on average should expect to lose $5 every time she plays if she plays the same lottery over and over. Not what she can expect from a single game. Mary has a 1 % chance of winning the lottery and if she wins, her gain is $490. She has a 99 % chance of losing $10.

At the country club John is asked: Which of the following games do you want to play?
   (A) Flip a coin and if you get heads you win $100
   (B) Toss a single die and if you get number 6 you win $600.
You don't have to pay anything to enter these games.

The games are the same as playing a lottery with 2 or 6 tickets. How should John choose? To answer this he needs to ask: "How many times am I going to play?" "Is it a one-time bet or a repeatable bet?" "What are the consequences if I lose or win?" Since probability means the number of times an event is likely to happen during a large number of trials, the expected value is the amount John should expect to win or lose per game if he made the same bet many times. If John plays this game over and over again he should play game B. Then he is likely to win $600 on each of about 1/6th of the rolls and nothing on each of about 5/6th of the rolls. The average amount he should expect to win per roll over a large number of rolls is $100.

But what happens if John can only play once? In game (A) he has one chance of winning and one of losing. He gets nothing at all from what happens 50% of the time and $100 from what happens 50% of the time. If he only has time for one game, the probability is 50% that he flips tails and gets nothing.

In game (B) John has one chance of winning and five of losing. He gets nothing at all from what happens 83.3% of the time; $600 from what happens 16.6% of the time. If he only has time for one game the probability is 83.3% that he rolls 1 to 5 and gets nothing. If John only plays once he should choose to play game (A) because the probability of losing in a once played game is less in game (A) than in game (B).

Most of our decisions in every-day life are one-time bets. Choices we face only once. Still, this is not the last decision we make. There are a large number of uncertain decisions we make over a lifetime. We make bets every day. So if we view life's decisions as a series of gambles, we should use expected value as a guide whenever appropriate. Over time, we will come out better.

John placed $38 dollar on the roulette table.
Mathematics and human nature make it impossible for us to beat the roulette wheel for any considerable length of time. If we play at a casino once we may be lucky and in the short run win some money, but we should expect to lose in the long run. The casino has the advantage.

There are 38 different numbers (including double zero) on the roulette wheel. When the croupier spins the wheel there is an equal chance of the ball landing in any one of the 38 slots. John puts $1 on a single number. If his number comes up, he wins $35. On average his expected value of a one dollar bet is a loss of 5.26 cents (1/38x$35 – 37/38x$1). Over the long run John loses an average of 5.26 cents for every dollar he places on the table. The odds are set so they average out in the casino's favor.

"If I just stay at the table long enough, the odds turn in my favor and I will win back everything I lost."
But this is what the casino wants us to believe. The casino can't predict the outcome of any particular bet but as soon as there are a large number of individual players making bets, the casino will make money. As a casino operator said: "What I love is the risk. Some nights we make money, and other nights we make more money."

Even if we win in the short run, human nature turns us into losers. Nearly all of those who win big continue to play until they have lost their gains, and perhaps more. This is well illustrated by Henry Howard Harper in his book, *The Psychology of Speculation:*

> It is said to be a proven fact that the chances are so much against the player, that a roulette wheel can be run at a profit, even if the percentage in favor of the house is entirely eliminated. This is due to the fact that the excitement of play causes a certain confusion of mind, and players are prone to do the wrong thing; for instance, double their bets when in an adverse run of luck and "pinch" them when luck is running favorably. Or, on the other hand, players who have pressed their advantage and doubled in a run of favorable luck will continue stubbornly to plunge long after their luck has changed. Precisely the same psychology applies to trading in stocks.

Chance has no memory
"My luck is about to change. The trend will reverse."
After a run of bad outcomes in independent events that appear randomly, we sometimes believe a good outcome is due. But previous outcomes neither influence nor have any predictive value of future outcomes. There is neither memory nor any sense of justice.

Mary flipped a coin and got 5 heads in a row. Is a tail due? It must be, since in the long run heads and tails balance out.
When we say that the probability of tossing tails is 50%, we mean that over a long run of tosses, tails come up half the time. The probability that Mary flips a head on her fifth toss is 50%. The coin has no sense of fairness. As the 19th Century French mathematician Joseph Bertrand said: "The coin has neither memory or consciousness." Mary committed the gambler's fallacy. This happens when we believe that when something has continued for a certain period of time, it goes back to its long-term average. This is the same as the roulette player when he bets on red merely because black has come up four times in a row. But black has the same chance as red to come up on the next spin. Each outcome is independent of the one before. Only in the long run will the ratio of red to black become equal.

Every single time Mary plays, the probability it lands on heads is 50% and lands on tails 50%. Even if we know that the probability is 50%, we can't predict if a given flip results in a head or tail. We may flip heads ten times in a row or none. The laws of probability don't count out luck.

Assume airplane crashes in the U.S. happen on average twice a year and seven months have passed without one. Does this mean that a crash is due? No, in all independent events that have random components in them, there is no memory of the past.

Controlling chance events

The craps table was filled with people tossing their die soft and asking for a low number. We believe in lucky numbers and we believe we can control the outcome of chance events. But skill or effort doesn't change the probability of chance events.

"Change tickets! Are you crazy! I would feel awful if my number comes up and I'd traded it away."
In one experiment a social psychologist found that people were more reluctant to give up a lottery ticket they had chosen themselves, than one selected at random for them. They wanted four times as much money for selling the chosen ones compared to what they wanted for the randomly selected ticket. But in random drawings it doesn't make any difference if we choose a ticket or are assigned one. The probability of winning is the same. The lesson is, if you want to sell lottery tickets, let people choose their own numbers instead of randomly drawing them.

Gains, losses and utility

The 18th Century Swiss mathematician Daniel Bernoulli said: "A gain of one thousand ducats is more significant to a pauper than to a rich man though both gain the same amount." This means that the desirability of an outcome is different for different people and at different stages in life. Our preferences change as our state of wealth changes.

Often when we make financial decisions we don't consider our state of wealth. Instead we judge a decision by evaluating gains and losses.

"Should I invest?
  "There is a 60% probability that I gain $10,000. There is a 40% probability that I lose $7,500."
  "Since I get much pleasure out of gains and the expected value ($3,000) is positive, I decide to invest."
Instead we should take the long-term view and think in terms of wealth and to what degree an outcome helps us achieve our goals.

  "What are the possible outcomes and their probability and utility in terms of total wealth?"
  "There is a 60% probability for a positive outcome. My wealth will then be

$1.010.000. There is a 40% probability for a negative outcome. My wealth will then be $992,500."

"The difference in pleasure with regards to my goals isn't much so I decide to decline."

Ask: What do I end up with? How much will I have if I succeed and how much will I have if I fail?

The consequences of low frequency events
Imagine the following scenario:

	Probability	Cost of consequence	Expected value
Outcome A	10%	-90	-9
Outcome B	90%	-10	-9

Both outcomes have the same expected value but differ hugely in their cost of consequences. We can't only look at how likely an unwanted event is to happen. We must also rate the magnitude of its consequences. Before taking an action, ask: What are the benefits and costs? What might go wrong? How can it go wrong? What is the probability and consequence of failure over time? How can the probability and consequence of failure be reduced?

What if the probability of success is high but the consequence of failure is terrible?

The consequences of being wrong
Take no chance whatsoever with food poisoning, and stay away from places where others have been recently killed, regardless of what the mathematical laws of probability tell you.
- Edward Wilson (Entomology Professor, from *Consilience*)

"Pascal's Wager" is French philosopher and mathematician Blaise Pascal's argument for believing in God. Pascal reasoned as follows: If we believe in God, and God exists, we would gain in afterlife. If we don't believe in God, and God exists, we will lose in afterlife. Independent of the probabilities of a God, the consequences of not believing are so awful, we should hedge our bet and believe.

Pascal suggests that we are playing a game with 2 choices, believe and not believe, with the following consequences:

	God does exist	God does not exist
Probability (p)	p	(1 - p)
Believe	Saved (good)	Inconvenience
Don't believe	Damned (bad)	Normal life

If God exists, and we believe God exists, we are saved. This is good. If we don't believe, and God is unforgiving, we are damned. If we believe but God doesn't exist, we miss out on some worldly pleasures. If God doesn't exist and we don't believe that God exists, we live a normal life.

Expected value of believing = p(the value of being saved) + (1-p)(the cost of inconvenience)

Expected value of not believing = p(the cost of being damned) + (1-p)(the value of living a normal life)

Pascal said: "If I lost, I would have lot little. If I won I would have gained eternal life." Our choice depends on the probabilities, but Pascal assumed that the consequences of being damned is infinite, meaning the expected value of believing is least negative and therefore he reasoned that believing in God is best no matter how low we set the probability that God exists.

John wants to make extra money and is offered to play Russian Roulette.

If John wins he gets $10 million. Should he play? There are 6 equally likely possible outcomes when he pulls the trigger - empty, empty, empty, empty, empty, bullet. This makes the probability 5/6 or 83%. This is the same as saying that John is playing a lottery with only 6 tickets where one ticket is lethal.

Should he play this game once? The probability is 83% that he gets $10 million. The probability is only 17% that he loses.

Let's look at the consequences: If John doesn't play and there was a bullet he is glad he didn't play. If he plays and there is a bullet, he dies. If he doesn't play and there was no bullet he loses the pleasure which the extra money could have bought him. If he plays and there is no bullet he gains $10 million which would buy him extra pleasure. To play is to risk death in exchange for extra pleasure. There is an 83% probability that John is right but the consequence of being wrong is fatal. Even if the probabilities favor him, the downside is unbearable. Why should John risk his life? The value of survival is infinite, so the strategy of not playing is best no matter what probability we assign for the existence of "no bullet" or what money is being offered. But there may be exceptions. Someone that is poor, in need of supporting a family who knows he will die of a lethal disease within 3 months might pull the trigger. He could lose 3 months of life, but if he wins, his family will be taken care of after his death.

We should never risk something we have and need for something we don't need. But some people pull the trigger anyway. This is what Warren Buffett said about the Long-Term Capital Management affair:

> Here were 16 extremely bright – and I do mean *extremely* bright – people at the top of LTCM. The average IQ among their top 16 people would probably be as high or higher than at any other organization you could find. And individually, they had decades of experience – collectively, *centuries* of experience – in the sort of securities in which LTCM was invested.
>
> Moreover, they had a *huge* amount of their *own* money up – and probably a very high percentage of their net worth in almost every case. So here were super-bright, extremely experienced people, operating with their own money. And yet, in effect, on that day in September, they were broke. To me, that's absolutely fascinating.
>
> In fact, there's a book with a great title – *You Only Have to Get Rich Once*. It's a great title, but not a very good book. (Walter Guttman wrote it many years ago.) But the title is right: You only have to get rich *once*.
>
> Why do very bright people risk losing something that's very important to them to gain something that's totally unimportant? The added money has no utility whatsoever – and the money that was lost had enormous utility. And on top of that, their reputation gets tarnished and all of that sort of thing. So the gain/loss ratio in any real sense is just *incredible…* Whenever a really bright person who has a lot of money goes broke, it's because of leverage… It's *almost* impossible to go broke without borrowed money being in the equation.

Six

Scenarios

Systems construction and planning processes

> *He that builds before he counts the cost, act foolishly;*
> *And he that counts before he builds, finds he did not count wisely.*
> - Benjamin Franklin

At the same time John started renovating his house, TransCorp started a billion-dollar project.
Why do house construction projects, start-ups or product development ventures take more time, money and effort than we expect? For example, one study found that of 3,500 projects executed, the project budget was often exceeded by 40 – 200%.

A project is composed of a series of steps where all must be achieved for success. Each individual step has some probability of failure. We often underestimate things that may cause a project to go wrong. Humans make mistakes, equipment fails, technologies don't work as planned, unrealistic expectations, biases, inexperience, wrong incentives, contractor failure, delays, wrong deliveries, changing requirements, random events, ignoring early warning signals are reasons for delays, cost overruns and mistakes. Often we focus too much on the specific project case and ignore what normally happens in similar situations (base rate frequency of outcomes – personal and others). Why should some project be any different from the long-term record of similar ones? Irish dramatist George Bernard Shaw said: "We learn from history that man can never learn anything from history."

The more independent steps that are involved in achieving a scenario, the more opportunities for failure and the less likely it is that the scenario will happen. We often underestimate the number of steps, people and decisions involved.

Add to this that we often forget that the reliability of a system is a function of the whole system. The weakest link sets the upper limit for the whole chain.

TransCorp wants to develop a new product.
The project is composed of 6 independent steps. Each step has an 80%

probability of success. Based on similar development programs performed under the same conditions, TransCorp estimates that 8 out of 10 times each step is successful. In 2 times out of 10 something happens that prevents each step from succeeding. But since each step is independent, the probabilities must be multiplied together. The probability the company finally succeeds in developing the product is 26% – meaning that TransCorp should expect success one time out of four. So even if each step had an 80% probability of success, when combined, the probability of product success decreases to 26%.

Every time we add another step to some system, the probability that the system works is reduced.

John is thinking of investing in a biotech start-up.
Professor and startup coach John Nesheim, who has been involved in some 300 plus startups, tell us in *High Tech Startup,* that only six out of one million high-tech ideas turn into a public company. This base rate frequency tells us there is a low prior probability of turning into a public company.

Take a biotech venture as an example. There are so many things that must go right before it becomes a business that generates money. Factors like technological virtue, product safety, cost-effectiveness, manufacturing, patent issues, product stability, regulatory matters, market assessment, competitive position, financial need (and availability), etc. How can we put a probability number on all these factors? And even if we can, these factors must all work to achieve the desired scenario. Ask: What is the prior probability of success for this type of venture before I consider this specific case?

Warren Buffett says on biotech:

> How many of those companies are making a couple of hundred million dollars a year? It just doesn't *happen*. It's not that *easy* to make lots of money in a business in a capitalistic society. There are people that are looking at what you're doing every day and trying to figure out a way to do it better, underprice you, bring out a better product or whatever it may be.

The compensation we need for taking a risk is really a function of the wanted outcome in relation to all possible outcomes. Take rolling a die as an example. How likely is it that we get a six four times in a row? If we have to invest $1 to play this game once, we need to get back $1,296 to go even. There are 1,296 outcomes and only one of them is favorable (6,6,6,6).

The more negative things that can happen – or positive things that must happen – the better compensated we must be for taking on the risk. Ask: What can happen and what are the consequences? Anticipate unforeseen obstacles.

If you do venture investments, follow the advice of Warren Buffett:

> You may consciously purchase a risky investment – one that indeed has a significant possibility of causing loss or injury – if you believe that your gain, weighted for probabilities, considerably exceeds your loss, comparably weighted, and if you can commit to a number of similar, but unrelated opportunities. Most venture capitalists employ this strategy. Should you choose to pursue this course, you should adopt the outlook of the casino that owns a roulette wheel, which will want to see lots of action because it is favored by probabilities, but will refuse to accept a single, huge bet.

We can demonstrate Buffett's advice mathematically. Suppose a start-up has a 40% probability of succeeding. The probability that 10 mutually independent start-ups (with the same probability of success) all succeed is 0.01% but the probability that at least one succeeds is 99.4%. Here we assumed that the fate of each venture is independent of the fate of the other. That one start-up fails make it no more likely that another start-up fails.

"How can we fund this venture if we don't present a great future?"
Consider bias from incentives. To sell in a venture, expected returns are often overestimated. Warren Buffett says, "We expect all of our businesses to now and then have ups and downs. (Only in the sales presentations of investment banks do earnings move forever upward.)"

Systems failure and accidents
On July 25th, 2000, a Concorde bound from Paris to New York crashed shortly after take off. All 109 people on board were killed, along with 4 on the ground.
A stray metal strip on the runway lost by another aircraft caused the event. As a result a tire burst. Its explosion sent pieces of rubber into the fuel tank, causing a fuel leak and fire.

We underestimate how likely it is that an event happens when it may happen one way or another. Accidents happen if they have opportunities to happen.

Astronomy Professor Carl Sagan said in *Carl Sagan*: "The Chernobyl and Challenger disasters remind us that highly visible technological systems in which enormous national prestige had been invested can nevertheless experience catastrophic failures."

System safety doesn't reside in one component but in the interactions of all the components. If one key component fails, the system may fail. Assume a space shuttle is composed of 2,000 independent parts, each with a working probability of 99.9%. All parts need to work for the shuttle to work. The probability that at least one of the parts doesn't work causing the shuttle to malfunction is 86% (many parts means many opportunities for failure).

Some systems are more prone to accidents than others because of the number of parts, their connections and interactions. The more variables we add to a system, the more complicated we make it and the more opportunity the system has to fail. The exception to this is systems that serve as a substitute if the present system breaks down. We must make sure that backup systems don't cause unwanted effects or that some parts share the same defects.

Separate between independent and dependent events. The probability that an airplane navigation system works is 99% and the probability that the back up navigation system works is 90%. The probability that the back up system fails is not influenced by whether the primary system fails or not. The probability that neither navigation system works is one tenth of a percent (0.01x0.1). Navigation system reliability is therefore 99.99% (at least one navigation system will work). But if the systems are dependent – the probability of the back up failing rises if the primary system fails – the overall probability of a system failure increases. We can't assume that events are independent of each other. What happens next in a chain of events may not be independent of the previous outcome. Subsystems may share something in common. For example, aircraft engines draw fuel from a common supply and a common pump. Dependence can also be caused by the fact that parts are of the same design, manufactured by the same company.

Unlikely things happen if enough time passes. An event that has one chance in 20 of happening in any given year (assume that the probability stay the same over time) is nearly certain to happen over 50 years (92.3%). If we reduce the probability to one chance in 40, the probability of the event happening at least once over 50 years is decreased to 71.8%.

Suppose there are 40 independent ways for a nuclear accident to happen in any given year, each with a probability of 1 in 1000. The probability that an accident happens in any given year is 3.9%. The probability that at least one nuclear accident happens during the next 10 years is 33%.

We might reduce the probability of accidents, but not eliminate them.

At 3:42pm, San Francisco was shaken by a major earthquake.
Based on frequency and scientific data, scientists estimated in 1999 that there is a 70% probability (±10%) of at least one 6.7 or larger ("major") earthquake hitting the Bay Area before 2030. The probability of a major earthquake

happening in any given year is therefore 3.9% (assuming the probability of a major earthquake happening in any given year stays the same). The probability that a major earthquake will happen at least once during the next 5 years is 18%.

Regardless of the factors that are considered in predicting earthquakes, chance plays a role in whether a large earthquake happens.

"Our technology was foolproof. How could this happen?"
Many systems fail because they focus on the machines, not the people that use them. For example, a study of anesthesiologists found that human error was involved in 82% of preventable accidents. The remainder was due to equipment failure.

Even if the probability that some technology works is 99.99%, human fallibility makes the system less reliable than technological reliability alone. Humans are involved in designing, execution and follow-up. Excluding ignorance and insufficient knowledge, given the complexity of human and non-human factors interacting, there is a multitude of ways in which things can go wrong.

In 1983 Korean airlines Flight 007 was shot down far into Russian territory for violating Russian air space. All 269 people on board were killed.
The plane had deviated close to 360 miles from its predetermined track. It was later shown that a chain of accidental events led the plane off track. It started when the plane left Anchorage, Alaska. The captain and crew were tired when the plane took off. A series of small events, each trivial, combined to cause a catastrophe.

Doctors sometimes make mistakes – both in diagnosing and treating patients. Surgical resident Atul Gawande tell us about some surgical mishaps in *Complications:*

> A general surgeon left a large metal instrument in a patient's abdomen, where it tore through the bowel and the wall of the bladder…a cancer surgeon biopsied the wrong part of a women's breast and thereby delayed her diagnosis of cancer for months. A cardiac surgeon skipped a small but key step during a heart valve operation, thereby killing the patient.

In the Harvard Medical Practice Study (1991), a random sample of 30,000 patients from 51 hospitals in the state of New York was selected. Medical records were examined to detect evidence of injuries caused by medical mismanagement. The study showed that 3.7% of patients (negligence accounting for 1%) had complications that either prolonged their hospital stay or resulted in disability.

Henry Ford said: "Don't find fault, find a remedy." Don't assign blame. Look for causes and preventive methods. Often it is better to prevent future errors by designing safety into systems than punishing individuals for past error. Blame does little to improve safety or prevent others from making the same mistake. For example, aviation assumes that errors of judgment happen and that it is better to seek out causes than assign blame. That is why the Federal Aviation Administration (FAA) has an Aviation Safety Reporting System (ASRS) for analyzing and reporting aviation incidents. FAA utilizes NASA as a third party to receive aviation safety reports. This cooperation invites pilots to report to NASA actual or potential deficiencies involving aviation safety. That NASA is the receiver ensures confidentiality and anonymity of the reporter and all parties involved in an incident. There has been no breach of confidentiality in more than 20 years of the ASRS under NASA management. Pilots who report an incident within ten days have automatic immunity from punishment.

Safety factor

"We always consider variability and unpredictability when setting safety factors. We act as if we were building a bridge. We are very conservative."

Ancient Rome used incentives in the design and construction of safe bridges. The designer of the bridge had to stand under it after completion while chariots drove over the top. This put both the designer's life and those who used the bridge at risk. This increased the probability that designers made sure the bridge held up.

Engineers and architects add a safety factor to accommodate uncertainty. This factor depends on the consequences of failure, how well the risks are understood, systems characteristics and degree of control.

Assume that accidents will happen and prepare for when people and technology don't work as planned. Systems should be designed to eliminate the probability of bad events or limit their consequences if they happen. We can borrow an idea from aviation where incidents are thoroughly investigated to learn what went wrong and how to do better next time – critical incident analysis. Ask: How do specific accidents evolve? What major factors contribute? Are there any common patterns?

We need to add a factor of safety for known and unknown risks. We have to consider break points, build in defense systems and contingency plans. We must also simplify and standardize equipment and processes and use checklists to decrease the likelihood of operator errors.

Seven

Coincidences and miracles

Coincidences

The most astonishingly incredible coincidence imaginable
would be the complete absence of all coincidences.
- John Allen Paulos (from *Beyond Numeracy*)

We underestimate how many opportunities there are for "unlikely" events to happen. Surprises and improbable events happen if they have enough opportunities to happen. There are many ways in which events may be linked together.

Getting 5 tails in a row is certain to happen somewhere, sometime to someone. The chances may be small that an event happens at a particular place, time or to a particular person. But with many places, over long periods of time or with many individuals, the seemingly improbable will happen. As Aristotle says: "It is likely that unlikely things should happen."

Someone flips tails 20 times in a row.
Amazing, isn't it? Seen as an isolated event it may seem unlikely. But with a large enough group to choose from, it is likely that it happens to someone. In a group of 1,048,576 people it happens to someone. In fact, in the U.S. a country with about 280 million people, one in a million chance events happen 280 times a day.

How likely is it that two people share the same birthday?
There are many opportunities for coincidences. For example, in a group of 23 people, the probability is 50.7% that two people share the same birthday. It is rather likely that events like this one happen since there are many ways that 2 people can share an unspecified birthday. Observe that the question is not how likely it is that 2 people share any particular birthday. The question is whether it is likely that 2 people share an unspecified birthday.

How many people have to be present at Mary's birthday dinner so that there is more than a 50% chance that one of the other guests has the same birthday as Mary? 183, since we now work with the restriction "two people must share a particular birthday."

Scale matters. When the numbers are large enough, improbable things happen. The more available opportunities or the longer the time, unlikely events happen.

Making up causes for chance events

Humans are pattern seeking, storytelling animals. We look for and find patterns in our world and in our lives, then weave narratives around those patterns to bring them to life and give them meaning.
- Michael Shermer (Publisher of *Skeptic*)

John tosses a single die six times and the result is either (A) 623512 or (B) 666111. Which alternative showed the correct outcome? Even if (A) looks like it has a pattern, in independent chance events, both A and B are equally likely to appear.

We look for causes when we see a pattern. We don't like uncertainty so we want to find reasons for all kinds of events – random or not. And if we don't find any, we construct them.

John rolls five dice and gets five sixes.
The probability that some roll contains any five specified numbers is very small or one in 7,776 (for example, 6x6x6x6x6). When we toss five dice there are precisely 7,776 different combinations of numbers that can appear. Every combination is equally likely and one of them is certain to happen every time we roll five dice. Even if one particular combination (five sixes) is improbable, no single combination is impossible. Any combination that happens is simply one out of a number of equally likely outcomes. It may have been improbable that John rolled five sixes, but not impossible.

Anything can happen if the number of possibilities is large. There are no mysterious forces, as described by the late Carl Sagan:

Occasionally, a vegetable or a pattern of wood grain or the hide of a cow resembles a human face. There was a celebrated eggplant that closely resembled Richard M. Nixon. What shall we deduce from this fact? Divine or extraterrestrial intervention? Republican meddling in eggplant genetics? No. We recognize that there are large numbers of eggplants in the world and that, given enough of them, sooner or later we'll come upon one that looks like a human face, even a very particular human face.

Believing in miracles

Inspector Gregory: "Is there any point to which you would wish to draw my attention?"
Sherlock Holmes: "To the curious incident of the dog in the night-time."
Inspector Gregoty: "The dog did nothing in the night-time."
"That was the curious incident," remarked Sherlock Holmes.
- Arthur Conan Doyle (from *Silver Blaze*)

Mary thinks about calling her friend Jill. Suddenly the phone rings and it is Jill.
Is something paranormal going on? No, Mary forgot about all the times Jill didn't call when Mary was thinking about her or someone else called or the times Jill called but Mary wasn't thinking of her.

What didn't happen is sometimes more important than what did happen.

We often see relationships where there are none. We consider cases where cause and effect is present and fail to consider cases involving no cause or no effect. For example, many people who use a certain treatment only consider cases with positive outcomes and therefore conclude that the treatment is effective. But we also have to look at the number of people who a) use the treatment and don't improve, b) don't use the treatment and improve, and c) don't use the treatment and don't improve.

Psychology Professor Thomas Gilovich says in *How We Know What Isn't So:* "With the body so effective in healing itself, many who seek medical assistance will experience a positive outcome even if the doctor does nothing beneficial. Thus, even a worthless treatment can appear effective when the base-rate of success if so high."

"The psychic predicted the tornado"

Amazing. It sounds too good to be chance. What we didn't know was that the psychic predicts a tornado every week. Often we don't notice the incorrect predictions, only the rare moments when something happens. We forget when they are wrong and only remember when they were right. And many times we want them to be right, so we hear what we want to hear and fill in the blanks.

"The art of prophecy is very difficult, especially with respect to the future", wrote Mark Twain. This is why it's important to remain skeptical of "future-tellers." Their right guesses are highly publicized but not all their wrong guesses. Like Harvard Professor Theodore Levitt says, "It's easy to be a prophet. You make twenty-five predictions and the ones that come true are the ones you talk about."

The future-tellers predictions are always far enough in the future that they never have to face the consequences when they're wrong. Or they make their forecasts so general they can apply to anyone or to any outcome so they can't be proved wrong.

Mary comes home after school and tell John: "My friend Alice witnessed a miracle." The 18th Century Scottish Philosopher David Hume suggested a test to analyze claims of miraculous events: "No testimony is sufficient to establish a miracle, unless the testimony be of such a kind, that its falsehood would be more miraculous than the fact which it endeavors to establish."

Hume suggests the following test: If the opposite of a given statement is more likely, the statement is probably false. Thus, isn't it more likely that the opposite, *"Alice didn't witness a miracle"* is true? Not because miracles are impossible but because the alternative explanation of illusion is more probable. How many things that are impossible must happen for a miracle to be true?

The German poet Johann Wolfgang von Goethe said: "Mysteries are not necessarily miracles." That an event can't be explained doesn't mean it is a miracle. No theory can explain everything. As Michael Shermer says, "My analogy is that the L.A.P.D. [Los Angeles Police Department] can solve, say, 90 percent of annual homicides. Are we to assume that the other 10 percent have supernatural or paranormal causes? No, of course not, because we all understand that the police cannot solve all murder mysteries."

Bertrand Russell said in *A History of Western Philosophy:* "Uncertainty, in the presence of vivid hopes and fears, is painful, but must be endured if we wish to live without the support of comforting fairy tales."

– Eight –

Reliability of case evidence

Prior probabilities

Does eyewitness identification or DNA evidence mean that a person is guilty? Does a positive medical test mean that a person has a disease?

In the late eighteenth century, the English Reverend Thomas Bayes, laid a foundation for a method of evaluating evidence. The French mathematician Pierre Simon de Laplace brought the method to its modern form. The method makes it possible to update the prior probability of an outcome in light of new evidence.

Bayes' theorem can be expressed as: The probability of an event H (the hypothesis) occurring given that event E (the evidence or data) has occurred or p(H|E) is equal to

$$\frac{p(H) \times p(E|H)}{[p(H) \times p(E|H)] + [p(\text{not } H) \times p(E|\text{not } H)]}$$

where p (H) is the prior probability (before the evidence or data), p(E|H) is the probability of E given H, and p(E|not H) is the probability of E given not H.

What is Bayes's theorem useful for? Let's demonstrate this with a modified version of the classic cab problem, originally developed by the psychologists Daniel Kahneman and Amos Tversky.

John testifies in court: "I witnessed the accident and the cab involved was green."
John's vision has been reliably tested and the tests establish that he can identify the color green correctly 80% of the time. John said "green" in 8 out of 10 cases when something was green and said "green" 2 times out of 10 when something was blue. This means that John misidentified the color 2 out of 10 times.

How trustworthy is John as an eyewitness? The reliability of any observation not only depends on the reliability of the observer – even if John has good eyes – but also on how likely his observation is true given prior probabilities.

First we ask: What is the prior probability of outcome – how probable is an event prior to considering the new evidence? How probable is it that a green cab was involved in an accident before we consider John's evidence? Assume that the relative frequency (the proportion of cabs of a certain color in a particular population at a specific point in time) of blue and green cabs gives us information about the prior probability of involvement in the accident. What was the proportion of blue and green cabs out of all cabs at the time of the accident? Assume there were a total of 100 cabs in town. 90 blue and 10 green.

The (posterior) probability the cab was green (H), given that John said it was green (E) is 10% x 80% / ((10% x 80%) + (90% x 20%)) = 30.8%.

	Given green	Given blue	Total
John says "green"	8 cabs (10 x 0.8)	18 (90 x 0.2)	26

If 10 out of 100 cabs are green and John is right 80% of the time, then he identifies 8 cabs as green. If John says green cab and it is not a green cab then he is likely to identify 18 of the 90 blue cabs as green. Out of a total of 26 cabs John has identified as green, only 8 are green. This means that the likelihood that the cab was green given John's testimony that "the cab was green" is 31% (8/26). It seems the cab involved is more likely to have been blue.

Before John testified the prior probability was only 10% that the cab involved was green. When he testified "green" the probability rose to 31%.

"Based on 50 years of accidents involving cabs, given the same proportion of color, 3 out of 4 times the cab involved was green."
Independent of the frequency of blue and green cabs, the appropriate prior probability may have been past evidence of accidents. What we want is the correct evidence that is representative for what was likely to happen before we considered the new evidence.

When we get new representative evidence, we must update the prior probability. Ask: What has happened in similar cases in the past? Are there any reasons this probability should be revised? Have the circumstances or the environment changed? The more uncertainty that surrounds a specific case, the more emphasis we must put on the prior probability.

How strong is the evidence?
One factor when evaluating evidence is the coincidental or random match probability. It answers the question: What is the probability that a person other than the suspect, randomly selected, will match a certain profile? For example, when evaluating DNA evidence a random match happens when two different people have the same DNA profile.

After five days of searching, the police found the missing woman strangled to death. John's brother, Bill, is on trial for her murder.

The forensic evidence against Bill is blood and tissue samples (analyzed using a DNA profile) taken from the crime scene, which match Bill's. Either Bill left the evidence or someone else did.

What is the probability of a coincidental match? How likely is it that a match occurs between the DNA profile found at the scene of the murder and a randomly chosen person? How likely is it that Bill's profile matches the profile of the person who did leave the evidence at the crime scene? How rare is this profile? The rarer the profile, the lower the probability that Bill's matches only by chance.

The prosecution's medical expert witness estimates (estimation of the frequency of the profile in the most appropriate comparison population) the probability that there would be such a match if Bill was innocent and the match was just a coincidence as only 1 in 20,000. This means that out of every 20,000 individuals, only one will have the same DNA profile as the one found at the murder scene. The prosecutor argues: *"There is only a one in 20,000 chance that someone other than Bill would by chance have the same profile as the one found on the murder scene. The probability is therefore only 1 in 20,000 that someone other than Bill left the evidence."* The figure had a dramatic impact on the media and the jury. Bill was found guilty and given a life sentence.

Where did justice go wrong? The prosecutor confused two probabilities. The probability that Bill is innocent given a match is not the same as the probability of a match given Bill is innocent. The prosecutor should have said: *"The probability is one in 20,000 that some person other than Bill would leave the same blood and tissue as that found on the crime scene."*

The jury also needs to consider prior (before the forensic evidence is considered) probabilities of guilt. The probability that Bill is the murderer can't only be calculated from the forensic evidence alone. Other evidence needs to be considered. What other data do the police have? What else is known about Bill? Does he have an alibi? Was he near the crime scene? Each piece of evidence must be considered together, and not in isolation. There may also have been a non-criminal explanation of how Bill left the blood and tissue samples.

Based on evidence prior to considering the forensic evidence the jury estimates there is a 10% probability that Bill is the source of the forensic evidence (90% that he is not and thus innocent). The probability of a match given Bill is guilty is 1 (sensitivity 100% i.e. no false negatives) because if Bill is the source of the forensic evidence and the laboratory test is accurate, his DNA profile will match. Combining this with the random match probability of one chance in 20,000 (that his DNA profile showed up at the crime scene just by chance) gives a posterior probability that Bill is the source of the forensic evidence of 99.96% (0.1/0.100045).

	Given guilty	Given innocent	Total
Match	10% x 100%	90% x 1/20,000	0.100045

One way of determining the prior probability is by asking: What is the population from which the murderer could have come? We need to know the appropriate comparison population to estimate this number. The murder has taken place in a city of 500,000 men. Assume any man in the city could have committed the crime. One of them is the murderer. Of the 499,999 people innocent, we can expect about 25 coincidental DNA matches. This means there are 26 men (25 + the murderer) who could have committed the crime. Since Bill is one of these 26, the probability that he is guilty given the forensic evidence, is only 3.8% (1/26).

But is this really true? It is only true if all men are equally likely to have committed the crime. For example, that they all had the same access to the crime scene.

The choice of appropriate comparison population also matters. How did the expert witness estimate the random match probability? What is the real prevalence of this profile? And does the random match probability mean that this profile would occur only once in 20,000 individuals? No, the calculated frequency is only an estimate that may be wrong in either direction.

DNA evidence is also easier to plant at a crime scene than for example fingerprints (easier to manufacture or distort). In *Scientific Conversations* by Claudia Dreifus, forensic mathematician Charles Brenner says about the O.J. Simpson case and DNA evidence: "The defense did something very clever from the DNA point of view: They said the evidence was planted. Their basic strategy was even if it matches, it was a plant. They gave up on the strategy of disproving the DNA evidence. There obviously was a match in the blood. They never denied it."

In the O.J. Simpson trial, the defense argued that fewer than one out of 1,000 wife abusers kill their wives. Therefore evidence of abuse is irrelevant and should not be admissible in a murder trial. But the appropriate probability is not the probability that a man who abuses his wife kills her. The relevant comparison population to consider is wives who have been abused by their husbands and thereafter been murdered by someone. The relevant question is therefore: What is the probability that a man killed his wife given that he abused her and given that she was actually killed by someone? And Nicole Brown Simpson was killed, not just abused.

The mathematician John Allen Paulos says in *Innumeracy* that given reasonable facts about murder and abuse, it has been shown that if a man abuses his wife or girlfriend and she is later killed, the abuser is the killer more than 80 percent of the time. But this doesn't mean that the probability that the husband or boyfriend is guilty of murder is 80%. It is just one piece of evidence among many that needs to be considered.

Do technical or human errors happen in testing?
Yes, people make errors when collecting and handling samples, in their interpretation of test results or in reporting test results correctly. This may cause false positives.

What is the frequency or probability of false positives?

John tested positive for a rare disease with a mortality rate of 80%. How scared should he be?
Are medical tests 100% accurate? What is the chance that anyone (belonging to the same risk group as John) actually has the disease given that they tested positive?

Reliability of case evidence depends both on how accurate the test is and the proportion of positive individuals in the population at a given time. Accuracy is composed of sensitivity (the probability of a positive test given a disease) and specificity (the probability of a negative test given no disease). Assume a population of 100,000 people.

The frequency of people with the disease in the population is 0.1% i.e. one person in 1,000 has the disease. Before the test John had a 0.1% chance of having the disease and a 99.9 % chance of not having the disease. If the test was 100% accurate, 100 people should test positive and 99,900 should test negative. These are the prior probabilities.

The test has a 97% sensitivity or true positive rate. This means that 97 out of 100 people with the disease correctly test positive. It also means that 3 people out of 100 with the disease wrongly test negative (false negatives).
The test has a 95% specificity or true negative rate. This means that 95 out of 100 people without the disease correctly test negative. 5% of the time the test is incorrect. 5% of the people without the disease or 4,995 people wrongly test positive (false positives).

Since John is told he tested positive, the information he needs is the frequency of people that test positive and have the disease (true positives) and the frequency of people that test positive but don't have the disease (false positives).

	Given disease	Given not disease	Total
Test positive	100 x 0.97 = 97	99,900 x 0.05 = 4,995	5,092

Out of every 1,000 people belonging to the same risk group as John, we can expect that 19 people have the deadly disease given they test positive (97/5,092). The probability that John has the deadly disease given he tested positive is about 1.9% or very low. Out of 5,092 tests most are false positives indicating the disease when there is no disease. John should get a second independent test.

The label "tested positive" can be scary but remember that the test is not the disease. A test could fall in the group of false positives. But which is worst? To belong to the group of false positives – diagnosed as having the disease without having it, or false negatives – diagnosed as not having the disease but having it?

The higher the prior probability or the more common a disease, the more reliable the outcome of the test. Conversely, the lower the prior probability or the more rare the disease, the less reliable the outcome of the test. Even a highly accurate test can yield an unreliable result if it tests for a rather uncommon disease. This assumes that the individual tested does not belong to a group of people at higher risk of having the disease.

Ask: What is the frequency of people with the disease in the relevant comparison population before I consider specific case evidence? How accurate is the medical test?

Estimating the frequency of false positives and false negatives are also important when evaluating the reliability of polygraph tests (used in criminal investigations or for screening employees) and identification systems.

In polygraph tests, false positives occur when innocent persons are found deceptive. False negatives occur when guilty persons are found non-deceptive.

In identification systems, a false positive occurs when a system accepts a match where there is none. A false negative occurs when a system fails to recognize a match where there is one.

The probability of false positives is also a factor to consider when evaluating the value of DNA profile evidence. This means that the jury in Bill's case also needs to consider the probability of a false positive. The jury must ask: What is the probability that the laboratory reports a match between two samples that don't match? A reported match doesn't necessarily mean a true match. Errors happen. A possible explanation for the forensic match may be error due to contamination (accidental or deliberate), mishandling the evidence, or switching the samples. For example, in one rape case, technicians from the Houston police crime laboratory told the jury that they found a DNA match between a rapist's DNA and a male suspect. The man was convicted in 1999 and sent to prison for 25 years. In 2003, the Houston Police Department said that the DNA was not from the convicted man.

How does a false positive probability of one in 100 affect the value of DNA evidence? The combined effect of the random match probability, and the false positive probability is $1/20000 + (1/100 \times (19999/20000)) = 0.01005$ or one in 99. This gives a posterior probability that Bill is the source of the forensic evidence of 91.7% (0.1/0.109045).

	Given guilty	Given innocent	Total
Match	10% x 100%	90% x 0.01005	0.109045

What are the posterior odds? The initial odds are 1:9. The posterior odds considering the random match probability are 2222:1. If the probability of a false positive is zero, then the posterior odds are 2222 to one in favor of Bill being the source.

The posterior odds considering the random match probability and false positive probability are 11:1. If the probability of a false positive is one in 100, then the posterior odds in favor of Bill being the source are 11 to one. False positives clearly influence the value of DNA evidence.

When evaluating case evidence we must consider the prior probability, the probability of a random match, and the probability of a false positive.

Nine

Misrepresentative evidence

Conditions, environments and circumstances change

People like to look for systems that have worked over the past 20 years or so. If you could make money based on what has worked the past 20 years, all of the richest people would be librarians.
- Warren Buffett

Can we use the past to indicate what might happen in the future? Often the past is a good guide to the future – but not always. Statistics are a record of the past, not a prediction of the future. We can't automatically assume that the future will mirror the past. Warren Buffett says: "Conditions relating to technology and all aspects of human behavior can make the future a lot different than the past."

We need to consider changes in conditions before using past evidence to predict likely future outcomes. For example, it's in the nature of businesses and economic conditions to change. Competition and demand changes. If there are more ways for creating competition or less demand, we have to change the equation.

We also make mistakes if we ignore that past performance may have been achieved under far different circumstances than today. As Warren Buffett says, "The same mistake that a baseball manager would were he to judge the future prospects of a 42-year-old center fielder on the basis of his lifetime batting average."

Warren Buffett said in 2002:

In the future, we won't come close to replicating our past record. To be sure, Charlie and I will strive for above-average performance and will not be satisfied with less. But two conditions at Berkshire are far different from what they once were: The, we could often buy businesses and securities at much lower valuations than now prevail [conditions change]; and more important, we were then working with far less money than we now have [scale matters]. Some years back, a good $10 million idea could do wonders for us...We need "elephants" to make significant gains now – and they are hard to find.

Management performance may also be conditioned on environment. What makes an individual successful in one environment does not guarantee success in another. Ask: What is the company's or managers ability to handle adversity?

"The number of deaths per thousand from cancer has increased."
Is the frequency of cancer death really increasing? Mathematician Horace Levinson tell us that we need to consider other factors before we conclude that the frequency of an event has changed:

> Cancer is now more accurately diagnosed than before…many deaths formerly listed under other diseases or under "cause unknown" are now listed as due to cancer…there is an increased number of post-mortem diagnoses, due to the increased number of autopsies…great improvements have been effected in the accurate reporting of cases of deaths and in collecting such data…the average length of life has increased, due above all to the decrease in infant mortality. As cancer is primarily a disease of later life, there has been a correspondingly increased proportion of the population "exposed" to it.

If conditions change, we must update our assumptions to reflect the present environment. Before we use the change as evidence for what is likely to happen, ask: What has changed? Are there more ways for some undesirable event to happen? Is the change permanent or temporary?

The single case or unrepresentative samples
Four out of five doctors recommend the drug.
This statement doesn't tell us anything if we don't know how many doctors were observed. Maybe it was just 10; an observation that can't be extrapolated to include all doctors. A small sample size has no predictive value. The smaller the sample is, the more statistical fluctuations and the more likely it is that we find chance events. We need a representative comparison group, sample size, and long enough periods of time.

Small samples can cause us to believe a risk is lower or higher than reality. Why? A small sample increases the chance that we won't find a particular relationship where it exists. A small sample may also increase the chance that we find a correlation where it doesn't exist.

Charles Munger gives an example of the importance of getting representative data – even if it's approximate:

> The water system of California was designed looking at a fairly short period of weather

history. If they'd been willing to take less perfect records and look an extra hundred years back, they'd have seen that they weren't designing it right to handle drought conditions which were entirely likely.

You see that again and again - that people have some information they can count well and they have other information much harder to count. So they make the decision based only on what they can count well. And they ignore much more important information because its quality in terms of numeracy is less - even though it's very important in terms of reaching the right cognitive result. All I can tell you is that around Wesco and Berkshire, we try not to be like that. We have Lord Keynes' attitude, which Warren quotes all the time: "We'd rather be roughly right than precisely wrong." In other words, if something is terribly important, we'll guess at it rather than just make our judgment based on what happens to be easily countable.

Chance and performance

No victor believes in chance.
- Friedrich Wilhelm Nietzsche

Past performance is no guarantee of future results. Consider evidence that describes what happens in most similar situations or to most people.

Sometimes a track record is not a good indicator of what is likely to happen in the future. It may show up by luck. Imagine a room filled with 1,000 monkeys. Each is trying to predict the direction (up or down) of interest rates. At the end of 10 predictions, one monkey has a perfect record of predicting the direction of interest rates. He is considered a genius and the greatest economist in history. Even if it was just by chance.

Sometimes we only see the good performers. Partly because winners have a tendency to show up (one monkey). Losers don't (999 monkeys). Often we aren't interested in the losers anyway. But we shouldn't be amazed to see winners if there is a large population to choose from. 10,000 monkeys and we find 10 geniuses.

When we measure performance we must consider both the number of successes (one monkey), the number of failures (999 monkeys), and the size of the relevant comparison population they came from (1,000 monkeys). The more people (or monkeys), involved in something where chance plays a role, the more likely it is that some people have great performances just by chance. An exception is in a group of high performers where we can observe some common characteristics that may be a causal factor and not luck.

The same mistakes may happen when people base their conclusions on mere effects and ignore the influence of chance. Think about 100 monkeys. They each roll a die once. Select those 16 monkeys (1/6x100) who rolled a six. As a cure for their "roll-a-six" tendency we give them a new drug. After taking the drug they roll the die again. Now only 2 or 3 monkeys (1/6x16) rolled a six. The rest were "cured." Our false conclusion: "The drug obviously worked."

A con artist sets up a trap. He calls John with a tip. "Watch this stock. It will go up."
After 3 correct predictions, John sends him his money. The con artist disappears.
What John didn't know was that the con artist made the same call to 80 people. He told half of them the stock would go up, and the other half the stock would go down. And one of his predictions is sure to be right. 40 people were impressed. At the second call 20 people were impressed and at his third and last call he was considered a genius by 10 people who all sent him their money.

Ignoring failures

Evidence must be drawn from the frequency of both success and failure over time. Often we only consider successes. The epidemiological literature refer to this as survival bias. Only the characteristics of the survivors of a disease or outcome under study are included in the study. Those who have died before the end of the study are excluded. If these are patients with more severe risk factors, the study reduces an apparent association between risk factors and outcomes. Survival bias is also common in all studies made after the outcomes have occurred (including back testing). They only focus on surviving cases/patients. The people who have died of the outcome under study are not in the sampling pool.

If we only study successes or survivors, a performance record may look better than it really is. Charles Munger says that we give too little attention to failures:

It is assumed by many business school graduates, and by almost all consultants, that a corporation can easily improve its outcome by purchasing unrelated or tenuously related businesses. According to this widely shared view, if only the obvious steps had been taken, if the right "mission statement" had been adopted and the right "experts" hired, then each railroad, instead of remaining bound in chains by new forms of competition and obsolete and hostile laws and union rules, would have become another Federal Express, another United Parcel Service, or even another brilliant performer in the mode of Emerson Electric.

Our experience, both actual and vicarious, makes us less optimistic about easy solutions through business acquisition. We think undue optimism arises because successful records draw too much attention. Many people then reason as I would if I forecasted good prospects in big-time tennis after observation limited to Ivan Lendl and Steffi Graf, or good prospects in the California lottery after limiting observations to winners. The converse is also true, only more so. Far too little attention is given to the terrible effects on shareholders (or other owners) of the worst examples of corporate acquisitions such as CBS-DuMont, Xerox-Scientific Data Systems, General Electric-Utah International, Exxon-Reliance Electric...and Avon Products.

In 1999, people said: "Internet businesses are doing great."
Often we see only the businesses that do well and ignore the failures. Especially in bull markets where successes get wide publicity. Ask: What is the relevant comparison population from which we measure 5-year performance (assume 100 Internet businesses)? How many are doing well (assume 5). How many are not performing well (assume 80). How many have gone out of business (assume 15). From this we can draw the conclusion that the above statement is false.

TransCorps technical department developed a new defense system and claims a success rate of 80%. When John observed 10 tests, he witnessed 8 failures and only 2 successes.
In 1992, Theodore Postol, a professor of science and national security at MIT, measured the effectiveness (not in terms of its psychological and political impact) of the Patriot anti-missile system in the Gulf War. Based on studying videotapes of 26 Patriot/Scud engagements involving 25 misses and 1 hit, he told the Committee on Government Operations that, "the video evidence makes an overwhelming circumstantial case that Patriot did not come close to achieving a 80 percent intercept rate in Saudi Arabia." The Pentagon reported firing 47 Patriot missiles at Scuds, at first claiming an 80% success rate. A congressional report later concluded that Patriots succeeded in downing only 4 Scuds.

If we assume that John's observations represent a valid random sample of tests, how likely is it that he would observe exactly 2 "hits" and 8 "misses" if the technical department's claim was true?

This is an example of a binomial experiment. It describes experiments with repeated, identical trials where each trial can only have two possible outcomes (e.g. success or failure). Assuming independent engagements, the probability is only 0.007%. If the departments claim was true, then John witnessed an event of a very low probability. It is more likely that their claim was false.

Variability

You can, for example, never foretell what any man will do, but you can say with precision what an average number will be up to. Individuals vary, but percentages remain constant. So says the statistician.
- Arthur Conan Doyle (from *The Sign of Four*)

When evaluating likely outcomes, look for average outcome, variability, and the probability of an extreme outcome and its consequences. Ask: How much do the outcomes fluctuate around the average? What factors contribute to past variability? Have they changed?

John has an option to play one of two games. Each game has three equally likely outcomes. The game may be one of chance, insurance, investing, etc.

	Outcomes	Average outcome	Probability	Expected value
Game 1	30 40 50	40	1/3 1/3 1/3	40
Game 2	0 20 100	40	1/3 1/3 1/3	40

If he plays each game over and over, the average outcome is 40 for both, so it shouldn't matter what game he chooses to play. But what about if John only plays this game once? He should play game 1 since it has less variability. What we mean with variability is how much the individual outcomes are spread out from the average outcome. The more spread out, the more variability.

John has been offered to invest in a private venture capital fund. The venture manager's track record is an average rate of return of 25% over the last five years.
This doesn't say much if we don't look at how the underlying performance was produced. By looking closely at how this return was produced John found that the venture manager had done 10 deals. One deal had been a spectacular success and the rest failures. Had this one deal been due to luck?
Remember that some people leave out data when reporting their performance.

Mary reads in the paper that the average price of a house is $1,000,000.
But this may cause her to get a false picture of reality. Assume there are 100 houses and 90 of them are priced at $500,000 and 10 "castles" at $5.5 million. We have to watch out for the variations.
A business executive tells us that his company had average earnings of $50 million over the last 3 years. But when we look closer we find great variability and a downward trend in the performance record: 1998: $100 million, 1999: $50 million, 2000: $0.

"We make an average profit of $100 on each customer."
What about the variability? Half the customers generate $200 and the other half -$100.
The normal distribution curve may help us find average outcome and

variations. It describes a random distribution of outcomes and variations from a large number of experiments.

There are many ways a set of outcomes can be distributed. But some outcomes are more frequent than others. A lot of characteristics resulting from random factors have a bell-shaped frequency distribution. This means that the most frequent outcomes will be in the middle of the distribution, and the other outcomes will fall on either side of the middle. The further away any outcome is from the middle, the less frequent it is.

Examples of normally distributed outcomes are heights or weights of adults (which depend on factors such as genes, diet, environment, etc.), temperatures, the length of life of a light bulb, etc. Take the heights of female adults as an example. If we randomly select one thousand adult females and measure their height, we end up with a distribution of outcomes that look like a bell-shaped curve. Their heights will be centered around their average length, and the breadth of the curve indicates how variable around this average the heights are.

Even the behavior of extreme events and values such as the very tallest or shortest individuals also follow their own curve. Catastrophic events fall in the tails of the curve, and are therefore the least predictable.

But sometimes the normal distribution curve may not give us a true picture of reality. If the number of experiments is large and independent, the curve tells us something, otherwise not. We also must watch for variations. One single extreme outcome can have a large impact. A few outcomes at the low end or high end could skew our picture of reality.

In repeated games and over the long run, the average dominates. The less number of times or the shorter the time, the more important it is to consider the variability. For an insurance company specializing in insuring unique events, the possible variability in outcomes is key. The more of the same game the insurance company plays (like auto insurance), the better the average becomes as a guide. This assumes that past average outcome is representative as a guide for the future.

Effects of regression

"Regression to the mean" is a notion worked out by Sir Francis Galton (Charles Darwin's first cousin). It says that, in any series of events where chance is involved, very good or bad performances, high or low scores, extreme events, etc. tend on the average, to be followed by more average performance or less extreme events. If we do extremely well, we're likely to do worse the next time, while if we do poorly, we're likely to do better the next time. But regression to the mean is not a natural law. Merely a statistical tendency. And it may take a long time before it happens.

Dissatisfied with the new employees' performance, John put them into a skill-enhancing program. He measures the employees' skills at the end of the program.
Their scores are now higher than they were on the first test. John's conclusion: "The skill-enhancing program caused the improvement in skill." This isn't necessarily true. Their higher scores could be the result of regression to the mean. Since these individuals were measured as being on the low end of the scale of skill, they would have shown an improvement even if they hadn't taken the skill-enhancing program. And there could be many reasons for their earlier performance – stress, fatigue, sickness, distraction, etc. Their true ability perhaps hasn't changed.

Our performance always varies around some average true performance. Extreme performance tends to get less extreme the next time. Why? Testing measurements can never be exact. All measurements are made up of one true part and one random error part. When the measurements are extreme, they are likely to be partly caused by chance. Chance is likely to contribute less on the second time we measure performance.

If we switch from one way of doing something to another merely because we are unsuccessful, it's very likely that we do better the next time even if the new way of doing something is equal or worse.

Part Two and Three dealt with reasons for misjudgments and ideas for reducing them. Before we enter Part Four let's conclude with how we can learn from past mistakes.

Post Mortem
Spanish-American philosopher George Santayana once said: "Those who cannot remember the past are condemned to repeat it." How can we understand what is happening to us without any reference to the past? We conveniently forget to record our mistakes. But they should be highlighted. We should confess our errors and learn from them. We should look into their causes and take steps to prevent them from happening again. Ask:

- What was my original reason for doing something? What did I know and what were my assumptions? What were my alternatives at the time?
- How did reality work out relative to my original guess? What worked and what didn't?
- Given the information that was available, should I have been able to predict what was going to happen?
- What worked well? What should I do differently? What did I fail to do? What did I miss? What must I learn? What must I stop doing?

Why don't we do post mortems? Charles Munger says:

You tend to forget your own mistakes when reputation is threatened by remembering. For that very reason, one very wise company – Johnson & Johnson – has a system whereby two years or so after they've made some big acquisition they have a post-mortem. And they bring back the original projections and the original reasons for doing the deal. They identify the people who made the arguments and what have you. Then they compare them with how the deal worked out.

Warren Buffett says:

Managers tend to be reluctant to look at the results of the capital projects or the acquisitions that they proposed with great detail only a year or two earlier to a board. And they don't want to actually stick the figures up there as to how the reality worked out relative to the projections. That's human nature.

But I think you're a better doctor if you drop by the pathology department occasionally. And I think you're a better manager or investor if you look at each decision that you've made of importance and see which ones worked out and which ones didn't – and figure your batting average. Then, if your batting average gets too bad, you better hand the decision-making over to someone else….

What guidelines and tools are there to better thinking? Charles Munger gives us some introductory remarks for Part Four:

Berkshire is basically a very old-fashioned kind of a place and we try to exert discipline to *stay* that way. I don't mean old-fashioned stupid. I mean the eternal verities: basic mathematics, basic horse sense, basic fear, basic diagnosis of human nature making possible predictions regarding human behavior. If you just do that with a certain amount of discipline, I think it's likely to work out quite well.

Part Four

Guidelines to better thinking

The brain can be developed just the same way as the muscles can be developed, if one will only take the pains to train the mind to think.
- Thomas Alva Edison (American inventor, 1847-1931)

ONE

Sun Tzu said in *The Art of War:* "The general who wins a battle makes many calculations in his temple before the battle is fought."

The purpose of this part is to explore tools that provide a foundation for rational thinking. Ideas that help us when achieving goals, explaining "why," preventing and reducing mistakes, solving problems, and evaluating statements.

The following 12 tools will be discussed.

1. Models of reality.
2. Meaning.
3. Simplification.
4. Rules and filters.
5. Goals.
6. Alternatives.
7. Consequences.
8. Quantification.
9. Evidence.
10. Backward thinking.
11. Risk.
12. Attitudes.

MODELS OF REALITY

Educated men are as superior to uneducated men as the living are to the dead.
- Aristotle

Learn, understand and use the big ideas that explain a lot about how the world works. When Charles Munger was asked what would be the best question he should ask himself, he said:

If you ask not about investment matters, but about your personal lives, I think the best question is, "Is there anything I can do to make my whole life and my whole mental process work better?"

And I would say that developing the habit of mastering the multiple models which underlie reality is the best thing you can do…It's just so much fun – and it works so well.

A model is an idea that help us better understand how the world works. Models illustrate consequences and answer questions like "why" and "how". Take the model of social proof as an example. What happens? When people are uncertain they often automatically do what others do without thinking about the correct thing to do. This idea helps explain "why" and predict "how" people are likely to behave in certain situations. Another use of models is from Sweden. Using models from racing (how mechanics change tires in a couple of seconds) and airports (air traffic control), a Swedish hospital anticipates shortening waiting lines for surgery.

Models help us avoid problems. Assume that we are told that the earth consists of infinite resources. By knowing the idea about limits, we know the statement is false. Someone gives us an investment proposal about a project that contradicts the laws of physics. How much misery can be avoided by staying away from whatever doesn't make scientific sense?

What characterizes a useful model?

If a model agrees with reality, it is most likely true. One idea from biology that agrees with reality is that "people on average act out of self-interest." But not the idea that "people's personalities can be evaluated by using the Rorschach ink-blot test." It can't predict people's personalities. Ask: What is the underlying big idea? Do I understand its application in practical life? Does it help me understand the world? How does it work? Why does it work? Under what conditions does it work? How reliable is it? What is its limitations? How does it relate to other models?

Charles Munger gives an example of a useful model:

Another model that I very much like, I've taken from E.O. Wilson, Harvard's great ant specialist biologist – and that's *autocatalysis* in chemistry. If you get a certain kind of process going in chemistry, it speeds up on its *own*. So you get this marvelous *boost* in what you're trying to do that runs on and on. Now, the laws of physics are such that it doesn't run on *forever*. But it runs on for a goodly while. So you get a huge boost. You accomplish A – and, all of a sudden, you're getting A + B + C for awhile…

Disney is an amazing example of autocatalysis… They *had* all those movies in the can. They owned the copyright. And just as Coke could prosper when refrigeration came, when the videocassette was invented, Disney didn't have to invent anything or do anything except take the thing out of the can and stick it on the cassette.

Which models are most reliable? Charles Munger answers:

> The models that come from hard science and engineering are the most reliable models on
> this Earth. And engineering quality control – at least the guts of it that matters to you and
> me and people who are not professional engineers - is very much based on the elementary
> mathematics of Fermat and Pascal: It costs so much and you get so much less likelihood
> of it breaking if you spend this much…
>
> And, of course, the engineering idea of a backup system is a very powerful idea. The
> engineering idea of breakpoints – that's a very powerful model, too. The notion of a critical
> mass - that comes out of physics - is a very powerful model. All of these things have great
> utility in looking at ordinary reality.

A valuable model produces meaningful explanations and predictions of likely
future consequences where the cost of being wrong is high.

A model should be easy to use. If it is complicated, we don't use it.

It is useful on a nearly daily basis. If it is not used, we forget it. And what use
is knowledge if we don't use it?

Considering many ideas helps us achieve a holistic view

Those who love wisdom must be inquirers into many things indeed.
- Heraclitus

What can help us see the big picture? How can we consider many aspects of an issue?
Use knowledge and insights from many disciplines. Most problems need to be
studied from a variety of perspectives. Charles Munger says, "In most messy human
problems, you have to be able to use *all* the big ideas and not just a few of them."

The world is multidisciplinary. Physics doesn't explain everything; neither
does biology or economics, etc. We need them all. For example, in a business it
is useful to know how scale changes behavior, how systems may break, how
supply influences prices, how incentives cause behavior, etc.

Since no single discipline has all the answers, we need to understand and use
the big ideas from all the important disciplines – mathematics, physics,
chemistry, engineering, biology, psychology, and use them in order of their
reliability. Charles Munger illustrates the importance of this:

> Suppose you want to be good at declarer play in contract bridge. Well, you know the
> contract – you know what you have to achieve. And you can count up the sure winners
> you have by laying down your high cards and your invincible trumps.

But if you're a trick or two short, how are you going to get the other needed tricks? Well, there are only six or so different, standard methods: You've got long-suit establishment. You've got finesses. You've got throw-in plays. You've got cross-ruffs. You've got squeezes. And you've got various ways of misleading the defense into making errors. So it's a very limited number of models. But if you only know one or two of those models, then you're going to be a horse's patoot in declarer play…

If you *don't* have the full repertoire, I guarantee you that you'll overutilize the limited repertoire you have – including use of models that are inappropriate just because they're available to you in the limited stock you have in mind.

We also need to understand how different ideas interact. Charles Munger says:

You get *lollapalooza* effects when two, three or four forces are all operating in the same direction. And, frequently, you don't get simple addition. It's often like a critical mass in physics where you get a nuclear *explosion* if you get to a certain point of mass - and you don't get anything much worth seeing if you *don't* reach the mass.

Sometimes the forces just add like ordinary quantities and sometimes they combine on a break-point or critical-mass basis… More commonly, the forces coming out of…models are *conflicting* to some extent. And you get huge, miserable trade-offs…So you [must] have the *models* and you [must] see the *relatedness* and the effects from the relatedness.

How can we learn an idea so it sticks in our memory? Samuel Johnson said: "He is a benefactor of mankind who contracts the great rules of life into short sentences, that may be easily impressed on the memory, and so recur habitually to the mind."

Richard Feynman answered the following question in one of his physics lectures:

If, in some cataclysm, all of scientific knowledge were to be destroyed, and only one sentence passed on to the next generations of creatures, what statement would contain the most information in the fewest words? I believe it is the *atomic hypothesis* (or the atomic *fact,* or whatever you wish to call it) that *all things are made of atoms - little particles that move around in perpetual motion, attracting each other when they are a little distance apart, but repelling upon being squeezed into one another.* In that one sentence, you will see, there is an *enormous* amount of information about the world, if just a little imagination and thinking are applied.

We can use the Feynman "one sentence explanation" when dealing with big ideas. "What sentence contains the most information in the fewest words?" An example of a one-sentence idea from psychology is: "We get what we reward for."

A sentence from physics is: "Energy is neither created nor destroyed – only changed from one form into another."

Another way to understand a model is to give it a "hook." Associate the model with a dramatic real-life story, analogy, individual, or picture. For example to remember social proof, we can think about the Genovese homicide in New York City (see Part Two).

A Chinese proverb says, "I forget what I hear; I remember what I see; I know what I do." Since the best way to learn something is by doing it, we must apply models routinely to different situations. Like any skill, this takes both repetition and discipline.

Search for explanations
What happens and why does it happen?
One way of forcing us to learn models to better deal with reality is to open our eyes and look at the things we see around us and ask "why" things are happening (or why things are not happening). Take some simple examples as "why do apples fall downward?" or "why do we fall down when we slip?" or "why don't we fall off the earth?" The English mathematician and physicist Sir Isaac Newton's law of gravitation can explain this.

Newton's 1st law tells us that an object in motion tends to continue in motion at a steady speed in a straight line, and an object at rest tends to stay at rest, unless the object is acted upon by an outside force.

This means that there are only 3 ways to change an object: an object at rest can start to move, an object in motion at a steady speed can go up or down in speed, and an object in motion in a straight line can change direction. And what is needed to change an object's motion? A force.

All change in motion happens in response to the action of force(s). By forces, we mean a push or a pull that acts on an object. When we open a door or throw a baseball, we are using forces (muscular effort). Almost everything we do involves forces.

Newton's 2nd law tells us that force is the product of mass and acceleration. Acceleration is any change in speed and/or direction. It depends on the mass (measures an object power to resist change in its state of motion) of an object and the magnitude and direction of the frce acting on it. The more force we use at a given mass, the greater the acceleration. But the more mass, the more an object resists acceleration. For example, the more force we use to throw a baseball, the greater the acceleration of the ball. If we increase mass, we have to add more force to produce the same rate of acceleration.

Newton's 3rd law is that forces work in pairs. One object exerts a force on a second object, but the second object also exerts a force equal and opposite in direction to the force acting on it – the first object. As Newton said in *Philosophiae Naturalis Principia Mathematica*: "If you press a stone with your finger, the finger is also pressed by the stone." If we throw a baseball, the ball also "throws" us or pushes back on our hand with the same force.

Now we come to the force of gravity. Influenced by Johannes Kepler's work on planetary motion and Galileo Galilei's work on freely falling objects, Newton found out that there was a force that attracts two objects to each other. Two factors influence the degree of attraction. Mass and distance. The greater the mass of two objects or the closer the distance between them, the greater the attraction between them. This also means that the greater the distance between the objects, the weaker the force of gravity. If we for example double the distance, the force is as fourth as strong.

Mathematically we can state the force of attraction or gravitation as equal to the mass of one object multiplied with the mass of the other object divided by the square of the distance between the objects. All this is multiplied with a constant (a number that doesn't change in value) – g (9.8 meters per second each second or $9.8m/s^2$). We can call g, the acceleration of gravity near the surface of the Earth.

It is the force of gravity that makes an apple fall toward the Earth.
The Earth attracts the apple with a force that is proportional to its mass and inversely proportional to the square of the distance between them. But Newton's third law says that the apple also exerts an equal and opposite force on the Earth. The force of attraction on the apple by the Earth is the same as the force of attraction on the Earth by the apple. So even if it looks to us like the apple falls to the Earth, both the Earth and apple fall toward each other. The force is the same but as we see from Newton's second law, not the acceleration. Their masses differ. The Earth's mass is so large compared to the apple that we see the apple "falling." Apples fall, starting at rest, to the Earth since they have less mass than the Earth, meaning they accelerate (change speed) more toward the Earth than the Earth does toward the apple. The Earth's great mass also explains why we fall toward the Earth when we slip.

The same force draws the Moon to the Earth. But what keeps the Moon in orbit around the Earth instead of crashing into the Earth?

Newton knew that there must be some force pulling the Moon toward the Earth. Otherwise according to the 1st law the Moon would continue in motion in a straight line at a steady speed instead of its more elliptical motion. Some force must continuously pull the Moon out of its straight-line motion and change its direction. And since the Moon's orbit is circular, this force must originate from the center of the Earth. Why? Newton knew that a centripetal force (any force directed toward a fixed center) controls objects going in a circle around a fixed point.

That force is gravity. It changes the Moons acceleration by continually changing its direction toward the center of the Earth causing the Moon to curve into circular motion. As the Moon moves horizontally in a direction tangent (the straight line that touches a curve) to the Earth, at each point along its path, gravity pulls it inward toward the center of the Earth and the result is a Moon in circular orbit.

The Moon's speed is great enough to ensure that its falling distance matches the Earth's curvature. The Moon remains at the same distance above Earth since the Earth curves at the same rate as the Moon "falls." By the time the Moon has fallen a certain distance toward Earth, it has moved sideways about the same distance. If its speed were much lower, the pull of gravity would gradually force the Moon closer to the Earth until they crash into each other. If its speed where much higher, the Moon would escape the force of gravity and move away from us.

The Moon doesn't accelerate as much as the apple, because of its distance to Earth (the force of gravity is weaker). The Moon in its orbit is about sixty times as far away from the Earth's center as the apple is.

Newton's law of gravitation isn't enough to describe the motion of objects whose speed is near the speed of light. Why? According to Albert Einstein's theory of relativity, the mass of an object is not a constant. It increases as its speed approaches the speed of light. Newton's theories and the theory of relativity also differ when gravitational fields are much larger than those found on Earth. Under most conditions, though, Newton's laws and his theory of gravitation are adequate.

The relative influence of gravity varies with size and scale.

Why does falling from a high tree not harm an insect?
In *Two New Sciences,* Galileo Galilei wrote: "Who does not know that a horse falling from a height of three or four cubits will break his bones, while a dog falling from the same height or a cat from a height of eight or ten cubits will suffer no injury?"

Imagine if a mouse, a horse and a human were to be thrown out of an airplane from 1,000 yards. What happens? The biologist J.B.S. Haldane said in *On Being the Right Size* (reprinted in The World of Mathematics): "You can drop a mouse down a thousand-yard mine shaft; and, on arriving at the bottom, it gets a slight shock and walks away, provided that the ground is fairly soft. A rat is killed, a man is broken, a horse splashes."

Physical forces act on animals differently. Gravity has a more powerful effect on bigger things, than on smaller things. Gravity is a major influence on us, but is of minor significance to smaller animals. Since human surface area is so small, gravitational forces act upon our weight. But gravity is negligible to very small animals with high surface area to volume ratios. The dominant force is then surface force. Haldane says: "Divide an animal's length, breadth, and height each by ten; its weight is reduced to a thousandth, but its surface only to a hundredth. So the resistance to falling in the case of the small animal is relatively ten times greater than the driving force [of gravity]."

Weight affects speed when air resistance is present.
On smaller scales, gravity becomes less and less important compared with air resistance. Throw a mouse off the plane and it floats down as frictional forces acting on its surface overcome the influence of gravity.

A falling object falls faster and faster, until the force of air drag acting in the opposite direction (arising from air resistance) equals its weight. Air drag depends on the surface area (the amount of air the falling object must plow through as it falls) and the speed of the falling object. Since a mouse has so much surface area compared to its small weight, it doesn't have to fall very fast before the upward-acting air drag builds up to its downward-acting weight. The net force on the mouse is then zero and the mouse stops accelerating.

The force of air resistance against the falling horse is much greater than the force against the mouse. This happens because the horse plows through more air than the mouse does. The heavier horse falls faster through the air, increasing air resistance even more. The horse falls faster than the human before the air drag equals its weight and will therefore reach the ground first.

The horse has a greater surface area than the mouse, but the mouse has a greater surface area for its volume than the horse has. A mouse obeys the same law of gravitation as a human, and also the same law of air-resistance. But gravitation is key for humans, while air-resistance is all-important for the mouse.

On the other hand, due to surface tension, the mouse will have problems when climbing from a pool of water. Haldane tells us a wet mouse has to carry its own weight of water. Imagine how hard it would be to get out of the bathtub if we carried on our body a weight of water equal to our weight.

These examples show how we can better deal with reality by observing and ask "why" things happen. So look around, ask questions and remember the words of inventor and engineer Charles Proteus Steinmetz: "There are no foolish questions and no man becomes a fool until he has stopped asking questions."

Assume that the big ideas are true until learning otherwise. All knowledge is subject to change as new evidence arrives. This mean we have to continuously learn and re-learn.

Keeping knowledge alive and adding knowledge over time comes with an extra benefit. "Just as iron rusts from disuse, and stagnant water putrefies, or when cold turns to ice, so our intellect wastes unless it is kept in use," wrote Leonardo da Vinci. Research by Neuroanatomy Professor Marian Cleeves Diamond at the University of California, Berkeley, reveals that a stimulating environment, curiosity and education is nourishment to the brain and therefore health. The more stimulation we give our brains, the better off we are. In *Psychology Today* (1984) she says, "I looked for people who were extremely active after 88 years of age. I found that the people who use their brains don't lose them. It was that simple."

Remember, knowing a definition or memorizing an idea is useless if we don't understand its meaning. The British mathematician and philosopher Alfred North Whitehead said in *The Aims of Education:* "Education should be useful, whatever your aim in life. It was useful to Saint Augustine and it was useful to Napoleon. It is useful, because understanding is useful."

Two

Meaning

Bad terminology is the enemy of good thinking.
- Warren Buffett

Words, definitions, propositions, statements, or goals don't tell us anything. We need to understand what they mean. It is the same with knowledge. Knowledge is only valuable if it's useful and something is only useful if we understand what it means.

Richard Feynman's father, Melville, taught his son, "the difference between knowing the name of something and knowing something," as told by Feynman in this anecdote:

> "See that bird?" he [Melville] says. "It's a Spencer's warbler." (I knew he didn't know the real name.) "Well, in Italian, it's a *Chutto Lapittida*. In Portuguese, it's a *Bom da Peida*. In Chinese, it's a *Chung-long-tah*, and in Japanese, it's a *Katano Tekeda*. You can know the name of that bird in all the languages of the world, but when you're finished, you'll know absolutely nothing whatever about the bird. You'll only know about humans in different places, and what they call the bird. So let's look at the bird and see what it's *doing* – that's what counts."

Doesn't this tell us something in the sense of learning? Words or names don't constitute knowledge. Knowing the name of something doesn't help us understand it. Since understanding implies action and accomplishment, one way of understanding is to see what happens. Feynman illustrates:

> There is a picture of a dog, a windable toy dog, and a hand comes to the winder, and then the dog is able to move. Under the last picture, it says "What makes it move?"...
>
> The answer I was trying to learn is that "energy makes it move." ...
>
> It would be equally well to say that "God makes it move," or "spirit makes it move," or "movability makes it move." (In fact equally well to say "energy makes it stop.")
>
> Look at it this way: That's only the definition of energy. It should be reversed. We might say when something can move that it has energy in it, but not "what makes it move is energy."...

If you ask a child what makes the toy dog move, if you ask an ordinary human being what makes a toy dog move, that is what you should think about. The answer is that you wound up the spring, it tries to unwind and pushes the gear around. What a good way to begin a science course. Take apart the toy, see how it works…

I think for lesson number one, to learn a mystic formula for answering questions is very bad.

Feynman gives another example of an empty definition: "the soles of your shoes wear out because of friction." Real knowledge is: "Shoe leather wears out because it rubs against the sidewalk and the little notches and bumps on the sidewalk grab pieces and pull them off."

Feynman provides a test we can do to check our understanding:

Without using the new word which you have just learned, try to rephrase what you have just learned in your own language. Without using the word *energy*, tell me what you know now about the dog's motion.

Understanding "meaning" requires that we observe and ask basic questions. Examples of some questions are:

- Meaning of words: What do the words mean? What is implied by them? Do they mean anything? An expression is always relative. We have to judge and measure it against something.
- Meaning of an event: Can we translate words, ideas or statements into an ordinary situation that tells us something? Albert Einstein said: "If you can't explain it simply, you don't understand it well enough." What is really happening using ordinary words? What is the explanation? What is it doing? What is accomplished? Under what conditions does it happen? What else does it mean?
- Causes: What is happening here and why? Is this working? Why or why not? Why did that happen? What caused it? Why does it work here but not there? How can it happen? What are the mechanisms behind? What makes it happen?
- Implications: What is the consequence of this observation, event, or experience? What does that imply?
- Purpose: Why should we do that? What is the purpose? Why do I want this to happen?
- Reason: Why is this better than that?
- Usefulness: What is the applicability of this? Does it mean anything in relation to what I want to achieve?

Danish physicist Niels Bohr said: "Never express yourself more clearly, than you are able to think." When describing something, tell it as it is and use words that people understand, and in terms of ideas with which they are familiar. Get to the point. Ask: What do I want to say? One reason for miscommunication can be that the words mean one thing to you and something else to the person you're talking to.

Ask "What happens?"

Why have Warren Buffett and Charles Munger successfully compounded the value of Berkshire Hathaway over 3000 times over the last 38 years? Why do many people lose money investing?

The reason we invest in an economic asset like a business, apartment building, farm, or bond is to make money. But what does that mean? What is making money? What happens when we make money?

Follow the cash. "How much cash do I get and when do I get it?"

What happens when we make money is that we get more money back in the future than we invest today. For example, we invest $100 and get back $150.

What determines our return from investing in an economic asset? The price we pay, how much money we get back, and when we get it back. It makes a huge difference if we get $150 back in 2 years or 10 years. The difference in yearly return is 22% versus 4%. Our return can be measured against the expected returns from other available investment opportunities. This means that the value of an economic asset is influenced by interest rates. If interest changes, value changes. The higher the rates, the less the value.

If we knew for certain we would get $10 in cash every year for 5 years and we use a risk-free government bond rate of 6% as the discount rate, then the asset has a value of about $42. This means that if we pay $42, we get a 6% average yearly rate of return. If we pay $30, our return rises to 20%. The larger the difference between an economic asset's value (e.g. $42) and the price we pay, the higher our yearly return becomes.

Warren Buffett says, "We use the risk-free rate merely to equate one item to another. In other words, we're looking for whatever is *the* most attractive. In order to estimate the present value of anything, we're going to use a number. And, obviously, we can always buy government bonds. Therefore, that becomes the yardstick rate…to simply compare all *kinds* of investment opportunities across the spectrum: oil wells, farms, whatever it may be."

Don't pay more than what you get back in value.
Benjamin Franklin said: "I conceive that great part of the miseries of mankind are brought upon them by the false estimates they have made of the value of things, and by their giving too much for their whistles." One of Francois Duc de la Rochefoucauld's maxims was: "The height of ability consists in a thorough knowledge of the true value of things."

The key question we should ask when investing money in economic assets is: What is the expected future cash we can take out and when does it appear? How else can we know what an asset may be worth and what kind of return we can expect at a given price? Warren Buffett says: "In the end, what you have to decide is whether you're going to value a business at $400 million, $600 million or $800 million – and then compare that with the price."

John wants to buy an ice cream store (it doesn't matter if it is a small ice cream store or 100 shares in a billion dollar business, the relevant reasoning is the same).
Is this a good deal? It depends on the price John pays, and the discounted value of the cash that can be taken out of the ice cream store during its remaining life. How much cash can John take out? When can he take it out? This depends on the amount and timing of the free cash flow that is generated by the store or how much cash he can take out (and when) without hurting the store's present position against competition.

Warren Buffett says of the "cash flow" numbers that are often set forth in Wall Street reports:

> These numbers routinely include (a) [reported earnings] plus (b) [depreciation, depletion, amortization, and certain other non-cash charges] – but do not subtract (c) [the average annual amount of capitalized expenditures for plant and equipment, etc.] Most sales brochures of investment bankers also feature deceptive presentations of this kind. These imply that the business being offered is the commercial counterpart of the Pyramids – forever state-of-the-art, never needing to be replaced, improved or refurbished.

Some cash is always needed for reinvestment in capital expenditures for plant and equipment and working capital merely to enable a business to stay in business or maintain its unit volume and long-term competitive position. A classic example is a retail store that needs to install air-conditioning because other stores have made the investment. It doesn't generate any extra business, but without it, the store may lose customers to competition.

Buffett also says that we have to watch out for certain figures: "When companies or investment professionals use terms such as "EBITDA" and "pro forma," they want you to unthinkingly accept concepts that are dangerously flawed."

He continues:

Trumpeting EBIDTA (earnings before interest, taxes, depreciation and amortization) is a particularly pernicious practice. Doing so implies that depreciation is not truly an expense, given that it is a "non-cash" charge. That's nonsense. In truth, depreciation is a particularly unattractive expense because the cash outlay it represents is paid up front, before the asset acquired has delivered any benefits to the business. Imagine, if you will, that at the beginning of this year a company paid all of its employees for the next ten years of their service (in the way they would lay out cash for a fixed asset to be useful for ten years). In the following nine years, compensation would be a "non-cash" expense – a reduction of a prepaid compensation asset established this year. Would anyone care to argue that the recording of the expense in years two through ten would be simply a bookkeeping formality?

But isn't it earnings that matter for stockholders? John Burr Williams wrote in his 1938 book, *The Theory of Investment Value:*

If earnings not paid out in dividends are all successfully reinvested at compound interest for the benefit of the stockholder…then these earnings should produce dividends later; if not, then they are money lost….Earnings are only a means to an end, and the means should not be mistaken for the end. Therefore we must say that a stock derives its value from its dividends, not its earnings, In short, a stock is worth only *what you can get out of it…* for we are discussing permanent investment, not speculative trading, and dividends for years to come, not income for the moment only.

Warren Buffett adds, "If somebody's reinvesting all their cash flow, they better have some very big figures coming in down the road because a financial asset has to give you back a lot more cash one day in order to justify your laying out cash for it now."

Is value a precise figure?
Warren Buffett says:

Intrinsic value is an estimate rather than a precise figure, and it is additionally an estimate that must be changed if interest rates move or forecasts of future cash flows are revised.

Two people looking at the same set of facts, moreover - and this would apply even to Charlie and me - will almost inevitably come up with at least slightly different intrinsic value figures.

Using precise numbers is, in fact, foolish; working with a range of possibilities is the better approach.

Is there a difference between how we value different businesses?
No matter whether a company makes telecom equipment, cars, or candy, it's still the same question: How much cash do we get and when? The name attached to the cash doesn't matter. Warren Buffett says:

> What you're trying to do is to look at all the cash a business will produce between now and judgment day and discount it back to the present using an appropriate discount rate and buy a lot cheaper than that. Whether the money comes from a bank, an Internet company, a brick company...the money all spends the same. Why pay more for a telecom business than a brick business? Money doesn't know where it comes from. There's no sense in paying more for a glamorous business if you're getting the same amount of money, but paying more for it. It's the same money that you can get from a brick company at a lower cost. The question is what are the economic characteristics of the bank, the Internet company or the brick company. That's going to tell you how much cash they generate over long periods in the future.

What if John needs to invest more cash in the store?
We have to consider the amount and timing of both cash into and from the store. As many investors in "growth" companies are well aware of, some businesses seem to need a never-ending supply of new cash. Warren Buffett says, "Growth can destroy value if it requires cash inputs in the early years of a project or enterprise that exceed the discounted value of the cash that those assets will generate in later years…Growth is simply a component – usually a plus, sometimes a minus – in the value equation."

But isn't it easy going wrong in estimating the amount and timing of future cash flows in and out of a business?
At Berkshire, they deal with this problem in two ways. Warren Buffett says:

> First, we try to stick to businesses we believe we understand. That means they must be relatively simple and stable in character. If a business is complex or subject to constant change, we're not smart enough to predict future cash flows. Incidentally, that shortcoming doesn't bother us. What counts for most people in investing is not how much

they know, but rather how realistically they define what they don't know. An investor needs to do very few things right as long as he or she avoids big mistakes.

Second, and equally important, we insist on a margin of safety in our purchase price. If we calculate the value of a common stock to be only slightly higher than its price, we're not interested in buying. We believe this margin-of-safety principle, so strongly emphasized by Ben Graham, to be the cornerstone of investment success.

Warren Buffett also says that, "we try…to keep our estimates conservative."

What can John reasonably expect the store to be worth?
How much should John pay for the store? What future free cash flow can rationally be expected? How much cash can John take out and when?

Warren Buffett says, "You'd try to figure out what you were laying out currently and what you're likely to get back over time, how certain you felt about getting it and how it compared to other alternatives." He continues: "For our discount rate, we basically think in terms of the long-term government rate…But in times of what seem like very low rates, we might use a little higher rate." Buffett also says, "And that discount rate doesn't pay you as high a rate as it *needs* to."

In 2003, Warren Buffett said, "We love owning common stocks – if they can be purchased at attractive prices…Unless, however, we see a very high probability of at least 10% pre-tax returns, we will sit on the sidelines."

Let's assume based on the store's history and expecting the same conditions in the future, John estimates that he can take out $300,000 in cash every year. Knowing he can always buy a risk-free government bond, John uses a bond rate of 6% as the discount rate. He also knows he can reinvest whatever cash he can take out from the store at 6%. The value of the store is then $5 million ($300,000/0.06).

Whatever he can pay below this figure increases his expected return. But since cash from a business can't be as certain as cash from a government bond, why should John pay $5 million? Why should John take time and effort investing in something that gives him the same return as doing nothing? And since John can't know for certain whether expected cash flows will turn out as he expects, he should buy the store at a price that gives him a huge margin of safety.

If John's required rate of return is 10%, the value of the store is $3 million. Each person should use his own required rate of return. But whatever discount rate we use, we should always require a substantial discount from the estimated value in order to justify making the investment.

We shouldn't engage in false precision. Warren Buffett says, "We believe that if you can pinpoint it, you're kidding yourself. Therefore, we think that when we make a decision there ought to be such a margin of safety – it ought to be so attractive – that you don't have to carry it out three decimal places." He continues: "We are very inexact…How certain we are is the most important part…You'd be amazed at how inexact we are." Charles Munger says, "We never sit down, run the numbers out and discount them back to net present value…The decision should be obvious."

We can use whatever discount rate we require and we can always compare investment opportunities with the long-term Treasury rate. But there is no point in calculating the value of the unpredictable. We need some certainty. Ask: How much confidence do I have in the numbers?

We can't compensate what we can't predict with a higher discount rate. Warren Buffett says:

> When we look at the future of businesses, we look at riskiness as being sort of a go/no-go valve. In other words, if we think that we simply don't know what's going to happen in the future, that doesn't mean it's risky for everyone. It means *we* don't know – that it's risky for *us*. It may not be risky for someone else who understands the business.
>
> However, in that case, we just give up. We don't try to predict those things. We don't say, "Well, we don't know what's going to happen. Therefore, we'll discount some cash flows that we don't even know at 9% instead of 7%." That is not our way to approach it.
>
> Once it passes a threshold test of being something about which we feel quite certain, we tend to apply the same discount factor to everything. And we try to only buy businesses about which we're quite certain.

Should John always take out whatever cash he can?
That depends on if the return for keeping the cash in the business is higher than the return John gets if he takes it out and invests somewhere else. Why should John want to take it out if he could reinvest the cash in the business at a higher return than 6%? And why should he not take the cash out if he can't reinvest it in the business at a higher return than 6%?

Here is a big difference between a company controlled by John and a public company where John only owns a part of the business. He doesn't control when to take the cash out. Both in private and public companies, cash may be reinvested at a mediocre return or into ideas that don't work. History has shown that many times reinvested cash has been wasted money and that a pay-out would have been better.

How much cash flow the store will generate is mainly determined by three variables: (1) Sales – how many units of ice cream will be sold at what price? (2) Operating costs – how much does it cost to make the ice cream and conduct the business? (3) Invested capital – how much capital is needed to conduct the business? To what degree is this capital financed with debt rather than equity and at what cost?

These variables determine what return the business earns on the capital that is invested in the store. Sales, costs, and capital need are largely determined by demand, competition from similar or substituting products, advantages against competition and their sustainability, cost and capital efficiency, and operational effectiveness in execution. What does this mean? Let's translate it into a simple question: Does the ice cream store have something people need or want now and in the future (demand), that no one else has (competitive advantage) or can copy or get now and in the future (sustainable) and can these advantages be translated into business value?

For example, why do customers choose to buy ice cream from this store rather than from somewhere else? Is it location, assortment, taste, service, price? What do they associate the store and its products with? What is important to customers? Why do they come back? Have their motivations changed over the years or are they likely to change over the next 10 years? What incentives can cause customers to switch to or away from the store? What threats are there?

Warren Buffett illustrates his thinking:

> If you and I were looking at the chewing gum business (and we own no Wrigley's, so I use it fairly often in class), you'd pick a figure that you would expect unit volumes of chewing gum to grow in the next 10-20 years and you'd give me your expectations about how much pricing flexibility Wrigley's has and how much danger there is that Wrigley's market share might be dramatically reduced – you'd go through all of that…We're evaluting the moat, the price elasticity that interacts with the moat in certain ways, the likelihood of unit demand changing in the future or management being either very bright with the cash that they develop or very stupid with it.

Can competitors make the store's product obsolete or copy its advantages?
If someone puts a store next to John's and customers don't see any difference between two stores products and services, then customers are likely to buy the ice cream in the store with the lowest prices.

Could John still make money having the lowest price? Yes, if demands exceeds supply or if John can produce and sell his ice cream at a lower cost than competition assuming of course competition doesn't want to run its business at a loss. John must run the store with extreme cost and capital efficiency relative to the competition. Lower costs and better use of capital allows him to keep the lowest price and still make money.

How important is store management?

How much cash and when John gets it is also a function of the ability and integrity of management. Management can influence owners' return by influencing the return of the business. It can influence where capital is being employed, and under what conditions money is to be reinvested.

When it comes to integrity, Warren Buffett says it best:

> One friend of mine said that in hiring they look for three things: intelligence, energy, and character. If they don't have the last one, the first two will kill you because, it's true, if you are going to hire somebody that doesn't have character, you had really better hope they are dumb and lazy, because, if they are smart and energetic, they'll get you in all kinds of trouble.

A business may look to have a huge margin of safety in price but without an able and honest management this margin may end up as an illusion. History is filled with stories about great businesses that were destroyed by poor management. Ask: Is the company equipped with a competent and honest management that focuses on value? Will they use free cash flow for the benefit of the owners?

But in some businesses, not even brilliant management helps. Warren Buffett shares his experiences:

> My conclusion from my own experiences and from much observation of other businesses is that a good managerial record (measured by economic returns) is far more a function of what business boat you get into than it is of how effectively you row (though intelligence and effort help considerable, of course, in any business, good or bad). Some years ago I wrote: "When a management with a reputation for brilliance tackles a business with a reputation for poor fundamental economics, it is the reputation of the business that remain intact." Nothing has since changed my point of view on that matter. Should you find yourself in a chronically-leaking boat, energy devoted to changing vessels is likely to be more productive than energy devoted to patching leaks.

Let's take another example of "what happens". This time we describe a model from chemistry and give an example of a misused word – entropy.

At 3.54 a.m. the city of Los Angeles woke up to a 6.5 earthquake.
Why does an earthquake crush so many structures and cause so many deaths? Why doesn't hot coffee stay hot? The answer to these questions gets to the heart of every spontaneous physical or chemical event in our lives. The warmth in a hot beverage is due to fast moving molecules. They collide with slower moving molecules in the (relatively colder) environment and cause the slower ones to speed up. Energy is spread out from the hot liquid to the cup, the air, and by the currents of the air, to distant places. That is the nature of energy.

The instant we drop a ball on the floor its energy becomes kinetic energy or energy due to movement. But the term isn't important. What happens is. All energy tends to spread, to become dispersed, if it is not hindered from doing so. That explains why iron rusts, why there are hurricanes, why objects break, etc. Why does a speeding truck running into a brick wall cause enormous destruction? Its kinetic energy not only tends to spread out; it spreads out catastrophically.

The same with the earthquake. Stress in the earth caused by the slow movement of the earth's crust floating on its hot molten energy-filled core suddenly spreads. Its potential energy is instantly changed to kinetic energy as the earth moves. When such gigantic energy spreads, it shakes everything for miles around an epicenter. Because of that energy dispersal, not only buildings collapse, but lives are cut short.

Our lives are based on energy dispersal. Each second, chemicals in our body (converted within us from the food we eat and oxygen we breathe) keep our hearts beating. Our lungs pump oxygen into us and carbon dioxide out. We are energy processing machines. We must keep spreading out energy so that we are warm and keep making chemicals so our hearts beat and muscles work and our lungs function. If these processes are seriously interrupted – as they are in any major accident like an earthquake – we die.

What does it mean (what happens) when we hear it was a magnitude 6.5 earthquake?
The Richter scale is a logarithmic scale developed by the geophysicist Charles F. Richter and measures the amplitude (size) of an earthquake from the recording of earthquake waves made on a seismograph. Each unit increase in the scale corresponds to a 10-fold increase in ground motion. A magnitude 7.5 earthquake produces 10 times more ground motion than a magnitude 6.5 earthquake. But since energy causes the damage, the important difference lies in the energy release. For every unit increase, energy release increases by a factor of about 32. A 7.5 earthquake releases about 32 times more energy than a 6.5.

Since 1900, the biggest earthquake in the U.S. occurred in Alaska in 1964. It had a magnitude of 9.2. What is the difference in strength or energy between a magnitude 9.2 earthquake and a 6.5 earthquake? About 11,220 times. This means that it would take 11,220 earthquakes of magnitude 6.5 to equal the energy released by a 9.2 earthquake. This explains the destructive power of big quakes.

"Follow the energy."

Entropy measures how much energy is spread out in any happening. Entropy is a misused word often used to explain all kinds of "disorder." Disorder is certainly characteristic of many of our situations in life – failed relationships, social problems, messy desks, etc. However, entropy has no relevance to these things. Only to the scientific measure of physical energy flow from being concentrated to being spread out.

A desk doesn't have a tendency to get messy by itself. Some outside energy is needed. It is the energy concentrated in our muscles that is being spread and causes our desks to be messed up. There is no energy being spread out in the papers themselves. As Chemistry Professor Frank Lambert says, "There isn't any 'tendency of objects to become disorganized' in nature any more than bank tellers have a 'tendency to give money to robbers' without a gun."

That energy tends to spread explains why metal rusts, why things break and wear down. Since energy always flows from being concentrated to less concentrated; physical objects and chemical systems deteriorate, break or become destroyed. But these things don't happen immediately or spontaneously. The repetition of time and energy must be considered. A small push (or activation energy) is needed to start a reaction. Gasoline needs a spark or flame to react with oxygen. We need a match to light a fire. For example, it took a single spark to initiate the reaction between hydrogen gas and oxygen, causing the Hindenburg to burn. It takes movements of wind and warm moisture from a tropical ocean to form a hurricane. It takes oxygen and moisture to make iron rust. It takes energy to make wood rot. And this process can be delayed. This happens if we for example paint iron to prevent rusting. Painting keeps oxygen away from the iron so a reaction can't happen.

These examples show how we by observing "what happens" can better understand reality.

SIMPLIFICATION

> *We have a passion for keeping things simple.*
> - Charles Munger

John fears that being simple reduces his importance.
Former General Electric CEO Jack Welch said: "You can't believe how hard it is for people to be simple, how much they fear being simple. They worry that if they're simple, people will think they're simple-minded. In reality, of course, it's just the reverse. Clear tough-minded people are the most simple."

Simplify the way we do things
> *It's amazing how people even today use a computer to do*
> *something you can do with a pencil and paper in less time.*
> - Richard Feynman (from *No Ordinary Genius*)

Make problems easier to solve. Turn complicated problems into simpler ones. Break down a problem into its components. Draw a picture of the problem. Put down on a paper the key factors and their relationship.

Use whatever works. Why? Because the result is what matters, not the method we use to arrive at it.

Make fewer and better decisions. Why? Because it forces us to think more on each decision and thereby reduces our chance of mistakes. Warren Buffett gives another compelling reason:

> Charlie and I decided long ago that in an investment lifetime, it's just too hard to make hundreds of smart decisions. That judgment became ever more compelling as Berkshire's capital mushroomed and the universe of investments that could significantly affect our result shrank dramatically. Therefore, we adopted a strategy that required our being smart - and not too smart at that - only a very few times.

William James said: "The art of being wise is the art of knowing what to overlook." Often we try to get too much information, including misinformation, or information of no use to explain or predict. We also focus on details and what's irrelevant or unknowable and overlook the obvious truths. Dealing with what's important forces us to prioritize. There are often just a few actions that produce most of what we are trying to achieve. There are only a few decisions of real importance.

More information doesn't equal more knowledge or better decisions. And remember that we not only have access to more information, but also misinformation.

In Arthur Conan Doyle's *The Reigate Puzzle,* Sherlock Holmes says: "It is of the highest importance in the art of detection to be able to recognize, out of a number of facts, which are incidental and which vital."

Turn off the noise or what's irrelevant and look at the big picture. Ask: Why am I doing this? What really matters? What is important for what I want to achieve? Don't collect data randomly. Start with why the particular information is needed in the first place.

When asked if he used a computer, Charles Munger said:

I'm a follower of what I call the Thomas Hunt Morgan school. Morgan was one of the great biologists in the history of the world who figured out a lot of genetics [Morgan established that chromosomes carried the units of inheritance] with very slender resources in a so-called "fly room" – first at Columbia and then at Caltech. And when Morgan reached Caltech, he did something that was very peculiar. He banned the Friden calculator – which was the computer of that age – from the biology department. Everybody else at Caltech used the Friden calculator endlessly for all kinds of statistical correlations and much else. Morgan *banned* it.

And they asked, "Why are you doing this?" He said, "I'm so located in life that I'm like a gold miner in 1848 who could just walk along the banks of the river and pick up enormous nuggets of gold with organized common sense. And as long as I can do his, I'm not going to use scarce resources in placer mining."

Well, that's the way I go at life. I think if you get the big points with organized common sense, it's amazing the placer mining you never have to do…

But is there still enormous gain to be made with organized common sense that doesn't require a computer? I think the answer is "yes." Are there dangers in getting too caught up in the minutiae of using a computer so that you miss the organized common sense? There are *huge* dangers. There'll *always* be huge dangers. People calculate too much and think too little.

Avoid certain things

> *There are things that we stay away from. We're like the man who said he had three baskets on his desk: in, out and too tough. We have such baskets – mental baskets – in our office. An awful lot of stuff goes in the "too tough" basket.*
> - Charles Munger

Deal with the situations in life by knowing what to avoid. Reducing mistakes by learning what areas, situations and people to avoid is often a better use of time than seeking out new ways of succeeding. Also, it is often simpler to prevent something than to solve it. Benjamin Franklin said: "An ounce of prevention is worth a pound of cure."

Warren Buffett describes how he and Charles Munger do it:

Easy does it. After 25 years of buying and supervising a great variety of businesses, Charlie and I have *not* learned how to solve difficult business problems. What we have learned is to avoid them. To the extent we have been successful, it is because we concentrated on identifying one-foot hurdles that we could step over rather than because we acquired any ability to clear seven-footers. The finding may seem unfair, but in both business and investments it is usually far more profitable to simply stick with the easy and obvious than it is to resolve the difficult.

We basically have the attitude that you can't make a good deal with a bad person. We don't try to protect ourselves by contracts or all kinds of due diligence - we just forget about it. We can do fine over time dealing with people we like and admire and trust.

And the bad actor will try to tantalize you in one way or another. But you won't win. It pays to just avoid him. We started out with that attitude. However, one or two experiences have convinced us even more so that that's the way to play the game.

Charles Munger follows up with:

I've heard Warren say since very early in his life that the difference between a good business and a bad one is that a good business throws up one easy decision after another, whereas a bad one gives you *horrible* choices – decisions that are extremely hard to make: "Can it work?" "Is it worth the money?"

One way to determine which is the good business and which is the bad one is to see which one is throwing management bloopers – pleasant, no-brainer decisions – time after time after time.

188

Focus leads to understanding and efficiency

Those who attain to any excellence commonly spend life in some
single pursuit, for excellence is not often gained upon easier terms.
- Samuel Johnson

It is impossible for our brain to think too many things at the same time and expect to do well.

Actions and decisions are simpler when we focus on one thing at the time. Publilius Syrus said: "To do two things at once is to do neither." If we only have one thing on which to focus, we tend to do it well and build knowledge. If we do one thing only and nothing else and do it over and over again, we get better and better.

Is focus important in business and for management? Warren Buffett says:

A… serious problem occurs when the management of a great company gets sidetracked and neglects its wonderful base business while purchasing other businesses that are so-so or worse…(Would you believe that a few decades back they were growing shrimp at Coke and exploring for oil at Gillette?) Loss of focus is what most worries Charlie and me when we contemplate investing in businesses that in general look outstanding. All too often, we've seen value stagnate in the presence of hubris or of boredom that caused the attention of managers to wander.

I *love* focused management… And when you lose that focus - it shows… GEICO actually started fooling around in a number of things in the early 1980s. And they paid a price for it – actually a very *big* price. They paid a direct price in terms of the cost for those things – because they almost all worked out badly. And then they paid an additional price in terms of the loss of focus on the main business.

Focus on what you can know and that makes a difference

Warren Buffett explains one of the reasons for his and Charles Munger's success in life and business:

There are two questions you ask yourself as you look at the decision you'll make. A) is it knowable? B) is it important? If it is not knowable, as you know there are all kinds of things that are important but not knowable, we forget about those. And it it's unimportant, whether it's knowable or not, it won't make any difference. We don't care. But there are enough things that are knowable and important that we focus on those things. And everything else, we forget about.

What's knowable and important? And what can be translated into useful action? Some important things we can't know. Like where the stock market is going. Other things we can know but they are not important.

Ask the right questions

The formulation of a problem is often more essential than its solution,
which may be merely a matter of mathematical or experimental skill.
- Albert Einstein

Sometimes it is harder to understand a problem than to solve it. Asking the important questions may help. Start with basic questions like: What does it mean? What is the simplest example? What is the number 1 question? How can I tell if the answer is right? Can I come up with an example that makes it clear what the problem is?

But it is not enough to ask the right questions. We must look at the right place and ask the right person. We can't rely too much on assumptions since we can't be sure that someone else's assumptions are the same as ours, unless we ask them to explain.

Patience

It's not that I'm so smart; it's just that I stay with problems longer.
- Albert Einstein

The best thinking is often done when there is no stress, time limit, threats, or judging. Thinking takes time and the simple truths often reveal themselves when we're doing something else.

We are more likely to solve a specific problem or gain new insight if we leave the problem alone for awhile and let our subconscious mind work. This is well illustrated by the physicists Albert Einstein and Leopold Infeld:

In nearly every detective novel since the admirable stories of Conan Doyle there comes a time where the investigator has collected all the facts he needs for at least some phase of his problem. These facts often seem quite strange, incoherent, and wholly unrelated. The great detective, however, realizes that no further investigation is needed at the moment, and that only pure thinking will lead to a correlation of the facts collected. So he plays his violin, or lounges in his armchair enjoying a pipe, when suddenly, by Jove, he has it!

Roger Lowenstein describes Warren Buffett in *Buffett: The Making of an*

American Capitalist: "Buffett's genius was largely a genius of character – of patience, discipline and rationality...His talent sprang from his unrivaled independence of mind and ability to focus on his work and shut out the world."

Have patience in waiting for opportunities. Resist the temptation to always do something. If we are in a hurry, it's easier to make misjudgments. This is key to investing. Warren Buffett says, "In allocating capital, activity does not correlate with achievement. Indeed, in the fields of investments and acquisitions, frenetic behavior is often counterproductive." He continues: "If you feel like you have to invest every day, you're going to make a lot of mistakes. It isn't that kind of a business. You have to wait for the fat pitch."

Charles Munger adds:

A few major opportunities, clearly recognizable as such, will usually come to one who continuously searches and waits, with a curious mind, loving diagnosis involving multiple variables. And then all that is required is a willingness to bet heavily when the odds are extremely favorable, using resources available as a result of prudence and patience in the past.

Four

Rules and filters

> *Rules are for the obedience of fools and the guidance of wise men.*
> - David Ogilvy (Advertising executive)

What can help us avoid problems and act as guidelines when making decisions? Based on our knowledge of reality and our personal situation we should establish some "what to do" and "what to avoid" rules.

Charles Munger gives an example of a rule:

> Any time anybody offers you *anything* with a big commission and a 200-page prospectus, don't buy it. Occasionally, you'll be wrong if you adopt "Munger's Rule". However, over a lifetime, you'll be a long way ahead - and you will miss a lot of unhappy experiences that might otherwise reduce your love for your fellow man.

Another rule comes from Benjamin Franklin: "To apply myself industriously to whatever business I take at hand, and not divert my mind from my business by any foolish project of growing suddenly rich; for industry and patience are the surest means of plenty."

One rule could be, *"Walk away from anything I don't understand or can't quantify or doesn't work. Only deal with people I trust."*

Warren Buffett provides us with guidelines on how to win in insurance, which applies to other areas as well:

> What counts in this business is underwriting discipline. The winners are those that unfailingly stick to three key principles:
> *1. They accept only those risks that they are able to properly evaluate (staying within their circle of competence) and that, after they have evaluated all relevant factors including remote loss scenarios, carry the expectancy of profit. These insurers ignore market-share considerations and are sanguine about losing business to competitors that are offering foolish prices or policy conditions.*
> *2. They limit the business they accept in a manner that guarantees they will suffer no aggregation of losses from a single event or from related events that will threaten their solvency. They ceaselessly search for possible correlation among seemingly-unrelated risks.*

3. They avoid business involving moral risk: No matter what the rate, trying to write good contracts with bad people doesn't work. While most policyholders and clients are honorable and ethical, doing business with the few exceptions is usually expensive, sometimes extraordinarily so.

I have known the details of almost every policy that Ajit [Ajit Jain] has written…and never on even a single occasion have I seen him break any of our three underwriting rules. His extraordinary discipline, of course, does not eliminate losses; it does, however, prevent foolish losses. And that's the key: Just as in the case of investing, insurers produce outstanding long-term results primarily by avoiding dumb decisions, rather than by making brilliant ones.

Filters

We really can say no in 10 seconds or so to 90%+ of all the things that come along simply because we have these filters.
- Warren Buffett

Filters help us prioritize and figure out what makes sense.

Let's take an example where we combine rules and filters. Reality often shows that one cause of problems is getting involved with wrong people. A rule could therefore be: "Avoid low quality people." As a consequence a filter may be: "Good track record and character traits." Then we look for clues and ask questions designated to answer the question: "High or low grade individual?"

Checklist procedures

Air carrier cockpit checklists to be reviewed in an effort to ensure that each list provides a means of reminding the crew, immediately prior to takeoff, that all items critical for safe flight have been accomplished.
- National Transportation Safety Board, 1969

Use checklist procedures. Together with other tools they help us reduce the chance of harm. Concentrate on the critical items. If we don't check for them we may get harmed. Pilots call these the "killer items."

Charles Munger suggests using models in a checklist fashion:

Generally speaking, I think you need mental models – and what I call checklist procedures – where you take a worthwhile list of models and run right down them: "Is this here? Is that here?" and so on and so on…Now if there are two or three items that are very important that aren't on your checklist – well, if you're an airplane pilot, you can crash.

Likewise, if you're trying to analyze a company without using an adequate checklist, you may make a very bad investment.

Some issues to think about when designing checklists are:
- Different issues need different checklists.
- A checklist must include each critical item necessary for "safety" and avoiding "accidents" so we don't need to rely on memory for items to be checked.
- Readily usable and easy to use.
- Agree with reality.

Avoid excessive reliance on checklists. Checklists work well as long as what may happen can be foreseen. But the unexpected sometimes happens. An unmentioned item may be the core cause of a problem.

Doing something according to pre-established rules, filters and checklists often makes more sense than doing something out of pure emotion. But we can't have too many rules, filters or items without thinking. We must always understand what we're trying to accomplish.

Goals

*Our plans miscarry because they have no aim. When a man does
not know what harbor he is making for, no wind is the right wind.*
- Lucius Annaeus Seneca

"Why doesn't our employee, Tom, perform well?"
Often we are surprised when people don't perform as we expect.

How does Tom perceive he is being measured and rewarded? What does he perceive is expected of him? Do we give him mixed messages? What skills, knowledge and information does he need? Does he have those? What response do we give him about his performance?

Tom: "I have the right knowledge and understand the goal. I also know how to achieve the goal and why my way makes the most sense. I have the authority to make the relevant decisions and can measure the outcome continuously. If I achieve the goal, I will be rewarded. I decide the amount of reward I will get. If I don't accomplish the goal, I lose my job. Since I have the responsibility, it is only right that I face the consequences."

Have goals that cause what we want to accomplish. Do we know what we want to achieve and why? As Aristotle said: "Are we not more likely to hit the mark if we have a target?" How can we make the right decision if we don't know what we want to achieve? Even if we don't know what we want, we often know what we don't want, meaning that our goal can be to avoid certain things.

Meaningful goals need to be backed by reasons as a way of testing that we set the right goal. Goals should be:
- Clearly defined. Don't say: "I want to have a better life." Be concrete. For example: "I want a new Volvo."
- Focused on results.
- Realistic and logical - what can and can't be achieved? Low goals may produce low performance and unrealistic goals may cause people to cheat.
- Measurable.
- Tailored to our individual needs.
- Subject to change.

Goals also need target dates and control stations measuring the degree to which the goal is being achieved.

Do we know what causes our goal to be achieved? We can't achieve what we want if we don't understand what makes it happen. And are we sure our goal is the right one for what we finally want to achieve?

Warren Buffett and Charles Munger elaborated on the issue of the energy crisis at the 2001 Berkshire Hathaway Annual Meeting:

> In power systems we need surplus of capacity. And how do we get that? By giving people an incentive for having extra capacity. A power business can't be punished for not having excess capacity and can't be rewarded for having less then what is needed.
>
> We need three things for this not to happen again. One is that we need reasonable efficiency in operations. Secondly, since it does tend to have in many situations monopoly characteristics, we want something that produced a fair return, but not a great return, on capital – enough to attract new capital. And third, we need a margin of safety or a little more capacity than needed. And we need the whole equation.

Always ask: What end result do I want? What causes that? What factors have a major impact on the outcome? What single factor has the most impact? Do I have the variable(s) needed for the goal to be achieved? What is the best way to achieve my goal? Have I considered what other effects my actions will have that will influence the final outcome?

Since big effects – bad or good – happen when many factors combine, we should use whatever factors necessary to achieve our goal.

Six

ALTERNATIVES

Search for available alternatives and have predetermined criteria to evaluate them.

When we know what we want, we need criteria to evaluate alternatives. Ask: What are the most critical (and knowable) factors that will cause my goal to be achieved? Try to use as few criteria as necessary to make your judgment. Then rank them in order of their importance and use them as filters.

A man is rushed to a hospital in the throes of a heart attack. The doctor needs to decide whether the victim should be treated as a low risk or high-risk patient.
Criteria don't have to be numerous or complicated. Professor Leo Breiman and colleagues at University of California, Berkeley, developed a method to classify high-risk heart attack patients using only a maximum of 3 variables. Blood pressure, age and sinus tachycardia (rapid heartbeat).

If a patient's minimum systolic blood pressure over the initial 24-hour period is less than 91, he is immediately classified as high risk. If not, the second variable is age. If the patient is over 62.5 years old, then one more variable - sinus tachycardia - is needed to classify him as high or low risk. If the patient displays sinus tachycardia he is classified as high risk. Thus, the doctor needs to answer three yes-no questions to reach a decision. The method is more accurate in classifying high risk heart attack patients than complex statistical classification methods.

At a press conference in 2001, when Warren Buffett was asked how he evaluated new business ideas, he said he used 4 criteria as filters.

- Can I understand it? If it passes this filter,
- Does it look like it has some kind of sustainable competitive advantage? If it passes this filter,
- Is the management composed of able and honest people? If it passes this filter,
- Is the price right? If it passes this filter, then we write a check

What does Warren Buffett mean by "understanding?" Predictability: "Our definition of understanding is thinking that we have a reasonable probability of being able to assess where the business will be in 10 years." He continues:

The only way *we* know how to make money is to try and evaluate businesses. And if we can't evaluate a carbon steel company, we don't buy it. It doesn't mean it isn't a good buy. It doesn't mean it isn't selling for a fraction of what its worth. It just means that we don't know how to evaluate it. If we can't evaluate the sense of putting in a chemical plant or something in Brazil, we don't do it…

We understand the product. We understand what it does for people. We just don't know [what its economics will be] 10 years from now…You can understand steel. You can understand homebuilding. But if you look at a homebuilder and try to think where the economics of it is going to be in five or 10 years, that's another question. It's not a question of understanding the product they turn out, the means they use to distribute it – all of that sort of thing – it's the predictability of the economics of the situation 10 years out.

Opportunity cost

If you've got two suitors who are really eager to have you and one is way
he hell better than the other, you do not have to spend much time
with the other. And that's the way we filter out buying opportunities.
- Charles Munger

"I weigh my use of capital and time against other available alternate uses."
One filter that can be used to measure choices against each other is opportunity cost. Our time and money are limited. If we make a decision to do one thing we are deciding not to do some other available thing. Every minute we choose to spend on one thing is a minute unavailable to spend on other things. Every dollar we invest is a dollar unavailable for other available investments. If we decide to spend money today instead of investing for the future we give up the opportunity to spend more in the future. If I decide to play golf today I miss the opportunity to finish this book on time. If I write, I miss the opportunity to spend time with my children. Since children grow up, this opportunity has a time limit.

Choices have costs. Even understanding has an opportunity cost. If we understand one thing well we may understand other things better. The cost of using a limited resource like time, effort and money for a specific purpose can be measured as the value or opportunity lost by not using it in its best available alternative use (assuming it achieves the same purpose).

Do you choose to work or go to college?
What is the real cost of choosing one alternative in favor of another? To use a somewhat changed example from Warren Buffett: What is the real cost of not

having a college education? What is the difference in income over a lifetime between having an education or not? If we ignore the non-economic benefits of having an education, this difference in income discounted to graduation day is the value of the education or the real cost of not having an education.

What is our time worth? Do we spend ten hours doing repairs on our house or do we use a carpenter? The real cost of doing the repairs ourselves is the money that we would have earned doing something else.

"Employ 3 more sales representatives in Montana."
Should TransCorp take the time, money and talent to build a market presence in Montana? The real cost of doing that is the value of the time, money and talent used in its best alternative use. Maybe increasing their presence in a state where they already have a market share is creating more value. Sometimes it is more profitable to marginally increase a cost where a company already has an infrastructure. Where do they marginally get the most leverage on resources spent? Always ask: What is the change of value of taking a specific action? Where is it best to invest resources from a value point of view?

John's return from the investment was a meager 1%.
The 10-year $100,000 investment in the private partnership promised a yearly return of 15%. John's next best available investment at the time was a long-term U.S. government bond yielding 6%. 10 years later reality kicked in. He got back $110,000. His yearly return was only 1%. If he hadn't made the investment back then, but had earned returns comparable with the government bond, John would now have $179,000 (pretax) instead of the $110,000 (pretax). His real cost of doing this investment was $69,000. The money invested tied him in other ways. This doesn't include the mental stress he experienced during the ride.

We all have a lot of things we like: our car, house, job, spouse, investments, etc. When we decide whether to change something, we should measure it against the best of what we already have.

A complementary filter to evaluate alternatives is to list their respective pros and cons and then weigh all the points. Charles Darwin did this in order to decide whether to marry.

We can also weigh alternatives the way Benjamin Franklin did. Make up a list of reasons for and against and assign them weights.

CONSEQUENCES

The key question of ecolate analysis is this: "And then what?" That is, what further changes occur when the treatment or experience is repeated time after time.
- Garrett Hardin (from *Filters Against Folly*)

Charles Munger points out that in a commodity business or in a business earning substandard returns,

All of the advantages from great improvements are going to flow through to the customers…the people who sell the machinery - and, by and large, even the internal bureaucrats urging you to buy the equipment - show you projections with the amount you'll save at current prices with the new technology. However, they don't do the second step of the analysis - which is to determine how much is going to stay home and how much is just going to flow through to the customer.

I've never seen a single projection incorporating that second step in my life. And I see them all the time. Rather, they always read: "This capital outlay will save you so much money that it will pay for itself in three years." So you keep buying things that will pay for themselves in three years. And after 20 years of doing it, somehow you've earned a return of only about 4% per annum. That's the textile business.

And it isn't that the machines weren't better. It's just that the savings didn't *go to you*. The cost reductions came through all right. But the *benefit* of the cost reductions didn't go to the guy who bought the equipment.

Whenever we install a policy, take an action or evaluate statements, we must trace the consequences. When doing so, we must remember four key things:

(1) Pay attention to the whole system,
(2) Consequences have implications or more consequences, some which may be unwanted,
(3) Consider the effects of feedback, time, scale, repetition, critical points and limits,
(4) Different alternatives have different consequences in terms of costs and

benefits. Estimate the net effects over time and how desirable these are compared to what we want to achieve.

Judge an action by its net consequences over time considering the whole system. Follow up changes in individual variables by determining how the rest of the system will respond over time. Changes in one variable may change the entire system. One change may cause another change causing another, etc. This includes considering short and long-term consequences since there may be a long time between an action and its full effects.

Charles Munger tell us about the Navy model - a rule with net benefits:

If you're a captain in the Navy and you've been up for 24 hours straight and have to go to sleep and you turn the ship over to a competent first mate in tough conditions and he takes the ship aground - clearly through no fault of *yours* - they don't court martial you, but your naval career is *over.*

Napoleon said he liked luckier generals - he wasn't into supporting losers. Well, the Navy likes luckier captains.

You can say, "That's too *tough*. That's not law school. That's not due process." Well, the Navy model is *better* in its context than would be the law school model. The Navy model *really* forces people to pay attention when conditions are tough - because they know that there's no *excuse*. Very simply, if your ship goes aground, your career is over.

"It doesn't *matter* whether it was your fault or not. Nobody's *interested* in your fault. It's just a *rule* that we happen to have - for the good of all, all effects considered."

I *like* some rules like that - I think that the civilization works *better* with some of these no-fault rules. But that stuff tends to be anathema around law schools. "It's not due process. You're not really searching for justice."

Well, I *am* searching for justice when I argue for the Navy rule - for the justice of fewer ships going aground. Considering the net benefit, I don't *care* if one captain has some unfairness in his life. After all, it's not like he's being court marshalled. He just has to look for a new line of work. And he keeps vested pension rights and so on. So it's not like it's the end of the world.

EIGHT

QUANTIFICATION

*Philosophy is written in this grand book – I mean the universe – which
stands continually open to our glaze, but it cannot be understood unless
one first learns to comprehend the language and interpret the characters
in which it is written. It is written in the language of mathematics, and
its characters are triangles, circles, and other geometric figures, without
which it is humanly impossible to understand a single word of it.*
- Galileo Galilei

Alfred North Whitehead said in *The Aims of Education:* "Through and through
the world is infected with quantity. To talk sense, is to talk in quantities. It is no
use saying that the nation is large, - How large? It is no use saying that radium is
scarce, - How scarce? You cannot evade quantity."

Most aspects of our life depend on our ability to quantify and understand
relationships, proportions, etc. What does math do? It helps us develop
consequences, and evaluate when things make sense. And math is stable. Two plus
two is four was true 1 million years ago and will be true 1 million years from today.

When we translate something into numbers we can make comparisons. How
can we evaluate if a decision is intelligent or not if we can't measure it against a
relevant and important yardstick?

Some things can't be measured exactly so estimating a range is the next best
alternative. J.M. Keynes said: "We'd rather be roughly right than precisely wrong."

Let's illustrate the importance of quantification with examples from the world
of business and investing.

How much capital is needed to produce a dollar of cash flow?
Does return on invested capital make a difference? Assume two businesses – X
and Y – generate the same cash earnings of $10 million and "perpetual" growth
of 5%. The difference lies in how much capital they use to produce these
earnings. X needs $100 million and Y $40 million. This means that their return
on invested capital is 10% respective 25%. This also means that they differ in the
free cash flow (after reinvesting) or distributable cash they generate. X generates

$5 million and Y $8 million. Return on invested capital makes a difference in value.

	Business X	Business Y
Invested capital	100	40
Free cash flow	10	10
Reinvested capital	-5	-2
Return on reinvested capital	10%	25%
Available cash flow for distribution	5	8
Value at 10% discount rate	100 (5/(0.1-0.05))	160

Warren Buffett describes what businesses are best to own:

> Leaving the question of price aside, the best business to own is one that over an extended period can employ large amounts of incremental capital at very high rates of return. The worst business to own is one that must, or *will,* do the opposite – that is, consistently employ ever-greater amounts of capital at very low rates of return.

Should higher earnings automatically impress us?
Warren Buffett gives an example from one of Berkshire's subsidiaries:

> While an increase in earnings from $8 million to $72 million sounds terrific – and usually is – you should not automatically assume that to be the case. You must first make sure that earnings were not depressed in the base year. If they were instead substantial in relation to capital employed, an even more important point must be examined: how much additional capital was required to produce the additional earnings?

We need to understand what is behind the numbers. Warren Buffett says that, "return on beginning equity capital" is "the most appropriate measure of single-year managerial performance. Informed use of that yardstick, however, requires, an understanding of many factors, including accounting policies, historical carrying values of assets, financial leverage, and industry conditions."

We can't expect to get a higher return on investment over time than the underlying business produces on its invested capital over time. Charles Munger says:

> Over the long term, it's hard for a stock to earn a much better return than the business which underlies it earns. If the business earns 6% on capital over 40 years and you hold it

for that 40 years, you're not going to make much different than a 6% return – even if you originally buy it at a huge discount. Conversely, if a business earns 18% on capital over 20 or 30 years, even if you pay an expensive looking price, you'll end up with a fine result.

Few companies can manage, over a ten to twenty-year period, to keep earning high returns on 20% or more on invested capital while reinvesting all or most of their earnings. Changes in the competitive arena, buyer habits, and the environment will make that almost a certainty.

Warren Buffett reveals the limits of earnings growth and how lofty predictions lead to dumb behavior:

> Examine the record of, say, the 200 highest earning companies from 1970 or 1980 and tabulate how many have increased per-share earnings by 15% annually since those dates. You will find that only a handful have. I would wager you a very significant sum that fewer than 10 of the 200 most profitable companies in 2000 will attain 15% annual growth in earnings-per-share over the next 20 years.

He continues:

> Finally, be suspicious of companies that trumpet earnings projections and growth expectations. Businesses seldom operate in a tranquil, no-surprise environment, and earnings simply don't advance smoothly (except, of course, in the offering books of investment bankers).
>
> Charlie and I not only don't know today what our businesses will earn *next year* – we don't even know what they will earn *next quarter*. We are suspicious of those CEOs who regularly claim they do know the future – and we become downright incredulous if they consistently reach their declared targets. Managers that always promise to "make the numbers" will at some point be tempted to *make up* the numbers.

Suddenly demand goes down and price competition rises.
How does a change in growth rate change business value? Business value is a function of the amount and timing of future cash flows. If cash flows decreases and/or appears further off in the future, business value declines.

Warren Buffett illustrates how valuations must change when growth expectations are revised:

> A few years ago the conventional wisdom held that a newspaper, television or magazine property would forever increase its earnings at 6% or so annually and would do so *without*

the employment of additional capital, for the reason that depreciation charges would roughly match capital expenditures and working capital requirements would be minor. Therefore, reported earnings (before amortization of intangibles) were also freely-distributable earnings, which meant that ownership of a media property could be construed as akin to owning a perpetual annuity set to grow at 6% a year. Say, next, that a discount rate of 10% was used to determine the present value of that earnings stream. One could then calculate that it was appropriate to pay a whopping $25 million for a property with current after-tax earnings of $1 million [1/0.1-0.06].

Now change the assumption and posit that the $1 million represents "normal earning power" and that earnings will bob around this figure cyclically. A "bob-around" pattern is indeed the lot of most businesses, whose income stream grows only if their owners are willing to commit more capital (usually in the form of retained earnings). Under our revised assumption, $1 million of earnings, discounted by the same 10%, translates to a $10 million valuation. Thus a seemingly modest shift in assumptions reduce the property's valuation to 10 times after-tax earnings.

Dollars are dollars whether they are derived from the operation of media properties or of steel mills. What in the past caused buyers to value a dollar of earnings from media far higher than a dollar from steel was that the earnings of a media property were expected to constantly grow (without the business requiring much additional capital), whereas steel earnings clearly feel in the bob-around category. Now, however, expectations for media have moved toward the bob-around model.

Do we pay the same price for a business financed with debt as for a business with no debt?

Assume Mary is interested in buying a furniture store. The business is stable with no growth, free cash flow of 15 and financed with 75 in equity. A price of 100 (15/0.15) will give her a 15% return. Does debt make a difference? Yes, the seller could then make extra money by leveraging the business before selling it. If the seller refinances the business with 50 in debt (and the business can borrow at 6% interest) and withdraws 50 as a dividend, income after interest would be 12 (15-3). If Mary then buys the store for 80 (12/0.15) the seller would have made an extra 30 (50+80-100) without any change in the underlying operations of the business.

Instead Mary should assume she acquires a debt-free business and adjust for 50 of debt and pay 50 (15/0.15-50). She should also correct (add to the price) for excess cash – cash or cash assets that aren't needed to conduct the business.

This is the same type of reasoning as when we buy a house. If we for example buy a house for $500,000 and put in $200,000 of our own saved money and mortgage the rest or $300,000, the price of the house is still $500,000.

"The synergies we expected from the merger never materialized. They were mere illusions."

Don't forget to quantify consequences when making acquisitions. Take the profit & loss statement and balance sheet of the acquiring company and the target company. Calculate what happens with volume, prices, cost, and invested capital when the companies combine considering consequences and behavioral changes of employees, suppliers, customers, and competition. How does business value change? Be realistic. Studies show that most mergers fail to generate value for the acquiring company's owners. The main reason is that the buyer paid too much for synergies that weren't real.

"Of one thing, however, be certain," says Warren Buffett, "If a CEO is enthused about a particularly foolish acquisition, both his internal staff and his outside advisors will come up with whatever projections are needed to justify his stance. Only in fairy tales are emperors told they are naked."

John reads the paper. A company announced a $10 million contract and its market capitalization jumped $1 billion.
Does this make sense? If we assume the contract generates a 15% profit margin, the implied market value increase is $1.5 million. And even a high-margin project can be a loser if it requires a lot of capital and human resources.

It is hard to grow from a large base – especially when there is little underlying market volume growth.
We can't expect a business to grow its free cash flow 20% every year if its base is a market share of 50% on a market with unit volume growth of 2% per year.

If present value is the same for different businesses, does the timing of the dividend matter?
Assume there are 2 different businesses – X and Y – with the following forecasted dividends. After year 5 the two companies close down.

Year	1	2	3	4	5
Dividends from X	10	10	10	10	10
Dividends from Y	0	0	0	0	61

All cash generated by X is each year distributed to its owners. The free cash flow generated by Y is reinvested and not paid out until after the five year period. Assuming we want a 10% return, the present value of X's respective Y's dividends are the same or about 38. But this assumes that we can reinvest our dividends from X at 10% so that we have 61 after 5 years. It also assumes that Y can reinvest their cash flow at rates that cause the dividend to be 61 after 5 years. But in both cases the future may turn out different than expected. The business environment may change and competition increase making the dividends from X and Y come out differently from what we expect. The more our calculation depends on cash flows far out in the future, the more opportunities there are for unwanted events, and the more uncertain our expected return.

Do the math!
We can do a simple exercise to test our possible return from investing in a company and if its market valuation makes sense. Just think about the math implicit.

Below are some examples where we have ignored dividends and options (in reality we need to properly account for options and make sure that the company's accounting reflects reality and the true operational performance.) Think of a stock as part of a business and remember that small changes in assumptions can dramatically change value.

John is thinking of buying 1,000 shares of stock in a public ice cream manufacturer with a market value of $1 billion and no debt or off-balance sheet obligations. How should John reason?

What is my estimated annual rate of return?
John projects the future value, and then compares that value with the present market value of $1 billion. What is his implied annual rate of return? Will the price paid give him an adequate return?

The business has initial cash earnings (earnings + amortization of goodwill) of $40 million and an assumed average annual growth rate in cash earnings of 10% for 10 years. This translates into $104 million in cash earnings in year 10. Assume the market pays an average multiple of 15 for this type of business. This implies $1.56 billion in market value in year 10. If John compares this figure with the present market value, his implied yearly return is 4.5%. John compares this return with the return from other available investment opportunities. A business may have a great track record, but if the math doesn't work, stay away.

What scenario achieves a 15% annual rate of return?
How much must the ice cream manufacturer earn to generate a 15% annual rate of return for John? If the present market value compounds at 15%, what does this imply and is it reasonable?

A present market value of $1 billion and an annual return of 15% imply $4 billion in market value in year 10. This is what $1 billion will grow to in 10 years if it grows 15% per year. An average multiple of 15 implies $270 million in cash earnings in year 10. This translates into an average annual growth rate in cash earnings of 21% (from a base of $40 million). A profit margin of 15% implies $1.8 billion in sales year 10. He can continue with implied future sales volume, number of users and usage, market share, etc.

John then asks: What causes this future value? What does this imply in numbers today? Is it reasonable regarding evidence of track record in growth, earnings, profit margins, market size/volume growth, market share, competitive advantage, etc? Which factor has the greatest impact on future cash earnings and thereby value? What forces can change this scenario? How can the company lose its advantages?

If the company doesn't make money today, what future free cash flow is implied by their market value if I want a 10% return?
In the midst of the Internet mania, Warren Buffett said:

> When we buy a stock, we always think in terms of buying the whole enterprise because it enables us to think as businessmen rather than stock speculators. So let's just take a company that has marvelous prospects, that paying you nothing now where you buy it at a valuation of $500 billion…For example, let's assume that there's only going to be a one-year delay before the business starts paying out to you and you want to get a 10% return. If you paid $500 billion, then $55 billion in cash is the amount that it's going to have to be able to disgorge to you year after year after year. To do that, it has to make perhaps $80 billion, or close to it, pretax. Look around at the universe of businesses in this world and see how many are earning $80 billion pretax – or $70 billion or $60 or $50 or $40 or even $30 billion. You won't find any.

Suppose an Internet auction site has a market value of $4 billion. It gives John no cash today. Then the company next year must be able to pay him $440 million in cash each year in perpetuity or close to $640 million pretax to justify its present market value. If the company isn't expected to pay him until the fifth year, then it has to pay him $586 million in cash per year in perpetuity.

What does the figure $640 million imply? Assume the site is open for business 250 days per year. That translates into pretax cash flows of $2.56 million per day or at an average commission of 2%, $128 million in sales transactions per day! Is that realistic?

Whether a business sells nails or telecom equipment, if more money is going out than coming in, on a present value basis, it is worthless. As Warren Buffett says, "Value is destroyed, not created, by any business that loses money over its lifetime, no matter how high its interim valuation may get."

He continues:

There's plenty of magic in short term in rising P/E multiples and the games people play with accounting and so on. But in the end, you can't get more out of a business between now and its extinction than the business makes. And actually you'll make something less depending on who your business managers are, how often there's turnover in the security and how much you pay the investment manager and so on.

Nine

Evidence

*It is undesirable to believe a proposition when there
is no ground whatsoever for supposing it true.*
- Bertrand Russell

Evidence helps us prove what is likely to happen or likely to be true or false. Evidence comes from facts, observations, experiences, comparisons, and experiments.

The methods of science

*There are in fact two things: science and opinion;
the former begets knowledge, the latter ignorance.*
- Hippocrates

"What experiment can I do to figure this out?"
In 1986, the space shuttle Challenger exploded on launch, killing all astronauts aboard. After the disaster, NASA put together a commission where Richard Feynman showed that the fuel booster rockets were not safe when the temperature was cold. The temperature at takeoff was 32 F. During a launch, vibrations causes the rocket joints to move. Inside the rocket joints there were rubber O-rings that are used in a certain key stage in the space shuttle's fuel delivery system.

Richard Feynman did a simple experiment with a rubber O-ring from the Challenger rocket. He squeezed the rings in a C-clamp and dipped them in a glass of ice water (32 F) and showed that the rubber didn't expand. Since there was no resilience in the rubber at 32 F, the O-ring could not fill the gap in the expanding rocket booster joints. It consequently caused an explosion of the booster and the space shuttle.

This also illustrates that an experiment doesn't have to be complicated.

Do what scientists do: Strive for objectivity. Scientists try to describe the world as it is, not as they want it to be. They seek to answer "why" and "how" questions by using methods of scientific integrity.

The 400-year old scientific method is the foundation of modern science and a reliable method for gaining knowledge about the world. It is composed of the following steps:

Observation – We observe a certain behavior and wonder what happens and why (what matters is what actually happens).

Guess why – We try to find an explanation for what we observed. We start with forming a hypothesis. A clearly stated possible explanation (of why or how something happens) that can be proved or disproved by testing it against observed facts. Maybe some rule or model will explain our observation. Our guess must be measurable and agree with nature and proven evidence.

Consequences – We work out all logical consequences of our guess and see what would be implied if our guess was right. If our guess is right, we should be able to predict what we will observe.

Test – "If I do this, what will happen?" Testability is key. We compare the implied consequences of our guess with evidence and experiment. We repeat the experiment against error, fraud, coincidence, and change in circumstances or environment. The more evidence that agrees with our guess, the more likely it is that we guessed right. If the guess disagrees with evidence, it is wrong. As Richard Feynman says:

> It does not make any difference how beautiful your guess is. It does not make any difference how smart you are, who made the guess, or what his name is - if it disagrees with experiment it is wrong.

Darwin realized that for an observation to be of any use, it must be tested against a theory, hypothesis or model. On board the HMS Beagle, in a letter to his friend Henry Fawcett, Darwin wrote:

> About thirty years ago there was much talk that geologists ought only to observe and not to theorize; and I well remember someone saying that at this rate a man might as well go into a gravel pit and count the pebbles and describe the colours. How odd it is that anyone should not see that all observation must be for or against some view if it is to be of any service!

We don't merely observe some behavior; we observe in light of some theory or with some background about what is important to look for or with some concrete goal in mind. It is the same when we search for information. Charles Munger says:

> …you have to have some idea of *why* you're looking for the information. Don't read annual reports the way Francis Bacon said you do science…where you just collect endless

[amounts of] data and then only later do you try to make sense of it. You have to start with some ideas of reality. And then you have to look to see whether what you're seeing fits in with that basic thought structure.

The philosopher Sir William of Occam in the 14th Century said: "Entities should not be multiplied unnecessarily." Occam's Razor is a way to explain an observation. If we face two possible explanations which make the same predictions, the one based on the least number of unproven assumptions is preferable. Occam doesn't rule out other explanations. As Albert Einstein said: "Things should be made as simple as possible, but not any simpler."

Finding evidence from the past
Study the past if you would divine the future.
- Confucius

John is thinking of hiring a new manager. Does the manager's past record matter? Warren Buffett says:

The best judgment we can make about managerial competence does not depend on what people say, but simply what the record shows. At Berkshire Hathaway, when we buy a business we usually keep whoever has been running it, so we already have a batting average. Take the case of Mrs. B. who ran our Furniture Mart. Over a 50-year period, we'd seen her take $500 and turn it into a business that made $18 million pretax. So we knew she was competent…Clearly, the lesson here is that the past record is the best single guide.

Then you run into the problem of the 14-year-old horse. Let's say you buy The Daily Racing Form and it shows that the horse won the Kentucky Derby as a four-year-old. Based on past performance, you know this was one hell of a horse. But now he's 14 and can barely move. So you have to ask yourself, "Is there anything about the past record that makes it a poor guidelines as a forecaster of the future?"

The following questions help us decide if past evidence is representative for the future:

Observation: Will past/present behavior continue? How long can it continue?

Explanation: Why did it happen in the past or why does it happen now? How did it happen? We must understand the reasons why a past outcome occurred. What are the key factors? This demands that we understand the equation – the key variables involved and their relationships. Start with a hypothesis. Compare the implied consequences of our explanation of causes with appropriate evidence – for and against.

Predictability: How predictive (representative) is the past/present evidence for what is likely to happen in the future? Are the conditions now and in the future likely to change? Make sure that the evidence isn't random. What worked in the past could have been the result of chance.

Continuation and Change: What is required to make the past/present record continue or to achieve the goal (look at the equation again)? What must happen? What must not happen? What forces can change it or cause what we don't want? Likely? Antidotes to what we don't want to happen?

Certainty and Consequences: How certain am I? What single event am I betting on must happen or not happen? What are the consequences of being wrong?

Falsify and disprove

> *All our commonsense ideas should always be open to criticism.*
> - Karl Popper (Austrian-born British philosopher, 1902-1994)

Scientific results always have some probability attached to them. Tomorrow may bring new evidence. Instead of verifying a statement, it is sometimes better to prove it false. A single piece of evidence in favor of a statement does not prove its truth – it only supports it. But a single piece of evidence against it will show that it is false. Albert Einstein said: "No number of experiments can prove me right; a single experiment can prove me wrong."

"All swans are white."
How could we test this statement? We could open our eyes, and go out looking for non-white swans. If we find one swan that is not white we have disproved the statement. The more swans we find to be white, the more support the statement has. But it is not proven. One black swan and the statement is rejected.

"The universe is no more than 10,000 years old."
What experiment can we do to falsify this statement? We can look up at the sky and observe stars that are millions of light-years away. This means we are seeing them as they were millions of years ago. Light left the stars millions of years ago spent all that time traveling towards us.

Michael Shermer says in *Why People Believe Weird Things:* "if the universe and Earth are only about ten thousand years old, then the modern sciences of cosmology, astronomy, physics, chemistry, geology, paleontology, paleoanthropology, and early human history are all invalid."

"The medical treatment worked. I'm cured."

How can we test whether a cure is due to treatment, good salesmanship, the power of suggestion, or the patient's imagination? Divide people in two groups. Make one group believe they are receiving the treatment, when they are not. Make the other group believe they are not receiving the treatment, when they are. Compare the effects.

To reduce error and bias, medical research uses randomized double-blind studies. Research subjects are randomly divided in two groups. Each subject has an equal chance to be assigned to each group. Neither the research subjects nor the researchers know who's getting the treatment or the placebo.

"There is no evidence that ghosts don't exist."

Some things can't be proven false. The fact that there is no evidence against ghosts isn't the same as confirming evidence that there are ghosts. What is true depends on the amount of evidence supporting it, not by the lack of evidence against it.

Disprove ideas. Charles Darwin always looked at the possibility that he was wrong:

> I had, also, during many years, followed a golden rule, namely, that whenever a published fact, a new observation or thought came across me, which was opposed to my general results, to make a memorandum of it without fail and at once: for I had found by experience that such facts and thoughts were far more apt to escape from the memory than favourable ones. Owing to this habit, very few objections were raised against my views which I had not at least noticed and attempted to answer…
>
> I think that I have become a little more skillful in guessing right explanations and in devising experimental tests; but this may probably be the result of mere practice, and of a larger store of knowledge. I have as much difficulty as ever in expressing myself clearly and concisely; and this difficulty has caused me a very great loss of time; but it has had the compensating advantage of forcing me to think long and intently about every sentence, and thus I have been led to see errors in reasoning and in my own observations or those of others.

"Since a lot of evidence agrees with my explanation, I must be right."

Not necessarily, the same evidence may agree with other explanations. Look for evidence that disproves your explanation.

Theories based on observations have priority over theories alone since observations can disprove theories. Galileo Galilei based his theories on observations in the debate whether the sun revolved around the Earth.

Engage in self-criticism. Explain the opposite of your beliefs. Ask: Assume I'm wrong, how will I know? Why may an opposite theory be correct? Assuming my answer is correct, what would cause me to change my mind? Then, look for that evidence.

Often we don't see our weaknesses and thus are not motivated to improve. Therefore, encourage the right people to give objective feedback that will help us improve.

Look back and measure how you are doing against your original expectations. Find your mistakes early and correct them quickly before they cause harm.

The next tool forces us to be objective. Charles Munger says on backward thinking:

> The mental habit of thinking backward *forces* objectivity - because one of the ways you think a thing through backward is you take your initial assumption and say, "Let's try and *disprove* it."
>
> That is *not* what most people do with their initial assumption. They try and *confirm* it. It's an automatic tendency in psychology - often called "first-conclusion bias". But it's only a tendency. You can train yourself away from the tendency to a substantial degree. You just constantly take your own assumptions and try and disprove them.

Ten

Backward thinking

*A lot of success in life and success in business comes from knowing
what you really want to avoid – like early death and a bad marriage.*
- Charles Munger

Avoid what causes the opposite of what you want to achieve.

"You must always invert," said the 19th Century German mathematician Karl
Jacobi when asked the secret of his mathematical discoveries. Whenever we try
to achieve a goal, solve problems, predict what is likely to happen or likely to be
true or false, we should think things through backwards.

*At the weekly meeting with his managers, John asked: "What actions could our
company take to destroy as much value as possible in as short time as possible?"*
"Treat the employees badly. Reward bad work. Don't appeal to the employee's self
interests but to a goal no one understands. Don't inform people what the
company stands for, what rules apply, and the consequences for breaking them.
Make sure people don't know their areas of responsibility. Put the right person in
the wrong place. Don't let people know if they achieve a goal. Everything should
be impossible to measure. Never tell people why something should be done.

Surround the CEO with confused, unmotivated subordinates. Give key
customers reasons to be angry. Late and wrong deliveries, delays, and arrogance
will help. Let the customers associate the business with misery and make sure that
this feeling gets reinforced at every contact with the company."

Thinking backwards, we can determine what actions must be avoided. As
Charles Munger says, "If you were hired by the World Bank to help India, it
would be very helpful to determine the three best ways to *increase* man-years of
misery in India - and, then, turn around and *avoid* those ways."

Instead of asking how we can achieve a goal, we ask the opposite question:
What don't I want to achieve (non-goal)? What causes the non-goal? How can I
avoid that? What do I now want to achieve? How can I do that? For example,
instead of searching for how John and Mary can improve their marriage, they ask:
"What qualities will destroy our marriage?" One quality is dishonesty. Now they

reinvert the question back and ask: "How can we improve our marriage?" Be honest. (See also Charles Munger's brilliant speech on prescriptions for guaranteed misery in Appendix One).

Charles Munger provides an enlightening example on how dumb systems cause dumb behavior:

> Let's say you have a desire to do public service. As a natural part of your planning, you think in reverse and ask, "What can I do to *ruin* our civilization?" That's easy. If what you want to do is to ruin your civilization, just go to the legislature and pass laws that create systems wherein people can easily cheat. It will work perfectly. Take the workers' compensation system in California. Stress is *real*. And its misery can be real. So you want to compensate people for their stress in the workplace. It seems like a noble thing to do.
>
> But the trouble with such a compensation practice is that it's practically impossible to delete huge cheating. And once you reward cheating, you get crooked *lawyers*, crooked *doctors*, crooked *unions*, etc. participating in referral schemes. You get a total *miasma* of disastrous behavior. And the behavior makes all the people doing it *worse* as they do it. So you were trying to help your civilization. But what you did was create enormous *damage*, net. So it's much better to let some things go uncompensated – to let life be hard – than to create systems that are easy to cheat.

"Don't think about the color red!"

If someone told you not to think of the color red, you might automatically think of that color. Why? Because in order to know what not to think about, your brain must first think about it. When John is on a golf course trying to hit over a water hazard in front of the green, he doesn't say to himself, "I don't want to hit the ball in the water," but instead "I want to hit the ball on the green." So when we tell people what to avoid, we should end with what we want them to achieve.

Study errors.

Marcus Porcius Cato wrote: "Wise men profit more from fools than fools from wise men; for the wise men shun the mistakes of the fools, but fools do not imitate the successes of the wise."

To reduce mistakes, we should study failures. Both in business and in life. We should look at their causes over time and see if they are unchanged. Knowledge about the causes behind failures helps us avoid new failures.

Often we learn more from understanding why something doesn't work than from why it does. Ask: Why did that happen? Why do certain businesses lose money or fail? Why do smart people engage in foolish behavior? Why do certain accidents happen? What was the mistake that caused bad performance? What circumstances were present? What's the lesson?

When we know this, we should ask: What people or businesses are doing things that history has proven causes failure? How can we best avoid what we don't want to happen? How can we create the best conditions to avoid mistakes? How can we prevent causes that can't be eliminated? How can we limit the consequences of what we want to avoid? How can we limit the probability of what we want to avoid?

We can organize the study of errors, by using a table like the one below.

What to avoid	Cause	Antidote
What were the mistakes?	Why did those happen?	What are the major risk factors? How do specific errors evolve? What factors contribute?
Stupidity/Irrationality	Big idea that helps explain and predict?	What is rational? How can I create the best conditions to make good decisions? What can be eliminated or prevented?

Turn the negative into an advantage.
In 1796, British physician Edward Jenner discovered vaccination. He noticed that milkmaids who had contracted a mild and usually non-lethal form of the pox virus – cowpox – seemed to be immune to the lethal form of the virus, smallpox. He then took samples of a milkmaid's lesions and inoculated a young boy with cowpox. The boy built up antibodies in his immune system that prevented him from getting smallpox and subsequently survived the epidemic.

Begin with the end in mind.
In the 4th Century the Greek mathematician Pappus of Alexandria wrote: "Let us start with what is being sought and assume that we already found it." Assume we've achieved our goal, then ask: What was the purpose? Was this what I wanted? If so, from which earlier position do I get there? What is needed to achieve this? Then work backward to the beginning. By working backwards we can easier see how and if something may work. An example of this is retrospective disease studies. Researchers study the disease then work backward to see what prior conditions are associated with it.

"We need discipline in schools."

What would be the consequences if this statement were false? Turn a statement backwards and show that the opposite is worse. What are the consequences? Unbelievable or negative? Suppose there was no discipline in schools, would there be more behavior we don't want?

When we believe we have arrived at the right judgment, we should consider what could cause the opposite of our prediction. Suppose we make a personality judgment and conclude that the individual is of good character and we want to enter a relationship. Ask: What can ruin this relationship? What causes me to misjudge character?

Other uses of backward thinking are: Study evidence that implies the opposite of what is normal and ask "why." Use "negative" rules – tell people what they can't do. Practice zero base thinking – start with a clean sheet of paper and ask: If we weren't already doing what we do, how can we best achieve our goal?

A doctor who believes a symptom is caused by too much of something can turn around and ask: What if it is due to the shortage of something else?

Next chapter is about risk or the possibility of loss. If we put our head in the lion's mouth, we shouldn't be surprised if it's bitten off.

Eleven

Risk

"Why do you want to buy this stock? What must happen for the investment to succeed? What is the downside?"

Reflect on what can go wrong. Ask: What is the potential downside? What should I worry about? What is the likelihood and magnitude of a possible loss? What's the worst thing that could happen? What can I do to prevent it? What will I do if it happens?

We need to look at the downside when we invest. According to *Forbes* Magazine, Charles Munger's way of reasoning is:

> The simple fact is that you can't tell whether an idea is likely to work unless you consider all the possible negatives... Okay, it's a good company. But is the price low enough? Is the management made up of people Munger and Buffett are comfortable with? If it is cheap enough to buy, is it cheap for the wrong reason or the right reason? As Munger puts it: "What's the flip side, what can go wrong that I haven't seen?"

Being wrong causes both an actual loss and an opportunity cost. When investing we can either lose our capital – we invest 10 and get back 5 – or we get an inadequate return – for example 3% versus 6% from a bond. What does Warren Buffett say about business risk?

> When we look at businesses, we try to look at businesses that are good businesses today and think about what can go wrong. We think of business risk in terms of what can happen five, 10 or 15 years from now that will destroy, modify or reduce the economic strengths we believe currently exist in the business. And for some businesses, that's impossible to figure – at least it's impossible for *us* to figure – and we don't even think about it. If we can think of very much that can go wrong, we just forget it.

Warren Buffett tells us how Berkshire reduces risk:

> In stocks, we expect every commitment to work out well because we concentrate on conservatively financed businesses with strong competitive strengths, run by able and

honest people. If we buy into these companies at sensible prices, losses should be rare. Indeed, during the 38 years we have run the company's affairs, gains from the equities we manage at Berkshire (that is, excluding those managed at General Re and GEICO) have exceeded losses by a ratio of about 100 to one.

Do we need to take a lot of risks to get ahead in life? Charles Munger tells a story:

I had a relative by marriage who died in his late 80s. And I don't think he ever had a loss. He only did about eight things in his lifetime. He started with a small poke, and if something wasn't a near cinch, he didn't do it. He lived well and died rich. I think it's possible for a great many people to live a life like that where there isn't much risk of disaster and where they're virtually sure to get ahead a reasonable amount. It takes a lot of judgement, a lot of discipline and an absence of hyperactivity. By this method, I think most intelligent people can take a lot of risk out of life.

The consequences of being wrong

If we can't tolerate a possible consequence, remote
though it may be, we steer clear of planting its seeds.
- Warren Buffett

John wants to buy another ice cream store.
The key variable he's betting on is that "Unit volume will increase." What are the consequences if he is wrong?

The worse the consequence of being wrong, the less inclined we must be to take a specific action or the more evidence we need in favor of something.

Ask: What is the cost of being wrong versus the benefit of being right compared to other investment opportunities? Cost: John may lose money, reputation, and experience mental stress. It will also take his focus away from other business. Benefit: Possibility to make more money over a period of time. Alternative: More time to concentrate on the present business or other opportunities.

Or stated another way: If I do this because I bet that unit volume will increase but I'm wrong (volume remains the same or decreases due to less demand and more competition or unfavorable environment) what are the consequences? Can I handle them? Are they reversible? If I don't do this because I bet that unit volume will go down or stay the same but I'm wrong, what are the consequences? In which alternative do I lose less?

Margin of safety

We try to arrange [our affairs] so that no matter
what happens, we'll never have to "go back to go."
- Charles Munger

We can't predict what is going to happen in life. Never underestimate the chance of rare events.

To protect us from all the unknowns that lie ahead we can either avoid certain situations, make decisions that work out for a wide range of outcomes, have backups or a huge margin of safety. For example, when investing money the following can guide us: know the underlying business value, don't use leverage, enter situations where the management is able and honest, and invest with a huge margin of safety.

How much margin of safety do we need? Warren Buffett answers:

If you understand a business – if you can see its future *perfectly* – then, obviously, you need very *little* in the way of margin of safety. Conversely, the more things that can happen, the more uncertainty there is, the more vulnerable the business is or the greater the possibility of change, the larger margin of safety you require…

If you're driving a 9,800 pound truck across a bridge that says it holds 10,000 pounds and the bridge is only about six inches above the ground, then you may feel OK. However, if the bridge is over the Grand Canyon, then you may want a little larger margin of safety. And, therefore, you may only drive a 4,000 pound truck across. So it depends on the nature of the underlying risk.

What else is important? We have a better chance of avoiding misjudgment and improving our lives if we have the right attitude and follow certain values.

In writer Janet Lowe's wonderful biography over Charles Munger, *Damn Right!*, we can learn some of Charles Munger's views on values and behavior from his stepson, Hal Borthwick:

Charlie drummed in the notion that a person should always "Do the best that you can do. Never tell a lie. If you say you're going to do it, get it done. Nobody gives a shit about an excuse. Leave for the meeting early. Don't be late, but if you are late, don't bother giving people excuses. Just apologize…Return your calls quickly. The other thing is the five-second no. You've got to make your mind up. You don't leave people hanging."

Twelve

ATTITUDES

Be happy while you're living, for you are a long time dead.
- Scottish proverb

Life is too short to waste. Time flies, whether we're having fun or not. Samuel Johnson said: "It matters not how a man dies, but how he lives. The act of dying is not of importance, it lasts so short a time."

We only have one life so we should try to create a life we enjoy. Comedian George Burns said: "You can either do what you love or love what you do. I don't see where there's any other choice."

We all have 24 hours in the day. We can't save time, only spend it wisely or foolishly. How do we use our time? What is the best use? What do we want out of life? Do we live in a way to make that possible? The shorter the list, the more likely it is to focus on things that matter. Know what we want and don't want. Do we do what we want to do or what others expect us to do? Who or what is most important in our life? Do we have a sense of meaning?

Part of avoiding misjudgments and improving our lives is having the right attitude toward life. Since people are different, there is no one-size-fits-all strategy. We each must figure out our own style. But there are guidelines that apply to us all.

We should act in a way that agrees with our nature, advantages and limitations and we should establish (and follow) some values.

How can we expect to succeed in a field we don't understand? We reduce the likelihood of making mistakes if we deal with things that agree with our nature, and things we understand and do well. We have a better chance solving problems and evaluating statements if they are within our area of competence. Confucius said: "To know that we know what we know, and that we do not know what we do not know; that is true knowledge." We must determine our abilities and limitations. We need to know what we don't know or are not capable of knowing and avoid those areas. As Warren Buffett says:

You have to stick within what I call your circle of competence. You have to know what you understand and what you don't understand. It's *not* terribly important how *big* the circle is. But it's *terribly* important that you know *where* the perimeter is.

Charles Munger adds:

We'd rather deal with what we understand. Why should we want to play a competitive game in a field where we have *no* advantage – maybe a *disadvantage* – instead of playing in a field where we have a clear *advantage?*

Each of you will have to figure out where *your* talents lie. And you'll have to use your advantages. But if you try to succeed in what you're worst at, you're going to have a very louse career. I can almost guarantee it. To do otherwise, you'd have to buy a winning lottery ticket or get very lucky somewhere else.

Ask: What is my nature? What motivates me? What is my tolerance for pain and risk? What has given me happiness and unhappiness in the past? What things and people am I comfortable with? What are my talents and skills? Do I know the difference between what I want and what I'm good at? Where do I have an edge over others? What are my limitations?

How can we do what is important if we don't have any values? If we don't stand for something, we fall for anything.

Be honest
Honesty is the first chapter of the book of wisdom.
- Thomas Jefferson (President and statesman, 1743-1826)

Act honorably. Listen to the words of Mark Twain: "Always do right. This will gratify some people and astonish the rest."

Honesty pays. Charles Munger says:

I'm proud to be associated with the value system at Berkshire Hathaway. I think you'll make more money in the end with good ethics than bad. Even though there are some people who do very well, like Marc Rich—who plainly has never had any decent ethics, or seldom anyway. But in the end, Warren Buffett has done better than Marc Rich—in money—not just in reputation.

Act with integrity and individuality. Heraclitus said: "The content of your character is your choice. Day by day, what you choose, what you think, and what you do is who you become. Your integrity is your destiny…it is the light that guides your way."

Every human being is unique so we have the right to be different. Why is integrity the real freedom? Because if we have nothing to hide we have nothing to fear.

Stay out of anything questionable and deal with honorable people. Use the Warren Buffett "front-page test:" "Would I be willing to see my action immediately described by an informed and critical reporter on the front page of my local paper, there to be read by my wife, children and friends?"

Treat people fairly

Lao-Tsu said: "Respond intelligently even to unintelligent treatment." Be nice to people and if they are not nice to you – don't be nasty – just avoid them in the future. Follow the advice of Charles Darwin – avoid controversies:

> I rejoice that I have avoided controversies, and this I owe to Lyell, who many years ago, in reference to my geological works, strongly advised me never to get entangled in a controversy, as it rarely did any good and caused a miserable loss of time and temper…
>
> All that I think is that you [letter to E. Haeckel] will excite anger, and that anger so completely blinds every one that your arguments would have no chance of influencing those who are already opposed to our views.

Don't take life too seriously

Life is too important to be taken seriously.
- Oscar Wilde (Anglo-Irish playwright and poet, 1854-1900)

Have perspective. Remember Samuel Johnson's words: "Distance has the same effect on the mind as on the eye." When we fail we should view it as a learning experience.

Have a positive attitude. Mayo Clinic researchers report that optimists report a higher level of physical and mental functioning than pessimists. Studies at the Mayo Clinic also show that optimists live about 20% longer than pessimists. Having a positive attitude also causes the body to produce pain-suppressing hormones, called endorphins, which work like morphine.

Warren Buffett says on the value of enthusiasm:

> I do think enthusiasm is a good quality to have generally. It has helped me… I like managers in our businesses that are enthusiastic. These people are enthusiastic about their work in the same way people can get enthusiastic about golf, and that translates into

results. If you are in a job that you are not enthusiastic about, find something else. You're not doing yourself any favor, and you're not doing your employer any favor and you're going to make a change anyway at some point. We're here on earth only one time, unless Shirley MacLaine is right, so you ought to be doing something that you enjoy as you go along, and can be enthusiastic about.

Have reasonable expectations

Blessed is he that expects nothing, for he shall never be disappointed.
- Benjamin Franklin

If we don't hope for much, reality often beats our expectations. If we always expect the best or have unreal expectations, we are often disappointed. We feel worse and make bad judgments.

Expect adversity. We encounter adversity in whatever we choose to do in life. Sherlock Holmes said in Arthur Conan Doyle's *The Hound of the Baskervilles:* "There is nothing more stimulating than a case where everything goes against you." Charles Munger gives his iron prescription for life:

Whenever you think that some situation or some person is ruining your life, it is actually *you* who are ruining your life…Feeling like a victim is a perfectly *disastrous* way to make go through life. If you just take the attitude that however bad it is in any way, it's *always* your fault and you just fix it as best you can – the so-called "iron prescription" – I think that really works.

When bad things happen, ask: What else does this mean? See life's obstacles as temporary setbacks, not disasters.

Live in the present.

The superior man does not waste himself on what is distant, on what is absent. He stands in the here and now, in the real situation.
- Confucius

Often we tend to emphasize the destination so much that we miss the journey. Stay in the present and enjoy life today. Blaise Pascal wrote:

Let each of us examine his thoughts; he will find them wholly concerned with the past or the future. We almost never think of the present, and if we do think of it, it is only to see what light it throws on our plans for the future. The present is never our end. The past and the present are our means, the future alone our end. Thus we never actually live, but hope to live, and since we are always planning how to be happy, it is inevitable that we should never be so.

Be curious and open-minded. Always ask "why"

Curiosity is one of the permanent and
certain characteristics of a vigorous mind.
- Samuel Johnson

Thomas Henry Huxley said: "Sit down before facts like a child, and be prepared to give up every preconceived Notion, follow humbly wherever and to whatever abysses Nature leads, or you shall learn nothing." A child is curious and asks "why?" As grown-ups we seem to forget the "why's" and accept what others say. We should all be children again and see the world as if through the eyes of a curious child without preconceptions.

The End

I confess that I have been as blind as a mole, but it is
better to learn wisdom late than never to learn it at all.
- Sherlock Holmes (Arthur Conan Doyle, *The Man with the Twisted Lip*)

I hope this book is helpful in both understanding and improving your thinking. I also hope that you will continue in your search for wisdom. We are still going to make misjudgments (at least I still do them), but we can improve.

CHARLES T. MUNGER HARVARD SCHOOL
COMMENCEMENT SPEECH
JUNE 13, 1986

Prescriptions for Guaranteed Misery in Life

Now that Headmaster Berrisford has selected one of the oldest and longest-serving trustees to make a commencement speech, it behooves the speaker to address two questions in every mind:

1) Why was such a selection made? and,
2) How long is the speech going to last?

I will answer the first question from long experience alongside Berrisford. He is seeking enhanced reputation for our school in the manner of the man who proudly displays his horse which can count to seven. The man knows that counting to seven is not much of a mathematical feat but he expects approval because doing so is creditable, considering that the performer is a horse.

The second question, regarding length of speech, I am not going to answer in advance. It would deprive your upturned faces of lively curiosity and obvious keen anticipation, which I prefer to retain, regardless of source.

But I will tell you how my consideration of speech length created the subject matter of the speech itself. I was puffed up when invited to speak. While not having significant public-speaking experience, I do hold a black belt in chutzpah, and, I immediately considered Demosthenes and Cicero as role models and anticipated trying to earn a compliment like Cicero gave when asked which was his favorite among the orations of Demosthenes. Cicero replied: "The longest one."

However, fortunately for this audience, I also thought of Samuel Johnson's famous comment when he addressed Milton's poem, *Paradise Lost,* and correctly said: "No one ever wished it longer." And that made me consider which of all the twenty Harvard School graduation speeches I had heard that I wished longer. There was only one such speech, that given by Johnny Carson, specifying Carson's prescriptions for guaranteed misery in life. I therefore decided to repeat Carson's speech but in expanded form with some added prescriptions of my own.

After all, I am much older than Carson was when he spoke and have failed and been miserable more often and in more ways than was possible for a charming humorist speaking at younger age. I am plainly well-qualified to expand on Carson's theme.

What Carson said was that he couldn't tell the graduating class how to be happy, but he could tell them from personal experience how to guarantee misery. Carson's prescriptions for sure misery included:

1) Ingesting chemicals in an effort to alter mood or perception;

2) Envy; and

3) Resentment.

I can still recall Carson's absolute conviction as he told how he had tried these things on occasion after occasion and had become miserable every time.

It is easy to understand Carson's first prescription for misery – ingesting chemicals. I add my voice. The four closest friends of my youth were highly intelligent, ethical, humorous types, favored in person and background. Two are long dead, with alcohol a contributing factor, and a third is a living alcoholic – if you call that living. While susceptibility varies, addiction can happen to any of us, through a subtle process where the bonds of degradation are too light to be felt until they are too strong to be broken. And I have yet to meet anyone, in over six decades of life, whose life was worsened by overfear and overavoidance of such a deceptive pathway to destruction.

Envy, of course, joins chemicals in winning some sort of quantity price for causing misery. It was wreaking havoc long before it got a bad press in the laws of Moses. If you wish to retain the contribution of envy to misery, I recommend that you never read any of the biographies of that good Christian, Samuel Johnson, because his life demonstrates in an enticing way the possibility and advantage of transcending envy.

Resentment has always worked for me exactly as it worked for Carson. I cannot recommend it highly enough to you if you desire misery. Johnson spoke well when he said that life is hard enough to swallow without squeezing in the bitter rind of resentment.

For those of you who want misery, I also recommend refraining from practice of the Disraeli compromise, designed for people who find it impossible to quit resentment cold turkey. Disraeli, as he rose to become one of the greatest Prime Ministers, learned to give up vengeance as a motivation for action, but he did retain some outlet for resentment by putting the names of people who wronged him on pieces of paper in a drawer. Then, from time to time, he reviewed these names and took pleasure in noting the way the world had taken his enemies down without his assistance.

Well, so much for Carson's three prescriptions. Here are four more prescriptions from Munger:

First, be unreliable. Do not faithfully do what you have engaged to do. If you will only master this one habit you will more than counterbalance the combined effect of all your virtues, howsoever great. If you like being distrusted and excluded from the best human contribution and company, this prescription is for you. Master this one habit and you can always play the role of the hare in the fable, except that instead of being outrun by one fine turtle you will be outrun by hordes and hordes of mediocre turtles and even by some mediocre turtles on crutches.

I must warn you that if you don't follow my first prescription it may be hard to end up miserable, even if you start disadvantaged. I had a roommate in college who was and is severely dyslexic. But he is perhaps the most reliable man I have ever known. He has had a wonderful life so far, outstanding wife and children, chief executive of a multibillion dollar corporation.

If you want to avoid a conventional, main-culture, establishment result of this kind, you simply can't count on your other handicaps to hold you back if you persist in being reliable.

I cannot here pass by a reference to a life described as "wonderful so far," without reinforcing the "so far" aspects of the human condition by repeating the remark of Croesus, once the richest king in the world. Later, in ignominious captivity, as he prepared to be burned alive, he said: "Well now do I remember the words of the historian Solon: "No man's life should be accounted a happy one until it is over."

My second prescription for misery is to learn everything you possibly can from your own personal experience, minimizing what you learn vicariously from the good and bad experience of others, living and dead. This prescription is a sure-shot producer of misery and second-rate achievement.

You can see the results of not learning from others' mistakes by simply looking about you. How little originality there is in the common disasters of mankind – drunk driving deaths, reckless driving maimings, incurable venereal diseases, conversion of bright college students into brainwashed zombies as members of destructive cults, business failures through repetition of obvious mistakes made by predecessors, various forms of crowd folly, and so on. I recommend as a memory clue to finding the way to real trouble from heedless, unoriginal error the modern saying: "If at first you don't succeed, well, so much for hang gliding."

The other aspect of avoiding vicarious wisdom is the rule for not learning from the best work done before yours. The prescription is to become as non-educated as you reasonable can.

Perhaps you will better see the type of non-miserable result you can thus avoid if I render a short historical account. There once was a man who assiduously mastered the work of his best predecessors, despite a poor start and very tough time in analytic geometry. Eventually his own original work attracted wide attention and he said of that work:

"If I have seen a little farther than other men it is because I stood on the shoulders of giants."
The bones of that man lie buried now, in Westminster Abbey, under an unusual inscription:
"Here lie the remains of all that was mortal in Sir Isaac Newton."

My third prescription for misery is to go down and stay down when you get your first, second, or third severe reverse in the battle of life. Because there is so much adversity out there, even for the lucky and wise, this will guarantee that, in due course, you will be permanently mired in misery. Ignore at all cost the lesson contained in the accurate epitaph written for himself by Epicetus: "Here lies Epicetus, a slave, maimed in body, the ultimate in poverty, and favored by the Gods."

My final prescription to you for a life of fuzzy thinking and infelicity is to ignore a story they told me when I was very young about a rustic who said: "I wish I knew where I was going to die, and then I'd never go there." Most people smile (as you did) at the rustic's ignorance and ignore his basic wisdom. If my experience is any guide, the rustic's approach is to be avoided at all cost by someone bent on misery. To help fail you should discount as mere quirk, with no useful message, the method of the rustic, which is the same one used in Carson's speech.

What Carson did was to approach the study of how to create X by turning the question backward, that is, by studying how to create non-X. The great algebraist, Jacobi, had exactly the same approach as Carson and was known for his constant repetition of one phrase: "Invert, always invert." It is in the nature of things, as Jacobi knew, that many hard problems are best solved only when they are addressed backward. For instance, when almost everyone else was trying to revise the electromagnetic laws of Maxwell to be consistent with the motion laws of Newton, Einstein discovered special relativity as he made a 180 degree turn and revised Newton's laws to fit Maxwell's.

It is my opinion, as a certified biography nut, that Charles Robert Darwin would have ranked near the middle of the Harvard School graduating class of 1986. Yet he is now famous in the history of science. This is precisely the type of example you should learn nothing from if bent on minimizing your results from your own endowment.

Darwin's result was due in large measure to his working method, which violated all my rules for misery and particularly emphasized a backward twist in that he always gave priority attention to evidence tending to disconfirm whatever cherished and hard-won theory he already had. In contrast, most people early achieve and later intensify a tendency to process new and disconfirming information so that any original conclusion remains intact. They become people of whom Philip Wylie observed: " You couldn't squeeze a dime between what they already know and what they will never learn."

The life of Darwin demonstrates how a turtle may outrun the hares, aided by extreme objectivity, which helps the objective person end up like the only player without blindfold in a game of pin-the-donkey.

If you minimize objectivity, you ignore not only a lesson from Darwin but also one from Einstein. Einstein said that his successful theories came from: "Curiosity, concentration, perseverance and self-criticism. And by self-criticism he meant the testing and destruction of his own well-loved ideas.

Finally, minimizing objectivity will help you lessen the compromises and burdens of owning worldly goods, because objectivity does not work only for great physicists and biologists. It also adds power to the work of a plumbing contractor in Bemidji. Therefore, if you interpret being true to yourself as requiring that you retain every notion of your youth you will be safely underway, not only toward maximizing ignorance, but also toward whatever misery can be obtained through unpleasant experiences in business.

It is fitting now that a backward sort of speech end with a backward sort of toast, inspired by Elihu Root's repeated accounts of how the dog went to Dover, "leg over leg." To the class of 1986:

Gentlemen, may each of you rise high by spending each day of a long life aiming low.

WISDOM FROM CHARLES T. MUNGER AND WARREN E. BUFFETT

On how to change people

Suppose you've got a client who really wants to commit tax fraud. If he doesn't push the tax law away beyond the line, he can't *stand* it. He can't shave in the morning if he thinks there's been any cheating he could get by with that he hasn't done. And there are people like that. They just feel they aren't living aggressively enough.

You can approach that situation in either of two ways: (A) you can say, "I just won't work for him," and duck it. Or, (B) you can say, "Well, the circumstances of my life require that I work for him. And what *I'm* doing for him doesn't involve my cheating. Therefore, I'll do it."

And if you see he wants to do something really stupid, it probably won't work to tell him, "What you're doing is bad. I have better morals than you."

That *offends* him. You're young. He's old. Therefore, instead of being persuaded, he's more likely to react with, "Who in the hell are you to establish the moral code of the whole world?"

But instead, you can say to him, "You can't do that without three other people beneath you knowing about it. Therefore, you're making yourself subject to *blackmail*. You're risking your *reputation*. You're risking your *family*, your *money*, etc."

That is likely to *work*. And you're telling him something that's *true*. Do you want to spend a lot of time working for people where you have to use methods like that to get them to behave well? I think the answer is *no*. But if you're hooked with it, appealing to *interest* is likely to work better as a matter of human persuasion than appeal to anything else. That, again, is a powerful psychological principle with deep biological roots.

I saw that psychological principle totally blown at Salomon. Salomon's general council *knew* that the CEO, Gutfreund, should have promptly told the Federal authorities all about Salomon's trading improprieties in which Gutfreund didn't participate and which he hadn't caused. And the general counsel urged Gutfreund to do it. He told Gutfreund, in effect, "You're probably not legally required to do that, but it's the right thing to do. You really should."

But it didn't work. The task was easy to put off - because it was unpleasant. So that's what Gutfreund did - he put it off.

And the general counsel had very little constituency within Salomon *except* for the CEO. If the CEO went down, the general counsel was going down with him. Therefore, his whole career was on the line. So to save his career, he needed to talk the dilatory CEO into doing the right thing.

It would've been child's play to get that job done right. All the general counsel had to do was to tell his boss, "John, this situation could ruin your *life*. You could lose your *wealth*. You could lose your *reputation...*" And it would have *worked*. CEOs don't *like* the idea of being ruined, disgraced and fired. (Lecture by Charles T. Munger to the students of Professor William Lazier at Stanford Law School, *Outstanding Investor Digest,* March 13, 1998, p.59.)

On some reasons to why managers don't make rational decisions

My most surprising discovery: the overwhelming importance in business of an unseen force that we might call "the institutional imperative." In business school, I was given no hint of the imperative's existence and I did not intuitively understand it when I entered the business world. I thought then that decent, intelligent, and experienced managers would automatically make rational business decisions. But I learned over time that isn't so. Instead, rationality frequently wilts when the institutional imperative comes into play.

For example: (1) As if governed by Newton's First Law of Motion, an institution will resist any change in its current direction; (2) Just as work expands to fill available time, corporate projects or acquisitions will materialize to soak up available funds; (3) Any business craving of the leader, however foolish, will be quickly supported by detailed rate-of-return and strategic studies prepared by his troops; and (4) The behavior of peer companies, whether they are expanding, acquiring, setting executive compensation or whatever, will be mindlessly imitated.

Institutional dynamics, not venality or stupidity, set businesses on these courses, which are too often misguided. After making some expensive mistakes because I ignored the power of the imperative, I have tried to organize and manage Berkshire in ways that minimize its influence. Furthermore, Charlie and I have attempted to concentrate our investments in companies that appear alert to the problem. (Warren Buffett, Berkshire Hathaway Inc., *Letters to Shareholders,* 1989, p.62.)

On the difficulty of replacing a CEO

Most organizations depend on the self-interest of the superior to weed out the second-rate inferior. If I'm a sales manager and I've got lots of lousy salesmen, it hurts *my* performance and it probably hurts my income to keep on the sub-par performers. It certainly hurts a football coach to keep a sub-par quarterback or any other player in there if he can get a better one. In almost all jobs, there is a reward or penalty system that causes the superior to think actively about whether the people beneath him are doing a first-class job and to do something about it if they aren't.

That works all the way up to the CEO. But the CEO's superiors are the directors of the publicly held company. And are the directors of the company going to suffer if the CEO is sub-par? Probably only if they're embarrassed. That's the way you hurt the superior in that case. You don't take away his directors' fee. And as a practical matter, you don't displace directors very often. So the only system that's comparable to the problem of the football coach or the sales manager is probably to hurt psychically the position of the inferior director – and that will work. Otherwise, the motivation to correct the CEO problem is not strong unless there's a big ownership among directors – and even that doesn't always work perfectly.

To change directors usually takes the action of big shareholders. It doesn't happen any other way. It's a very awkward situation for a management or a group of directors, who have somehow selected other weak directors, to make changes. It goes against all the natural societal norms to walk up to some guy at a meeting – who isn't causing any harm and is sitting there like a potted palm – and turn to him and say, "We've all thought it over. And you're really not any good." It just doesn't happen. (Warren Buffett, Berkshire Hathaway annual meeting, 1993, *Outstanding Investor Digest,* June 30, 1993, p.32.)

On the kind of people we should do business with

I have been asked by a number of people just what secrets the Blumkins [Nebraska Furniture Mart] bring to their business. These are not very esoteric. All members of the family: (1) apply themselves with an enthusiasm and energy that would make Ben Franklin and Horatio Alger look like dropouts; (2) define with extraordinary realism their area of special competence and act decisively on all matters within it; (3) ignore even the most enticing propositions falling outside of that area of special competence; and (4) unfailingly behave in a high-grade manner with everyone they deal with. (Mrs. B boils it down to "sell cheap and tell the truth".) (Warren Buffett, Berkshire Hathaway Inc., *Letters to Shareholders,* 1984, p.87.)

We really don't want to buy into any organization that we felt would be lacking that quality [intellectual honesty] in the first place - because we really don't believe in buying into organizations to change them. We may change the comp system a little or something of the sort…

We want people joining us who already are the type that face reality and that basically [not only] tell us the truth, but tell themselves the truth - which is even more important. Once you get an organization that lies to itself - and there are plenty that do - I just think you get into all kinds of problems. And people know it throughout the organization and they adopt the norms of what they think is happening up above them. Particularly in a financial organization - really in any organization, but particularly in a financial organization – that is death over time. We wouldn't buy into something that we felt had that problem with the idea that we would correct it - because we wouldn't. We've had a little experience with some organizations that have had that sort of problem. And it's not correctable - at least based on the life span of humans. It's too much to commit to. (Warren Buffett, Berkshire Hathaway annual meeting, 2000, *Outstanding Investor Digest,* OID.Com, continued from December 18, 2000 & Year End 2000 Editions.)

We find it meaningful when an owner *cares* about whom he sells to. We like to do business with someone who loves his company, not just the money that a sale will bring him (though we certainly understand why he likes that as well). When this emotional attachment exists, it signals that important qualities will likely be found within the business: honest accounting, pride of product, respect for customers, and a loyal group of associates having a strong sense of direction. The reverse is apt to be true, also. When an owner auctions off his business, exhibiting a total lack of interest in what follows, you will frequently find that it has been dressed up for sale, particularly when the seller is a "financial owner." And if owners behave with little regard for their business and its people, their conduct will often contaminate attitudes and practices throughout the company. (Warren Buffett, Berkshire Hathaway Inc., 2000 *Annual Report,* p.7.)

234

On picking up the right character traits

<u>Buffett:</u> It *does* pay to have the right models…I think that it just stands to reason that if you copy the people that you look up to – particularly if you do it at an early enough age…If you influence the role models of a five-year old or an eight-year old or a ten-year old, then it's going to have a huge impact.

And of course, virtually everybody starts out with their initial models being their parents. So they are the ones that are going to have a *huge* effect on 'em. And if that parent turns out to be a great model, I think it's going to be a huge plus for the child. I think it beats a whole lot of other things in life to have the right models around…

But you've got to start early. It's very tough to change behavior later on. I tell the students in classes, "Just pick out the person you admire the most in the class, and sit down and write the reasons why you admire him and then try and figure out why you can't have the same qualities." After all, they're not like the ability to throw a football 60 yards or run the 100 in ten seconds flat or something like that. They're qualities of personality, character and temperament that *can* be emulated.

And you can apply the reverse of it following Charlie's theory: You can find the people you don't like and say, "What *don't* I like about these people?" It takes a little strength of character, but you can look inwards and say, "Have I got some of that in me?"

It's not complicated. Ben Graham did it, Ben Franklin did it. And nothing could be more simple than to try and figure out what you find admirable and then decide that the person you *really* would like to admire is *yourself.* And the only way you're going to do it is to take on the qualities of other people you admire.

<u>Munger:</u> Also, there is no reason to look only for *living* models. The eminent dead are in the nature of things some of the best models around. And if a model is all you want, you're really better off not limiting yourself to the living. Some of the very best models have been dead for a long time. (Berkshire Hathaway annual meeting, 2000, *Outstanding Investor Digest,* Year End 2000 Edition, pp.62-63.)

On overconfidence

About 99% of American management thinks that if they're wonderful at doing one thing that they'll be wonderful at doing something else. They're like a duck on a pond when it's raining – they're going up in the world. They start thinking that they're the ones that are causing themselves to rise. So they go over to some place where it isn't raining and they just sit there on the ground. But nothing happens. Then they usually fire their number two in command or hire a consultant. They very seldom see what really happens is that they have left their circle of competence…

If you take the CEOs of America's largest corporations, they do not know what their circle of competence is. That's one of the reasons they make so many dumb acquisitions. They rise to the top of the business because they're great salesmen, great production people or whatever. All of a sudden, they're running a multi-billion dollar business and their job is to allocate capital and to buy businesses. They've never bought a business in their life. They don't know what it's all about.

So they usually do one or two things. Either they set up an internal department, hire a bunch of guys and have them tell him something to do. Of course, the guys know if they don't tell him something to do, then there will be no jobs. So you can imagine what activity takes place then. Or they go out and hire investment bankers who get paid by the transaction. (Warren Buffett, lecture at Stanford Law School, March 23, 1990, *Outstanding Investor Digest,* April 18, 1990, pp.13-14.)

On some reasons to why bad lending happen so often

Granting the presence of perverse incentives, what are the operating mechanics that cause widespread bad loans (where the higher interest rates do not adequately cover increased risk of loss) under our present system? After all, the bad lending, while it has a surface plausibility to bankers under cost pressure, is, by definition, not rational, at least for the lending banks and the wider civilization. How then does bad lending occur so often?

It occurs (partly) because there are predictable irrationalities among people as social animals. It is now pretty clear (in experimental social psychology) that people on the horns of a dilemma, which is where our system has placed our bankers, are extra likely to react unwisely to the example of other people's conduct, now widely called "social proof." So, once some banker has apparently (but not really) solved his cost-pressure problem by unwise lending, a considerable amount of imitative "crowd folly," relying on the "social proof," is the natural consequence. Additional massive irrational lending is caused by "reinforcement" of foolish behavior, caused by unwise accounting convention in a manner discussed later in this letter. It is hard to be wise when the messages which drive you are wrong messages provided by a mal-designed system…

Many eminent "experts" would not agree with our notions about systemic irresponsibility from combining (1) "free-market" pricing of interest rates with (2) government guarantees of payment. If many eminent "experts" are wrong, how could this happen? Our explanation is that the "experts" are over-charmed with an admirable, powerful, predictive model, coming down from Adam Smith. Those discretionary interest rates on deposits have a "free-market" image, making it easy to conclude, automatically, that the discretionary rates, like other free-market processes, must be good. Indeed, they are appraised as remaining good even when combined with governmental deposit insurance, a radical non-free-market element.

Such illogical thinking displays the standard folly bedeviling the "expert" role in any soft science: one tends to use only models from one's own segment of a discipline, ignoring or underweighing others. Furthermore, the more powerful and useful is any model, the more error it tends to produce through overconfident misuse.

This brings to mind Ben Graham's paradoxical observation that good ideas cause more investment mischief than bad ideas. He had it right. It is so easy for us all to push a really good idea to wretched excess, as in the case of the Florida land bubble or the "nifty fifty" corporate stocks. Then mix in a little "social proof" (from other experts), and brains (including ours) often turn to mush. It would be nice if great old models never tricked us, but, alas, "some dreams are not to be." Even Einstein got tricked in his later years…

We think current accounting for many high-interest-rate loans has terrible consequences in the banking system. In essence, it "front ends" into reported income revenues that would have been deferred until much later, after risky bets were more clearly won, if more

236

conservative accounting had been employed. This practice turns many a banker into a human version of one of B.F. Skinner's pigeons, since he is "reinforced" into continuing and expanding bad lending through the pleasure of seeing good figures in the short term. The good figures substitute nicely in the mind for nonexistent underlying institutional good, partly through the process, originally demonstrated by Pavlov, wherein we respond to a mere association because it has usually portended a reality that would make the response correct. (Charles Munger, Wesco Financial Inc., 1990 *Annual Report*. Berkshire Hathaway Inc., *Letters to Shareholders,* 1987-1995, pp.205-208.)

On the value of attacking problems early

One of the problems in society is that the most important issues are often these incremental type things. The world is not going to come to an end because tomorrow there are 200 or 250 thousand more people on the planet than there were today. That's about the number it grows every day. There is nothing apocalyptic about it. People will go on making apocalyptic projections. But, it is like eating about 300 calories more each day than you burn up; it has no effect on you today. You don't get up from the table and all of a sudden everybody says, "My God, you look fat compared to when you sat down!" But, if you keep doing it over time, the incremental problems are hard to attack because that one extra piece of pie doesn't really seem to make a difference. The 250,000 people tomorrow don't seem to make any difference, but the cumulative effects of them will make a huge difference over time, just like overeating will make a huge difference over time. The time to attack those problems is early. (1994 Lecture of The E. J. Faulkner Lecture Series, A Colloquium with University of Nebraska-Lincoln Students by Warren E. Buffett, p.21.)

On the value of math

53% of the world's stock market value is in the U.S. Well, if U.S. GDP [gross domestic product] grows at 4-5% a year with 1-2% inflation – which would be a pretty good, in fact it would be a *very* good result – then I think it's very unlikely that corporate profits are going to grow at a greater rate than that. Corporate profits as a percent of GDP are on the high side already – and corporate profits can't constantly grow at a faster rate than GDP. Obviously, in the end, they'd be greater than GDP.

It's like somebody said about New York – that it has more lawyers than people. You run into certain conflicts as you go along if you say profits can get bigger than GDP. So if you have a situation where the best you can hope for in corporate profit growth over the years is 4-5%, how can it be reasonable to think that equities – which, after all, are a capitalization of those corporate profits – can grow at 15% a year? It's *nonsense,* frankly…

The other day, I looked at the *Fortune* 500. And the companies on that list earned $334 billion and had a market capitalization of $9.9 trillion at year end – which would probably be up to at least $10.5 trillion now. Well, the only money investors are going to make in the long run is what the businesses make. There's nothing added. The government doesn't throw in anything. Nobody's adding to the pot. People take *out* from the pot in terms of frictional costs – investment management fees, brokerage commissions and all of that. But $334 billion is all that the investment earns.

If you own a farm, what the farm produces is all you're going to get from the farm. If it produces $50 an acre of net profit, you'll get $50 an acre of net profit. And there's nothing about it that transforms that in some miraculous form. If you owned all of the *Fortune* 500 – if you owned 100% of it – you'd be making $334 billion. And if you paid $10.5 trillion for that, well, that's not a great return on investment.

Then you might say, "Can that $334 billion double in five years?" Well, it *can't* double in five years with GDP growing at 4% a year or some number like that. It would just produce things so out of whack in terms of experience in the American economy that it won't happen. Any time you get involved in these things where if you trace out the mathematics of it, you bump into absurdities, then you better change your expectations somewhat. (Warren Buffett, Berkshire Hathaway annual meeting, 1999, *Outstanding Investor Digest,* December 10, 1999, p.52.)

On advantages of scale

In terms of which businesses succeed and which businesses fail, advantages of scale are ungodly important. For example, one great advantage of scale taught in all of the business schools of the world is cost reductions along the so-called experience curve. Just *doing* something complicated in more and more volume enables human beings, who are trying to improve and are motivated by the incentives of capitalism, to do it more and more *efficiently.*

The very nature of things is that if you get a whole lot of volume through your joint, you get better at processing that volume. That's an enormous advantage. And it has a lot to do with which businesses succeed and fail....

Let's go through a list - albeit an incomplete one of possible advantages of scale. Some come from simple geometry. If you're building a great spherical tank, obviously as you build it bigger, the amount of steel you use in the surface goes up with the square and the cubic volume goes up with the cube. So as you increase the dimensions, you can hold a lot more volume per unit area of steel. And there are all kinds of things like that where the simple geometry - the simple reality - gives you an advantage of scale.

For example, you can get advantages of scale from TV advertising. When TV advertising first arrived - when talking color pictures first came into our living rooms - it was an unbelievably powerful thing. And in the early days, we had three networks that had whatever it was - say 90% of the audience.

Well, if you were Proctor & Gamble, you could afford to use this new method of advertising. You could afford the very expensive cost of network television because you were selling so damn many cans and bottles. Some little guy couldn't. And there was no way of buying it in part. Therefore, he couldn't use it. In effect, if you didn't have a big volume, you couldn't use network TV advertising - which was the most effective technique.

So when TV came in, the branded companies that were already big got a *huge* tail wind. Indeed, they prospered and prospered and prospered until some of them got fat and foolish, which happens with prosperity - at least to some people....

And your advantage of scale can be an informational advantage. If I go to some remote place, I may see Wrigley chewing gum alongside Glotz's chewing gum. Well, I know that Wrigley is a satisfactory product, whereas I don't know anything about Glotz's. So if one is

$.40 and the other is $.30, am I going to take something I don't know and put it in my mouth - which is a pretty personal place, after all - for a lousy dime?

Another advantage of scale comes from psychology…We are all influenced - subconsciously and to some extent consciously - by what we see others do and approve. Therefore, if everybody's buying something, we think it's better. We don't like to be the one guy who's out of step.

Again, some of this is at a subconscious level and some of it isn't. Sometimes, we consciously and rationally think, "Gee, I don't know much about this. They know more than I do. Therefore, why shouldn't I follow them?"

The social proof phenomenon which comes right out of psychology gives huge advantages to scale - for example, with very wide distribution, which of course is hard to get. One advantage of Coca-Cola is that it's available almost everywhere in the world.

Well, suppose you have a little soft drink. Exactly how do you make it available all over the Earth? The worldwide distribution setup - which is slowly won by a big enterprise - gets to be a *huge* advantage…. And if you think about it, once you get enough advantages of that type, it can become very hard for anybody to dislodge you.

There's *another* kind of advantage to scale. In some businesses, the very nature of things is to sort of cascade toward the overwhelming dominance of one firm.

The most obvious one is daily newspapers. There's practically no city left in the U.S., aside from a few very big ones, where there's more than one daily newspaper.

And again, that's a scale thing. Once I get most of the circulation, I get most of the advertising. And once I get most of the advertising and circulation, why would anyone want the thinner paper with less information in it? So it tends to cascade to a winner-take-all situation. And that's a separate form of the advantages of scale phenomenon.

Similarly, all these huge advantages of scale allow greater specialization within the firm. Therefore, each person can be better at what he does…

On the subject of advantages of economies of scale, I find chain stores quite interesting. Just think about it. The concept of a chain store was a fascinating invention. You get this huge purchasing power - which means that you have lower merchandise costs. You get a whole bunch of little laboratories out there in which you can conduct experiments. And you get specialization.

If one little guy is trying to buy across 27 different merchandise categories influenced by traveling salesmen, he's going to make a lot of dumb decisions. But if your buying is done in headquarters for a huge bunch of stores, you can get very bright people that know a lot about refrigerators and so forth to do the buying.

The reverse is demonstrated by the little store where one guy is doing all the buying. It's like the old story about the little store with salt all over its walls. And a stranger comes in and says to the store owner, "You must sell a lot of salt." And he replies, "No, I don't. But you should see the guy who *sells* me salt." (Lecture by Charles T. Munger to the students of Professor Guilford Babcock at the University of Southern California School of Business on April 14, 1994, *Outstanding Investor Digest,* May 5, 1995, pp.52-54.)

On disadvantages of scale

For example, we - by which I mean Berkshire Hathaway - are the largest shareholder in Capital Cities/ABC. And we had trade publications there that got murdered - where our competitors beat us. And the way they beat us was by going to a narrower specialization.

We'd have a travel magazine for business travel. So somebody would create one which was addressed solely at corporate travel departments. Like an ecosystem, you're getting a narrower and narrower specialization.

Well, they got much more efficient. They could tell more to the guys who ran corporate travel departments. Plus, they didn't have to waste the ink and paper mailing out stuff that corporate travel departments weren't interested in reading. It was a more efficient system. And they beat our brains out as we relied on our broader magazine.

That's what happened to *The Saturday Evening Post* and all those things. They're gone. What we have now is *Motorcross* - which is read by a bunch of nuts who like to participate in tournaments where they turn somersaults on their motorcycles. But they *care* about it. For them, it's the principal purpose of life. A magazine called *Motorcross* is a total necessity to those people. And its profit margins would make you salivate. Just think of how narrowcast that kind of publishing is. So occasionally, scaling *down* and intensifying gives you the big advantage. Bigger is not always better.

The great defect of scale, of course, which makes the game interesting - so that the big people don't always win - is that as you get big, you get the bureaucracy. And with the bureaucracy comes the territoriality - which is again grounded in human nature.

And the incentives are perverse. For example, if you worked for AT&T in my day, it was a great bureaucracy. Who in the hell was really thinking about the shareholder or anything else? And in a bureaucracy, you think the work is done when it goes out of your in-basket into somebody's else's in-basket. But, of course, it isn't. It's not done until AT&T delivers what it's supposed to deliver. So you get big, fat, dumb, unmotivated bureaucracies.

They also tend to become somewhat corrupt. In other words, if I've got a department and you've got a department and we kind of share power running this thing, there's sort of an unwritten rule: "If you won't bother me, I won't bother you and we're both happy." So you get layers of management and associated costs that nobody needs. Then, while people are justifying all these layers. It takes forever to get anything done. They're too slow to make decisions and nimbler people run circles around them.

The constant curse of scale is that it leads to big, dumb bureaucracy - which, of course, reaches its highest and worst form in government where the incentives are *really* awful. That doesn't mean we don't need governments - because we do. But it's a *terrible* problem to get big bureaucracies to behave. (Lecture by Charles T. Munger to the students of Professor Guilford Babcock at the University of Southern California School of Business on April 14, 1994, *Outstanding Investor Digest,* May 5, 1995, p.53.)

On how to get worldly wisdom

I've long believed that a certain system – which almost any intelligent person can learn – works way better than the systems that *most* people use. As I said at the U.S.C. Business School, what you need is a latticework of mental models in your head. And you hang your actual experience and your vicarious experience (that you get from reading and so forth) on this latticework of powerful models. And, with that system, things gradually get to fit together in a way that enhances cognition.

And you need the models – not just from one or two disciplines, but from *all* the important disciplines. You need the best 100 or so models from microeconomics, physiology, psychology particularly, elementary mathematics, hard science and engineering [and so on].

You don't have to be a huge expert in any of those fields. All you've got to do is take the really *big* ideas and learn them early and well.

You *can't* learn those 100 big ideas you really need the way many students do – where you learn 'em well enough to bang 'em back to the professor and get your grade and then you empty them out as though you were emptying a bathtub so you can take in more water next time. If *that's* the way you learn the 100 big models you're going to need, [you'll be] an "also ran" in the game of life. You have to learn the models so that they become part of your ever-used repertoire. (Lecture by Charles T. Munger to the students of Professor William Lazier at Stanford Law School, *Outstanding Investor Digest,* December 29, 1997, p.24.)

On what something really mean

By its nature, the U.S. is running a substantial merchandise trade deficit. If you buy more from the rest of the world than you're selling them – which is what happens by definition when you're running a trade deficit – you have to balance the books. They have to get something – some capital asset – in exchange: They may get a government bond. They may get a piece of a U.S. business. But they have to get *something.*

The *key* thing in economics, whenever someone makes an assertion to you, is to always ask, "And *then* what?" Actually, it's not such a bad idea to ask it about *everything.* But you should always ask, "And then what?"

So when you read that the merchandise trade deficit is $9 billion, what *else* does that mean? It means that somehow we must also have traded $9 billion of capital assets – (future) claims on *our* production – and given them to somebody else in the world. So they *have* to invest. They don't have any choice. And when somebody says, "Won't it be terrible if the Japanese sell all of their government bonds?" Well, they *can't* without getting *another* American asset in exchange. There's simply no other way to *do* it. They could sell it to the French, but then the French have the same problem.

So trace *through* the transactions on the circle whenever you talk about any specific action in economics. (Warren Buffett, Berkshire Hathaway annual meeting, 1997, *Outstanding Investor Digest,* August 8, 1997, p.23.)

On setting goals

There are two lines of thought….. A whole bunch of management gurus say you need B-HAGs – bold, hairy, audacious goals. That's a technique of management – to give the troops a goal that looks unattainable and flog them heavily. And according to that line of thought, you will do better chasing a B-HAG than you will a reasonable objective.

And there's some *logic* in that – because if you tell your kid A-minuses are fine and he likes partying around the beer keg and can easily get A-minuses, you may *well* get a lower result than you would if you gave him a different goal.

Then there's another group that says that if you make the goals unreasonable enough, human nature being what it is, people will cheat. And you see that in the public schools –

where they say you've got to have the reading scores better so we are going to pay the teachers based on the reading scores getting better. So the teachers start helping students cheat to pass the reading tests. So human nature being what it is, if the goals are unreasonable enough, you will cause some cheating in your corporation - or even within your top management.

I can't *solve* that problem. There are two factors that are at war. You don't want the cheating - which is bad long term and bad for the people who are doing the cheating. However, you *do* want to maximize the real performance. And the two techniques are at *war.*

What people generally do is give people the unreasonable goal and tell 'em, "You can't cheat." That's basically the goal at General Electric. They say, "We don't want any excuses… But don't cheat….. If you can't handle those two messages, why, perhaps you'd be happier flourishing somewhere else." That is American system in many places.

I've got no answer to that tension. Low goals do cause lower performance and high goals increase the percentage of cheating. Each organization has to find its own way. (Charles Munger, Wesco Financial annual meeting, 2000, *Outstanding Investor Digest,* December 18, 2000, p.54.)

On 3 timeless ideas for investing

His [Benjamin Graham] three basic ideas – and none of them are complicated or require any mathematical talent or anything of that sort – are:

(1) that you should look at stocks as part ownership of a business,

(2) that you should look at market fluctuations in terms of his "Mr. Market" example and make them your friend rather than your enemy by essentially profiting from folly rather participating in it, and finally,

(3) the three most important words in investing are "margin of safety" – …always building a 15,000 pound bridge if you're going to be driving 10,000 pound truck across it…

So I think that it comes down to those ideas - although they sound so simple and commonplace that it kind of seems like a waste to go to school and get a Ph.D. in Economics and have it all come back to that. It's a little like spending eight years in divinity school and having somebody tell you that the ten commandments were all that counted. There is a certain natural tendency to overlook anything that simple and important. (Warren Buffett, speech at New York Society of Security Analysts, December 6, 1994, *Outstanding Investor Digest,* May 5, 1995, p.3.)

On how to evaluate businesses

Leaving aside tax factors, the formula we use for evaluating stocks and businesses is identical. Indeed, the formula for valuing *all* assets that are purchased for financial gain has been unchanged since it was first laid out by a very smart man in about 600 B.C. (though he wasn't smart enough to know it was 600 B.C.).

The oracle was Aesop and his enduring, though somewhat incomplete, investment insight was "a bird in the hand is worth two in the bush." To flesh out this principle, you must answer only three questions. How certain are you that there are indeed birds in the bush? When will they emerge and how many will there be? What is the risk-free interest rate (which we consider to be the yield on long-term U.S. bonds)? If you can answer these three questions, you will know the maximum value of the bush - and the maximum number of the birds you now possess that should be offered for it. And, of course, don't literally think birds. Think dollars.

Aesop's investment axiom, thus expanded and converted into dollars, is immutable. It applies to outlays for farms, oil royalties, bonds, stocks, lottery tickets, and manufacturing plants. And neither the advent of the steam engine, the harnessing of electricity nor the creation of the automobile changed the formula one iota – nor will the Internet. Just insert the correct numbers, and you can rank the attractiveness of all possible uses of capital throughout the universe. (Warren Buffett, Berkshire Hathaway Inc., 2000 *Annual Report,* p.13.)

On commodity businesses

Businesses in industries with both substantial over-capacity and a "commodity" product (undifferentiated in any customer-important way by factors such as performance, appearance, service support, etc.) are prime candidates for profit troubles. These may be escaped, true, if prices or costs are administered in some manner and thereby insulated at least partially from normal market forces. This administration can be carried out (a) legally through government intervention (until recently, this category included pricing for truckers and deposit costs for financial institutions), (b) illegally through collusion, or (c) "extra-legally" through OPEC-style foreign cartelization (with tag-along benefits for domestic non-cartel operators).

If, however, costs and prices are determined by full-bore competition, there is more than ample capacity, and the buyer cares little about whose product or distribution services he uses, industry economics are almost certain to be unexciting. They may well be disastrous.

Hence the constant struggle of every vendor to establish and emphasize special qualities of product or service. This works with candy bars (customers buy by brand name, not by asking for a "two-ounce candy bar") but doesn't work with sugar (how often do you hear, "I'll have a cup of coffee with cream and C & H sugar, please").

In many industries, differentiation simply can't be made meaningful. A few producers in such industries may consistently do well if they have a cost advantage that is both wide and sustainable. By definition such exceptions are few, and, in many industries, are non-existent. For the great majority of companies selling "commodity" products, a depressing equation of business economics prevails: persistent over-capacity without administered prices (or costs) equals poor profitability.

Of course, over-capacity may eventually self-correct, either as capacity shrinks or demand expands. Unfortunately for the participants, such corrections often are long delayed. When they finally occur, the rebound to prosperity frequently produces a pervasive enthusiasm for expansion that, within a few years, again creates over-capacity and a new profitless environment. In other words, nothing fails like success.

What finally determines levels of long-term profitability in such industries is the ratio of supply-tight to supply-ample years. Frequently that ratio is dismal. (It seems as if the most recent supply-tight period in our textile business - it occurred some years back - lasted the better part of a morning.)

In some industries, however, capacity-tight conditions can last a long time. Sometimes actual growth in demand will outrun forecasted growth for an extended period. In other cases, adding capacity requires very long lead times because complicated manufacturing facilities must be planned and built. (Warren Buffett, Berkshire Hathaway Inc., *Letters to Shareholders,* 1982, pp.56-57.)

On paying cash out or keeping it in the business

When we have capital around, we have three questions…First, "Does it make more sense to pay it out to the shareholders than to keep it within the company?" The sub-question on that is, "If we pay it out, is it better off to do it via repurchases or via dividend?" The test for whether we pay it out in dividends is, "Can we create more than a dollar of value within the company with that dollar by retaining it rather than paying it out?"

And you never *know* the answer to that. But so far, the answer, as judged by our results, is, "Yes, we can". And we think that prospectively we can. But that's a hope on our part. It's justified to some extent by past history, but it's not a certainty.

Once we've crossed *that* threshold, then we ask ourselves, "Should we repurchase stock?" Well, obviously, if you can buy your stock at a significant discount from conservatively calculated intrinsic value and you can buy a reasonable quantity, *that's* a sensible use for capital.

Beyond that, the question becomes, "If you have the capital and you think that you can create more than a dollar, how do you create the most value with the least risk?" And that gets to *business* risk…I can determine it by looking at the business, the competitive environment in which it operates and so on.

So once we cross the threshold of deciding that we can deploy capital so as to create more than a dollar of present value for every dollar retained, then it's just a question of doing the most intelligent thing you can find. And the cost of every deal that we do is measured by the *second* best deal that's around at a given time – including doing more of some of the things we're already in. (Warren Buffett, Berkshire Hathaway annual meeting, 2001, *Outstanding Investor Digest,* Year End 2001 Edition, pp.38-39.)

On how to avoid problems

We handle negotiations way different than anybody. When we bought See's Candy, I spent an hour there. Every business we've bought on one call. On the Borsheim's deal, I dropped over to Ike Friedman's house for half an hour. He showed me some figures that weren't audited penciled on a piece of paper.

If I need a team of lawyers and accountants, it isn't going to be a good deal…. We've never had an extended negotiation with anybody about anything. That's just not our style. If it's going to be that way, I don't want to deal with them - because it's going to ruin my life sooner or later. So we just walk away. (Warren Buffett, lecture at Stanford Law School, March 23, 1990, *Outstanding Investor Digest,* April 18, 1990, p.18.)

<u>Buffett:</u> Some businesses are a lot easier to understand than others. And Charlie and I don't like difficult problems. If something is difficult to figure… We'd rather multiply by 3 than by π.

Munger: That's such an obvious point. Yet so many people think that if they just hire somebody with the appropriate labels, they can do something very difficult. That is one of the most dangerous ideas a human being can have. All kinds of things can create problems by causing complexity. The other day I was dealing with a problem - it was a new building. And I said, "This problem has three things I've learned to fear - an architect, a contractor and a hill."

If you go through life like that, I think you'll at least make *fewer* mistakes than people who think they can do anything, no matter how complex, by just hiring somebody with a credible label. You don't have to hire out your thinking if you keep it simple…

Buffett: If you get into some complicated business, you can get a report that's 1,000 pages thick and you can have Ph.D.'s working on it. But it doesn't mean anything. What you'll have is a report. But you won't have any better understanding of that business and what it's going to look like in 10 or 15 years. The big thing to do is to avoid being *wrong*. (Berkshire Hathaway annual meeting, 1994, *Outstanding Investor Digest,* June 23, 1994, p.23.)

On the real risk of investing

In our opinion, the real risk that an investor must assess is whether his aggregate after-tax receipts from an investment (including those he receives on sale) will, over his prospective holding period, give him at least as much purchasing power as he had to begin with, plus a modest rate of interest on that initial stake. Though this risk cannot be calculated with engineering precision, it can in some cases be judged with a degree of accuracy that is useful. The primary factors bearing upon this evaluation are:

1) The certainty with which the long-term economic characteristics of the business can be evaluated;
2) The certainty with which management can be evaluated, both to its ability to realize the full potential of the business and to wisely employ its cash flows;
3) The certainty with which management can be counted on to channel the rewards from the business to the shareholders rather than to itself;
4) The purchase price of the business:
5) The levels of taxation and inflation that will be experienced and that will determine the degree by which an investor's purchasing power return is reduced from his gross return. (Warren Buffett, Berkshire Hathaway Inc., *Letters to Shareholders,* 1993, p.135.)

On the difficulty of developing a fair social system

Let's just say, Sandy, that it was 24 hours before you were born, and a genie appeared, and said "Sandy, you look like a winner. I have enormous confidence in you, and what I'm going to do is let you set the rules of the society into which you will be born. You can set the economic rules, the social rules, and whatever rules you set will apply during your lifetime, and your children's lifetimes."

And you'll say, "Well, that's nice, but what's the catch?"

And the genie says, "Here's the catch. You don't know if you're going to be born rich or poor, white or black, male or female, able-bodied or infirm, intelligent or retarded. All you know is that you're going to get one ball out of a barrel with, say, 5.8 billion balls in it." You're going to participate in what I call the Ovarian Lottery. And it's the most important thing that will happen to you in your life, but you have no control over it. It's going to determine far more than your grades at school or anything else that happens to you.

Now, what rules do you want to have? I'm not going to tell you the rules, and nobody will tell you; you have to make them up for yourself. But they will affect how you think about what you do in your will and things of that sort. That's because you're going to want to have a system that turns out great quantities of goods and services, so that your kids can live better than you did, and so that your grandchildren can live better than your kids. You're going to want a system that keeps Bill Gates and Andy Grove and Jack Welch working long, long after they don't need to work. You're going to want the most able people working more than 12 hours a day. So you've got to have a system that incentives them, and that turns out goods.

But you're also going to want a system that takes care of the bad balls, the ones that aren't lucky. If you have a system that is turning out enough goods and services, you can take care of them. You want a system where people are free of fear to some extent. You don't want people worrying about being sick in their old age, or fearful about going home at night. So you'll try to design something, assuming you have the goods and services to solve that sort of thing. You'll want equality of opportunity - a good public school system - to make you feel that every piece of talent out there will get the same shot at contributing. And your tax system will follow from your reasoning on that. And what you do with the money you make is another thing to think about it. As you work through that, everybody comes up with something a little different. I just suggest you play that little game. (Warren Buffett, "Buffett & Gates on Success", KCTS/Seattle, May 1998, transcript p.12.)

For other issues regarding investing, business economics and managing, read the annual reports of Berkshire Hathaway Inc. (www.berkshirehathaway.com) and subscribe to *Outstanding Investor Digest.* (www.oid.com)

Probability

Probability is a way of thinking about how likely a specific event is to happen. Blaise Pascal and Pierre Fermat developed the fundamental principles of probability in a series of letters exchanged starting in the year 1654.

Definitions

Experiment is the process of obtaining an observation. For example: *Toss a coin twice and observe what happens.*

Outcome is the possible result of the experiment. All possible outcomes of the experiment are called the sample space. *The experiment of tossing a coin twice results in one of four possible outcomes – Tail/Tail, Head/Head, Head/Tail, or Tail/Head.*

Event is a set of outcomes of the experiment. One event would be: *Observe at least one head. This event consists of the three outcomes HH, HT, TH.* A compound event is an event composed of two or more separate events.

Independent events – two events A and B are independent if no event can influence the probability of the other. *Event A: observe one head when flipping a coin. Event B: observe one tail when flipping another coin. Each flip is independent of the other since whatever happens to the first coin cannot influence the flip of the second or tell us what outcome is likely to happen when we flip the second coin.*

Mutually exclusive events – two events are mutually exclusive if they cannot happen at the same time i.e. they have no outcomes in common. *A single coin is tossed. There are two events: observing a head or observing a tail. Observing a head excludes the possibility of observing a tail.* Two events are non-mutually exclusive if they have one or more outcomes in common. *A single die is tossed. Event A: observe a four. Event B: observe an even number. These events have one outcome in common since an "even number" consists of the numbers 2, 4, and 6.*

Probability – a number between 0 and 1 that measures how likely an event is to happen over the long run. A probability of 1 means an event happens with certainty and a probability of 0 means it is impossible for an event to happen.

Expectation is the average value we expect to see if we perform an experiment many times.

Arithmetic mean of a set of numbers is usually called the average of these numbers. *To find the mean of the numbers 1,8,6,4,7, we add the numbers together – 26 – and divide by 5 = 5.2.*

Variability shows the variability of outcomes or how concentrated or spread out the outcomes are around the arithmetic mean – how different from the average. The standard deviation measures the variability.

Population – the total number of something – outcomes, objects, events, etc. It is a group that has at least one characteristic in common from which our sample of data is selected.

Sample – a representative and randomly taken part of the population. The larger the sample, the better our estimate of the probability. But observe that what is essential is the absolute size of the sample, not its proportion of the population. A random sample of 3,000 from the entire U.S. is more predictive than a sample of 40 from a large high school. A random sample is one in which every item in the population is equally likely to be chosen.

How do we decide the probability of an event?

The laws of probability tell us what is likely to happen over a large number of trials. This means we can expect to make reasonable predictions what on average are likely to happen over the long run, but we can't predict the outcome of a particular event.

There are three ways to measure probability: the logical way, the relative frequency way, and the subjective way.

The logical way

The logical way can be used in situations where we know the number of outcomes and where all these outcomes are equally likely. For example in games of chance, we find the probability by dividing the number of outcomes that are favorable to the event (yield the outcome we look for) with the total number of possible outcomes. Observe that this definition can only be applied if we can analyze a situation into equally likely outcomes.

What is the probability that we observe one head when tossing a coin? The number of equally likely favorable outcomes is one (head) and the total number of possible equally likely outcomes is two (head and tail) and therefore the probability is $\frac{1}{2}$ or 50%.

Relative frequency

When an experiment can be repeated many times, probability is the proportion of times the event happened in relation to an infinite number of experiments. In most cases we don't know the probability of an event. Why? Because we can't know all the outcomes. We must then try to estimate the long-term relative frequency by performing experiments or by finding representative information about how often an event happened in the past.

By representative we mean that the information must be based on the relative frequency of historical data over a large number of independent experiments or observations of the same reference class under essentially the same conditions. The reference class is the one for which the distribution of outcomes is known or can be reasonable estimated. The more relevant cases we examine, the better our chance is to estimate correctly the underlying probability.

Conduct an experiment to test how likely it is that you toss head. Toss a coin 1000 times and observe what happens. If you got heads 400 times the relative frequency or the fraction between the number of tossed heads (number of times the events happened) and the total number of tosses (number of experiments) is 400/1000. Toss a coin 2000 times and observe what happens. If you got heads 900 times the relative frequency is 900/2000. The more tosses, the less the difference will be between an events theoretical probability and the relative frequency with which it happens. In this case it will move towards the value $\frac{1}{2}$.

What is the frequency of losses? How are losses distributed over time? What is their magnitude? Insurance companies use relative frequencies. They base their premiums on an estimate of how likely it is that a specific event that cause them to pay happen. If they assume the past is a representative guide for the future they try to find out the relative frequency of a specific "accident" by observing past frequencies of specific accidents.

Suppose the probability that a given house will burn is 0.3%. This means that the insurance company found historical data and other indicators about a large number of houses (for example the reference class is "50 years of data of fires in a given area") and discovered that, in the past, 3 out of 1,000 houses in a given area will burn. It also means that, assuming there are no changes in the causes of these fires, we can predict approximately the same proportion of fires in the future.

An insurance company knows that in a given year a certain percentage of their policyholders will have an accident. They don't know which ones, but they diversify their risk by insuring many individuals. What is unpredictable for one person can be predictable for a large population. But they must make sure the events are independent and that not a single event or a confluence of independent events affects multiple policyholders causing the insurer to pay out on many claims at one time. For example, an insurance company who provides fire insurance to a number of buildings in a single block may face ruin if a large fire happens.

Subjective probability

If an experiment is not repeatable or when there is no representative historical relative frequency, or comparable data, the probability is then a measure of our personal degree of belief in the likelihood of an event happening. We have to make a subjective evaluation or a personal estimation using whatever information is available. But we can't just assign any number to events. They must agree with the rules of probability.

A New York Rangers supporter might say, "I believe that the NY Rangers have a 90% chance of winning their next match since they have been playing so well."

Rules of probability

When two events are independent (no event can influence the probability of the other), the probability that they both will happen is the product of their individual probabilities. We can write this as: Both A and B will happen = P(A) x P(B).

A company has two independent manufacturing processes. In process one, 5% of the produced items are defective, and in process two, 3%. If we pick one item from each process, how likely is it that both items are defective? 0.15% (0.05 x 0.03).

This rule is changed if the events are dependent. In many situations the probability of an event depends on the outcome of some other event. Events are often related in a way so that if one event happens, it makes the other event more or less likely to happen. For example, if we toss a die and event A is: observe an even number, and event B: observe a number less than 4, then given we know B has happened, the probability is 1/3. This is called a conditional probability or the probability that an event happen given that some other event has happened. Conditional probabilities involve dependent events. The conditional probability of A given B is 1/3 since we know B was either 1,2 or 3 and only 2 implies event A.

What is the probability that there are two boys in a two-child family given that there is at least one boy? Ask: What can happen or what are the number of outcomes that are equally likely to happen? Boy/Boy - Girl/Girl - Boy/Girl - Girl/Boy. Since we already know that there is "at least one boy", we can rule out scenario "Girl/Girl." The probability is therefore 1/3 or 33%.

What is the probability that there are two boys in a two-child family given that the first-born is a boy? The number of outcomes that are equally likely to happen are: Boy/Boy - Girl/Girl - Boy/Girl - Girl/Boy. Since we already know that the older child is a boy, we can rule out scenario GB and GG. The probability is 50%.

A problem in conditional probability that has caused many mathematics professors problems, is the Monty Hall Dilemma. The columnist Marilyn vos Savant (*Parade* 1990, Sept 9, p. 13.) asked the following problem:

"Suppose you're on a game show, and you're given the choice of three doors. Behind one door is a car; behind the others, goats. You pick a door, say No. 1, and the host, who knows what's behind the doors, opens another door, say No. 3, which has a goat. He then says to you, 'Do you want to pick door No. 2?' Is it to your advantage to switch your choice?"

How would you answer? Assume we always have the opportunity to switch. Make a table of possible outcomes and test in how many outcomes it pays to switch doors.

Door 1	Door 2	Door 3
Car	Goat	Goat
Goat	Car	Goat
Goat	Goat	Car

Assume you choose door number 1. What are then the consequences if the car is in door 1, 2 or 3?

Car behind door	Host opens door	You switch	You don't switch
1	2	Lose	Win
2	3	Win	Lose
3	2	Win	Lose
		2/3	1/3

We should always switch doors since we win 2/3 of the time. They key to this problem is that we know ahead of the game (conditional) that the host knows what is behind each door and always opens a door with a goat behind it.

When two events are mutually exclusive (can't both happen at the same time), the probability that one or the other will happen is the sum of their respective probabilities. We can write this as: Either A or B will happen = P(A) + P(B).

What is the probability that we get either a two or a four when a single die is tossed once? There are 6 outcomes and the two events ("getting a two" and "getting a four") have no outcomes in common. We can't get both a two and a four on the same toss. How many favorable outcomes are there or in how many ways can we get a two? In one out of six. In how many ways can we get a four? In one out of six. The probability that we get a four or a six is 1/6 + 1/6 = 33%.

When two events are non-mutually exclusive (both can happen at the same time), the probability that at least one of them will happen is equal to the sum of the probabilities of the two events minus the probability that both events happen. We can write this complementary rule as: P(A) + P(B) – P(A and B).

Assume that the probability a Los Angeles teenager owns a surfing board is 25%, a bicycle 85%, and owning both 20%. If we randomly choose a Los Angeles teenager, the probability that he or she owns a surfing board or a bicycle is (0.25 + 0.85) – 0.20 = 90%. These events had two outcomes in common since the teenager could have both a surfing board and a bicycle.

Sometimes it is easier to deal with problems if we turn them backwards. The probability of an event not happening is 1 minus the probability it will happen. If the probability of an event A is 30%, then the probability that the event won't happen is 70% because "not event A" is the complement of the event A. The sum of probability of an event happening and probability of the same event not happening is always 1.

What is the probability that we get at least one six in four rolls of a single die? We turn the question around and calculate the probability of "not getting any sixes in four rolls of a die". There are four independent events – not getting a six on the first throw…second…The probability of each one is 5/6 since there are five outcomes (1,2,3,4,5) which results in the event "no six" and each is independent of what happened before. This means that the probability of not getting any sixes are 5/6 x 5/6 x 5/6 x 5/6 or 48.2%. Therefore "the probability of getting at least one six" is 1 – 0.482 or 51.8%.

Counting possible outcomes
The multiplication principle says that if one event can happen in "n" different ways, and a second event can happen independent of the first in "m" different ways, the two events can happen in nm different ways.

Suppose there are 4 different flights between Los Angeles and New York, 3 between New York and Boston and 5 between Boston and Bermuda. The number of itineraries assuming we can connect between any of the stated flights are 4 x 3 x 5 = 60.

Permutations or rearrangements mean the different ways we can order or arrange a number of objects.

We have 3 hats to choose from – one black, one white and one brown. In how many ways can we arrange them if the order white, black and brown is different from the order black, white and brown? This is the same as asking how many permutations there are with three hats, taken three at a time. We can arrange the hats in 6 ways: Black-White-Brown, Black-Brown-White, White-Black-Brown, White-Brown-Black, Brown-White-Black, Brown-Black-White.

Another way to think about this: We have three boxes in a row where we put a different hat in each box. We can fill the first box in three ways, since we can choose between all three hats. We can then fill the second box in two ways, since we now can choose between only two hats. We can fill the third box in only one way, since we have only one hat left. This means we can fill the box in 3 x 2 x 1 = 6 ways.

Another way to write this is 3! If we have n (6) boxes and can choose from all of them, there are n (6) choices. Then we are left with n-1 (5) choices for box number two, n-2 (4) choices for box number three and so on. The number of permutations of n boxes is n!. What n! – Factorial – means is the product of all numbers from 1 to n.

Suppose we have a dinner in our home with 12 people sitting around a table. How many seating arrangements are possible? The first person that enters the room can choose between twelve chairs, the second between eleven chairs and so on, meaning there are 12! or 479,001,600 different seating arrangements.

The number of ways we can arrange r objects from a group of n objects is called a permutation of n objects taken r at a time and is defined as n! / (n-r)!

A safe has 100 digits. To open the safe a burglar needs to pick the correct 3 different numbers. Is it likely? The number of permutations or ways of arranging 3 digits from 100 digits is 970,200 (100!/(100-3)!). If every permutation takes the burglar 5 seconds, all permutations are tried in 56 days assuming a 24-hour working day.

Combinations means the different ways we can choose a number of different objects from a group of objects where no order is involved, just the number of ways of choosing them.

In how many ways can we combine 2 flavors of ice cream if we can choose from strawberry (S), vanilla (V), and chocolate (C) without repeated flavors? We can combine them in 3 ways: SV, SC, VC. VS and SV are a combination of the same ice creams. The order doesn't matter. Vanilla on the top is the same as vanilla on the bottom.

The number of ways we can select r objects from a group of n objects is called a combination of n objects taken r at a time and is defined as n! / r!(n-r)!

The number of ways we can select 3 people taken from a group of 10 people is 120 (10!/3!(10-3)!).

The binomial distribution

Suppose we take a true-false test with 10 questions. We don't know anything about the subject. All we can do is guess. To pass this test, we must answer exactly 5 questions correct. Are we likely to do that by guessing?

How should we reason? Ask: How many equally likely independent outcomes are there when we guess? There are 2 possible outcomes. Either we are right or wrong. If the test only had one question, the probability that we guess the right answer is 50%. The probability that we guess the wrong answer is also 50% (1- the probability of guessing the right answer).

What is the total number of equally likely outcomes? Since every question has 2 possible outcomes and there are 10 questions there are a total of 2^{10} outcomes or 1,024 possible true-false combinations. We can answer the test in 1,024 different ways. What is the number of favorable outcomes? There is only one way we can answer all 10 questions right (or wrong). They all have to be right (or wrong). The chance of getting all 10 answers right or wrong by guessing is therefore 1 in 1024. This means that if we took the test 1,024 times and guessed randomly at the answers each time, just once in 1,024 times should we expect to get all 10 answers right or wrong.

In how many ways can we be right on 5 questions? Let's go back to combinations and ask: in how many ways can we select 5 questions if we can choose from 10 questions? There are 252 ways (10!/5!(10-5)!) we can answer 10 questions to get exactly a score of 5. Since each guess has a 50% probability of being right and there are 10 questions and we want to be right on exactly 5 of them and there are 252 equally likely ways we can answer 5 questions, then the probability that we answer exactly 5 questions right is $(0.5)^5$ x $(0.5)^5$ x 252 = 24.6%

How likely is it then that we answer at least 5 questions correctly? This probability must be higher since we also can answer 6, 7, 8, 9 or 10 questions correct. Therefore we must add the probability that we guess 6, 7, 8, 9, and 10 questions correct.

In how many ways can we be right on 5 questions? 10!/5!(10-5)! = 252 ways
In how many ways can we be right on 6 questions? 10!/6!(10-6)! = 210 ways
In how many ways can we be right on 7 questions? 10!/7!(10-7)! = 120 ways
In how many ways can we be right on 8 questions? 10!/8!(10-8)! = 45 ways
In how many ways can we be right on 9 questions? 10!/9!(10-9)! = 10 ways
In how many ways can we be right on 10 questions? 10!/10!(10-10)! =   1 way
                                        Total = 638 ways

Since each guess has a 50% probability of being right and there are 10 questions and we want to be right on at least 5 of them and there are 638 equally likely ways we can answer at least 5 questions, the probability that we answer at least 5 questions right is $(0.5)^5$ x $(0.5)^5$ x 638 = 62.3%.

The example illustrated a binomial experiment. The probability distribution for a binomial experiment is: Number of possible ways of selecting k things from n things (observing k successes in n trials) x (probability of success)^k (1 - probability of success)$^{n-k}$

If we put in the above figures we get: 252 x $(0.5)^5$ x $(0.5)^5$ + 210 x $(0.5)^6$ x $(0.5)^4$ + 120 x $(0.5)^7$ x $(0.5)^3$ + 45 x $(0.5)^8$ x $(0.5)^2$ + 10 x $(0.5)^9$ x $(0.5)^1$ + 1x $(0.5)^{10}$ x $(0.5)^0$ = 62.3%

Binomial experiments have the following characteristics: An event that is repeatable or the experiment consists of n number of identical and independent trials. There are only two outcomes in every trial – success/failure, right/wrong, present/absent, 0/1 etc. and the probabilities of success and failure are constant in every trial.

Examples of binomial experiments are firing a projectile at a target (hit/miss), developing a new drug (effective/not effective), closing a sale (sale/no sale) etc.

We toss a single die 5 times. How likely is it that you will roll exactly 3 sixes? What is success? Rolling a 6 on a single die. What's the probability of rolling a 6 on a single die? 1/6 (there are 6 outcomes and one of them is a success). What is the probability of failure? 1-1/6 = 5/6. What is the number of trials? 5. What is the number of successes out of those trials? 3. In how many ways can you roll three sixes (successes) in 5 trials? 5!/3!(5-3)! = 10 → Probability = 10 x $(1/6)^3$ x $(5/6)^2$ = 3.2%

A boat has three independent engines and needs at least two to work properly. The probability that each engine works properly is 98%. The probability that all three engines work is 94.1%

(0.98^3). The probability that at least one engine fails (either engine 1, 2 or 3) is therefore 5.9% (this is the same as the probability that exactly 1 engine fail + exactly 2 engines fails + exactly 3 engines fails).

What is the probability that at least 2 engines work? Let's go back to combinations and the binomial distribution: probability (3 engines work) + probability (2 engines work) = 3!/3!(3-3)! x $(0.98)^3$ x $(0.02)^0$ + 3!/2!(3-2)! x $(0.98)^2$ x $(0.02)^1$ = 99.8816%. The probability that at least two engines will fail is therefore 0.1184%. The boat will fail to work in 1 out of 845 times.

Let's add a backup engine. What is now the probability that at least 2 engines work? Probability (4 engines work) + probability (3 engines work) + probability (2 engines work) = 4!/4!(4-4)! x $(0.98)^4$ x $(0.02)^0$ + 4!/3!(4-3)! x $(0.98)^3$ x $(0.02)^1$ + 4!/2!(4-2)! x $(0.98)^2$ x $(0.02)^2$ = 99.996848%. The probability that at least three engines will fail is therefore 0.003152%. The boat will now only fail in 1 out of 31,726 times.

Binomial probabilities assume independence. It may be that the failure of one engine increases the failure probability of a second engine. For example, the failure of one engine increases the load on which the second engine is run. Using one engine causes more stress and wear to the second engine, etc.

Calculations to some of the examples

Page

129   The possible number of ways we can choose 6 numbers out of 49 are 49!/(49-6)!6! =13,983,816.

24 hours equals 1,440 minutes. One 365-day year equals 525,600 minutes. 14 million minutes equals about 27 years.

138   The probability we succeed is $(0.8)^6$ or 26%.

139   The probability that 10 mutually independent start-ups all succeed is 0.01% (0.4^{10}) but the probability that at least one succeeds is 99.4% $(1 - 0.6^{10})$.

140   The probability that at least one of the parts don't work is 86.5% $(1 - 0.999^{2000})$. Assuming independence, the probability of system failure (where at least one part must fail for the system to fail) is 1 minus the reliability of the system.

140   Assuming independence, the probability of system failure (where both navigation systems must fail for the system to fail) is the product of the probabilities of primary and back up system failing.

140   An event that has one chance in 20 of happening in any given year is nearly certain to happen over 50 years $(1 - 0.95^{50} = 92.3\%)$. If there is a 5% chance that an event happens in any given year, then the chance that it won't happen is 95%. The chance that it won't happen over 50 years is 7.7%. This means that the probability that the event happens at least once is 92.3%.

254

140 The probability that at least one accident will happen in any given year is 3.9% (1 – 0.999^{40}). The probability that at least one accident will happen during the next 10 years is 33% (1 - 0.961^{10}).

141 The probability of a major earthquake happening in any given year (assumed to be a constant) is therefore 3.9% ($(1-p)^{30}$ = 30%). The probability that a major earthquake will happen at least once during the next 5 years is 18% (1 - 0.961^{5}).

143 In a group of 1,048,576 (2^{20}) people it happens to someone. In fact, in the U.S. a country with 280 million people, one in a million chance events happen 280 times a day (1/1,000,000 x 280 million).

143 1 person has 365 possible birthdays if we assume that there are 365 days to choose from and that all birthdays are equally likely to happen. When there are 2 persons in a group the second person can choose among 364 possible birthdays that are not shared with the first person. The second person only shares 1 day with the first person. The chance that 2 persons share birthdays is therefore 1 out of 365 or 0.27%. When there are 3 people in a group it is easier to find the likelihood that 2 of them share a birthday by first finding out how likely it is that no one of these 3 people share birthdays. When there are 3 people in a group the third person can choose among 363 possible birthdays that are not shared with any of the first 2 persons. This means that the chance that the third person will not share birthday with any of the first 2 persons is 363 out of 365 or 99.45%.
To find the probability that multiple events happen, we multiply the individual probabilities together. The probability that no one in a group of 3, share birthday is therefore: 365/365 x 364/365 x 363/365 = 99.18%. Therefore, the probability that 2 people in a group of 3 share birthdays is 1 – 0.9918 or 0.82%. Let's repeat this procedure for a group of 23 people:

$$\frac{365 \times 364 \times 363 \times \ldots\ldots 343}{365^{23}} = 49.3\%.$$

Therefore, the probability that 2 people in a group of 23, share birthdays is 1 – 0.493 or 50.7%.

156 At the end of 10 predictions, one monkey has a perfect record of predicting the direction of interest rates (1,000 x 0.5^{10}).

158 The number of ways to get 2 successes in 10 trials are 10!/ (10-2)!2! or 45. The probability is 45x $(0.8)^2$ x $(0.2)^8$ or 0.007%.

CHECKLISTS

Helpful for achieving goals, making choices, solving problems, evaluating what is likely to be true or false etc.

Use notions
- Use the big ideas that underlie reality
- Understand what something really means
- Simplify
- Use rules and filters
- Know what I want to achieve
- Find and evaluate alternatives
- Understand consequences and their consequences on the whole
- Quantify
- Search for and base things on evidence
- Think things through backward
- Remember that big effects come from large combinations of factors
- Evaluate the consequences if I'm wrong

What is the issue?
- What's the question? What is this really about?
- What's the essence or nub of the issue? What is then the key question?
- Relevant? Solvable? Important? Knowable? Predictability? Utility – applicability?
- Do I understand what the subject is all about? In order to have an opinion on a subject I need some relevant data and basic knowledge about the subject, otherwise just say: "I don't know".
- Is my judgment here better than others?
- What must I predict here and is it predictable?
- Is a decision needed? What happens if I don't deal with this? Is this something I can do anything about? Should "I" do this?
- Over what period of time am I considering this issue? Where am I at present? From whose point of view?
- Simplify by deciding big "no-brainer questions" first and begin from where I am.

Understand what it means
- Translate words and ideas in terms I understand. Do I understand what words and statements really mean and imply? Does it mean anything? Will it help me make useful predictions on what is likely to happen?

- Do I understand how and why something works and happens? What is it doing? Why does it do that? What is happening? How and why is this happening? What is the consequence of this (observation, finding, event, experience...)?
- Definitions and implications?
- Is it important and knowable?

Filters and Rules
- Use filters incl. rules and default rules – what test(s) can I make?
- Adapt to my psychological nature, abilities, advantages, and limitations
- Consider values and preferences and therefore priorities and what I want to avoid

What do I specifically and measurable want to achieve and avoid and when and why?
- What future "value" do I want to achieve? Target numbers? Target effects? Time horizon?
- Assume I have already reached my target. What would this imply in numbers and effects? What must then have been achieved? Is it (target) reasonable? Is it reasonable if I reverse this to the present?
- Do I have ways to measure to what degree my goal is being achieved? Key variables or components of yardstick?
- If I achieve this what will happen? Do I want that to happen?
- Can I break my goal into short-term goals with deadlines?
- What is my real reason for doing this? Is it because I want to or because I have to? Have I stated my goal from internal and external realities or am I biased now or influenced by some psychological forces?
- Can I express my goal in a way that makes it easier to see how it is going to be achieved?
- Is this the true goal for what I want to achieve?

What is the cause of that?
- To achieve my goal I must understand what causes my goal to be achieved
- What is the equation for goal and what evidence do I have for that?
- What don't I want to achieve? What causes non-goal and what can I do to avoid that? What must I not do or what must I avoid?
- What variables influence the system? What are the critical forces and variables, the ones that account for the main outcome? What is the key unknown? What is the certainty with which I can evaluate, optimize ... the different variables?
- Which variables are dependent on other variables (or situation, environment, context, timing, behavior) and which ones act independently of each other?
- What force causes a variable to be achieved? What produces the force(s)? Are there short- and long-term forces? What is their relative strength? How do they combine and interact and what are the effects? How can I get many forces to operate together in the same direction? What lack of force would destroy the system? What produces this force? How predictable are they? What can the forces in place rationally expect to cause? What forces are temporary and which ones are permanent? How will the system change as the forces that act on the variable change?

257

- How resistant is the system to a change in the variables and/or forces? What are the likely wanted and unwanted short- and long-term consequences (on numbers and effects) of changes (up/down) – scale, size or mass, strength, intensity, length, time horizon, environment, participants etc. – in the variables or forces? What happens when a number of small causes operate over a long time? What are the consequences if a force acts on the variable over a long time? Which force could change it? What is needed to create a critical mass? What forces when added can create a critical mass? How? Will something else happen when I change a variable or force? What must happen for a force to change? Can a change produce other consequences (observe that I am interested in effects on the whole system and the final outcome)? Does a change in one variable make a dramatic difference in outcome? Will the properties also change? What are the consequences if the relation between the variables changes? What is the change point? Barriers? Catalyst? Tipping point? Inflection point? Break point? Limits? Is there a time lag before effects happen? Feedback? What can speed up the cause? What are the critical points when the effects get reversed? What can I change in the equation and what can others change? How? Who? When? Which variables must I change to achieve goal? How can I measure the amount of change? Degree of sensitivity if I change the assumptions? Effects on goal and path? What will happen if I hold one variable constant? If I at the same time increase one variable and decrease another? Net effect? If I change one variable or force at a time? What is it in the environment that can change the situation? What other advantages and disadvantages can I achieve if I optimize one of the variables? What must happen to cause a change in outcome? Is it still a variable if I change the conditions?
- Are there exceptions to the equation and why? What conditions are required to achieve goal? Has my goal different cause short-term and long-term? Is the cause time-dependent? Can I deduce the cause by observing the effects? Have I looked upon the system from different angles and viewpoints? What does the measurement of the subject depend on?
- What is the major constraint that limits the goal from being achieved?

What available alternatives do I have to achieve my goal?
- Judge alternatives in terms of goal, subject in question, rules and filters, cause and effect, human behavior, evidence, counter evidence, simplicity and opportunity cost of money, time, other resources, effort, understanding, risk and of mental stress.
- What evidence (incl. models) do I have that these alternatives are most likely to achieve goal?
- Are they depending on time horizon or event?
- What are the likely consequences of each action? What possible outcomes can happen? Likelihood? How desirable is each consequence?
- Do I forego any future opportunities if I make a specific action now?

What are the consequences?
- Find out which alternative are most likely to achieve my goal by estimating their likely consequences
- If I do this, what will happen? Why will this not happen?
- What are the likely (logical) wanted and unwanted (or unintended) consequences

258

(quantitative and qualitative) and consequences of consequences (immediate and over the course of a long period) of each alternative/event (proposition) factoring in relevant variables?

- What are the different scenarios and outcomes that can happen? What is likely to happen short and long-term based on the evidence?
- What can help me make predictions on consequences or if something is likely to be true or false?
- What must happen for the goal to be achieved? How likely is it that the necessary events will happen and happen to me? What does the probabilities favor? What will happen if I reverse the proposition?
- What are the uncertainties that can significantly influence the outcome? What unintended consequences are there due to repeating effects, complications…? Is the net effect positive? Does the consequences predict anything else? What else does this mean?
- What are the consequences if this is true or false?
- Have I considered the whole system from different viewpoints? Have I considered social, financial, physical and emotional consequences? What are others likely to do? What are my experiences of earlier behavior? What happens when others do the same?

Bias
- Is there any reason for bias due to self-interest or psychological influences that may cause misjudgment?
- Is this a biased statement or a fact? What are factual judgments and what are value judgments?
- How reliable is he? Is he competent enough to judge? Credentials? What is his purpose with this? Does he have any motive to lie? How does he know that this is true?

The hypothesis
- Based on what I want to achieve; test statement implied by goal or statement for consequences.
- For every alternative ask: Is this alternative likely to achieve my goal (true)? For proposition ask: Is this proposition likely to be true?
- How can I test (testability) if this is true? Can I try to prove it is false before I try to see if it's true?
- What do I need to know if I shall test this statement? I must first find out the equation for what causes the statement to be true so I know what is the most important I need to know the future true outcome of and then search for the evidence for and against that this will be achieved. What is the statement that should be proved?
- What is the simplest hypothesis?

Look for evidence and judge the evidence
- How likely is it that the key cause (for goal, non-goal, and proposition) will be achieved?
- When evaluating statements or true/false, look for meaning, motives, causes, consequences and evidence for and against.
- If this were true what would the consequences then imply? Are the consequences of it not being true illogical or unbelievable? Does it have any predictability?

- How and where can I find the representative evidence if this is true? What is given? What are unquestionable truths? Will the test or other ways of measure give the same results when repeated (reliable)? Can I test for consequences (verifiable)? Is the evidence based on what is known and have I interpreted the data correct (valid)? What evidence do I have? Evidence against? What grounds do I have for accepting that evidence? Weight of evidence? What is the quality of the evidence? How credible is the evidence? Dependent on time, environment? Too small sample? Does the statement agree with the available evidence? Does it violate any scientific laws or laws of nature?
- What representative information do I have? What is happening by observation? Can I do an experiment to confirm my guess? Does it agree with experiment?
- What is the track record (case rate, base rate frequency, variability, average rate, degree of randomness, my own experiences, environment, players, and other relevant factors for the case) on what happened (worked and not) in the past? Is there any reason to believe that this record isn't representative for what is likely to happen in the future? What can make the future a lot different than the past? What's been permanent and what hasn't?
- How long can this continue? What is the major cause(s) now? What force(s) can make it continue, initiate a change, or stop it and why? Is it likely?
- If I get evidence that is the opposite of my previous convictions I must ask: How does this happen? What is going on here? What evidence do I have? What grounds do I have for accepting the evidence?

Disprove my (or others) conclusion by thinking like a prosecutor
- Consider causes for misjudgments
- How can I test and prove that my idea and conclusion is wrong? What reasons are there why I might be wrong? Where can I find the evidence that suggest I am wrong? How credible is my evidence? What facts and evidence disagree with my conclusion/idea?
- What major assumptions have I built the case on? Are they built on reality? Are their consequences logical? Has anyone proved that my assumptions are right? What are the consequences if my beliefs and assumptions are wrong?
- What have I ignored or overlooked? Better alternatives? Have I ignored evidence? Have I taken into account the limitations when humans are involved? What factors are uncertain and why? Have I just projected present trends? What have I misinterpreted? Have I used the right definitions? Did I consider and combined all the relevant factors? Have I used the appropriate measure/yardstick? Did I go wrong in the measurement? Have I confused cause and correlation? What about if my goal is shaped by what I believe is true but it isn't? Are there random or systematic errors? What other causes can explain my results? Have I considered the whole system and that interacting parts sometimes can vary in unexpected and unwanted ways?
- Bias for my own ideas? Is my ego getting in the way of making an intelligent decision? Will I really beat the historical average/record? Have I looked for contrary effects?
- What do I not see? What is the significance of this? Does an inversion of the assumption lead to a logical absurdity? Is the opposite more likely? Is there any contrary evidence? What evidence can prove it is false (or not achieving goal)? What experimental (or experience,

observation…) evidence are there that it's false? More evidence in favor of that? What causes it to be false?

- Meaning? Can I show that the consequences of it being true are unbelievable? What is the implied effect if I trace it out mathematically? Would the opposite of the statement be more likely? If yes, the proposition is probably false.

What is the downside?
- How can I be hurt? What could possible go wrong? What can turn this into a mistake? What would the consequences be?
- How often do things go wrong? Surprise factors? What can happen that will dramatically change the outcome?
- What is the worst thing that could happen - the nightmare scenario? How likely is that? What will I do if it does? What are the consequences if things go from bad to worse? And what are then the consequences?
- What are the consequences if I get two or three forces acting in concert against me? Which alternatives net effects are least worse?
- Execution risk?
- What do I least like? What am I least sure of?
- Can an advantage give me unwanted consequences? How do I lose an advantage?
- How can I structure the "system" to minimize the influence of negatives? Antidotes to what I don't want happen? Do I have a backup plan for surprises? Can I correct it? What rules can I install to achieve goal and avoid non-goal? Is there a built-in safety factor?

What are the consequences if I am wrong?
- What key thing am I betting on? Do I risk what is important for me for something of relative low utility for me?
- What is the cost (dollars, time, mental stress etc) of being wrong weighted against the benefit or value of being right compared to the next best available opportunity?
- If I do this because I believe the consequences are in my best interest/it's true but I turn out wrong/it is false, what are the short- and long-term consequences (actual loss and opportunity cost loss) for my goal and can I handle them and/or reverse them?
- If I don't do this because I believe the consequences is not in my best interest/it's false but I turn out wrong/it's true, what are the short- and long-term consequences for my goal and can I handle them and/or reverse them?
- If I don't take a decision at all now because I don't believe it is necessary but I am wrong, what are the short- and long-term consequences for my goal and can I handle them and/or reverse them?

What is the value?
- What is the utility or preference of each of these alternatives to me? Which alternative is most likely to achieve my goal and ultimate objective? Is it really more attractive than the other choices I have?
- What can I use as criteria to judge my alternatives against each other?

- What do I like best if I weigh the alternatives against each other by assigning their characteristics numerical values?
- Will it make a difference? Make an impact? How willing am I to accept certain outcomes?

What yardstick can be used to measure progress or to measure things against?
- What yardstick(s) do I use? What is the yardstick by which the decision is made?
- How can I easily measure to what degree my goal are being achieved? What indicators can I track?
- Does the "system" give people an incentive to behave in a way so that my goal will be achieved? Or does it work against the goal?

How act now?
- Can I execute? What specific action(s) do I have to do (must do) now? What do I need to do first?
- Who is going to do what, where, when, why and how?
- Have I decided on where the critical points (time and effects) are?
- Have I installed some kind of control stations and rules? Why is this the right rule? What are the consequences if I don't install this rule (or change my way of doing something)? What administrative and practical actions must I do due to the rule? How much time will it take to follow the rule? Can I control how I follow the rule? Can I install a time-limited rule? Where does the rules not work?

Have I made an active decision?
- Am I prepared to change the decision to reflect new information or new insights on what works and not?
- Is another decision contingent on a specific event happening? Have I evaluated the issue as it exists today? Is the underlying rationale for the decision still there? What new evidence is there that can change the likelihood? Does my way of measuring progress give any clue of what is likely to happen in the future? Events – relevant or irrelevant? Does it make any difference for my goal (independent of time horizon)?

Post mortem or learning from mistakes
- How well did it or didn't it work out? Did I act? Did I do what I said? What did I think at the time? Original reasons compared to reality?
- Why did I go wrong? How? Where? Opportunity cost?
- How can I figure out if this is going to continue? Have I acted on my mistakes? How act to not repeat? What should I have done and didn't do? What should I concentrate on? What must I improve? What must I learn?

What exactly is the problem?
- What do I want to achieve? Why don't I achieve my goal? What happen? How does it happen? Where does it happen and not? When does it happen and not? Who's affected?
- What causes my goal? What interferes with the factors that cause my goal? Symptoms or

core cause? What is the single most important limiting factor for reaching my goal? What principles or assumptions do I base this on? What are the consequences if they are wrong? Assuming no limitations, what would be the best course of action? Other consequences?

WHAT ARE THE LIKELY CONSEQUENCES CONSIDERING HUMAN BEHAVIOR?

What is causing me to do this?

What are my present environment and my state of mind? What is rewarding for me to do/say if I want to avoid pain? What do I perceive to be the consequences for me? Are they painful or pleasurable? What psychological tendencies will influence me? Are they likely to cause a misjudgment?

What is the context?

What does the environment and participants (incl. size) look like? Who is the decision-maker and what are his criteria for making decisions? Who benefits and who pay? Who is responsible for outcome? Who and what are influencing the participant's perception of reality?

Can I judge him?

Can I judge his character? What are his experiences? What temporary or permanent characteristics influence him (age, cultural background, health, mood…)? What environmental (present internal and external) or situational factors influence him? Does he want to sell me something?

What is in his self-interest to do?

What is logical for him to do? What is rewarding for him to do if he want to avoid pain? What does he perceive as painful? What does he fear and why? What does he want more of or what does he not want to be taken away? What "resources" motivates him? His health, job, family, position, reputation, status, power? What would give him an incentive or disincentive? What reward or penalty system causes his behavior? What is he rewarded (perceived) for doing? What is he punished (perceived) for doing? How is he measured? How does he perceive the consequences of non-goal? Is it to his advantage/interest to believe (or not to believe) something?

What are the psychological tendencies and shortcuts that influence him and can cause misjudgment?

What bias affects his conclusions? What external influences is there, that will likely influence him? What temptations are there that appeal to his self-interest? What activates his behavior?

What are the consequences?

What are the consequences for me? Will my goal still be achieved? Is what is rewarding for him also rewarding for me? Is the system set up so that the relevant participant's interest coincides with my goal? Does it "pay him" to make the wrong decision? Does he understand the consequences of his behavior? What are the short-and long-term consequences for him? What are the lines of responsibility? Does he have the responsibility for the consequences? What happens when others do the same?

What system would I like to have if the roles were reversed?
How would I like to be treated if the roles were reversed? What would cause me to do the things I want him to do? What are the behavioral tendencies I can use to change his behavior? How shall I behave if I want to guarantee non-goal? Can I now turn around and avoid those?

Is this the right system?
Can I appeal to his self-interest? Can I appeal to fear of losing reputation, money, status, family..? Can I change his present associations to pain? How can I organize the system to minimize certain influences? Have I told him what I expect? Have I inspected what is done? Have I supported things done well? Does he have the necessary skills, knowledge and the relevant information? Does he know what is expected of him? Does he know the goal, how he will reach it and why that is the best path? Can he measure his progress? Is it related to his daily activities? Does he have the responsibility and the authority? Is his reward aligned with the goal? What rules can I install that will consider human weaknesses? Can I install a reverse rule? What changes must be made? Who will call for them? How likely is that? What are his values? His goals? What does he consider to be result? What is his perception of the consequences if he behave like we want him to and if he doesn't?

Business evaluation
Filter 1 – Can I understand the business – predictability?
- *Reasons for demand* – How certain am I that and can explain why people are likely to continue buy this type of product or service in the future? What has happened in the past and what is likely to happen in the future? Cyclically in demand? Capacity versus demand?
- *Return characteristics* – Industry and company return characteristics and change over the last ten years?
- *Industry structure* – No of competitors and size? Who dictate the terms in this industry? What is needed to make money in this industry? Position within the industry? Do I know who is going to make the money in this market and why?
- *Real Customer* – Who decides what to buy and what are his decision-criteria?

Filter 2 – Does it look like the business has some kind of sustainable competitive advantage?
- *Competitive Advantage* – How certain am I that and can explain why they are likely to buy the product or service from the company rather than from someone else? Are the reasons virtually unchanged from what they were ten years ago? Are these motivations likely to be unchanged over the next ten years?
- *Value* – How strong and sustainable is this advantage? Have the advantages become stronger and more durable over the years? What can destroy or reduce them? Barriers to entry? Brand loyalty? Vulnerable to change in demand or prices? Easy to copy? Short product

life cycle? Customer cost and incentive to switch supplier? Annual cost differential against competition? Capital investments needed? Bargaining power? Obsolescence risk? New customer alternatives? Change in buying habits or power? Competitor potential to undercut prices assuming same cost structure? What is needed to make sure the advantages stay sustainable? Growth opportunities left? Untapped unit volume demand? Pricing power?

- *Profitability* – Can the advantage be translated into profitability and why? How does the company make money? How much capital is needed to produce incremental revenues? Business model – how make money? Financial characteristics – return on capital (operating margins and capital turnover), gross margins, sales growth, cost- and capital structure and efficiency? Normalized free cash flow? Advantages of scale? Critical variable?

Filter 3 – Able and honest management?
- Is the management composed of competent and honest people that understands and focuses on creation of value?

Filter 4 – Is the price right?
- Can I buy at a price that provides a good return with a huge margin of safety measured against other available alternatives and with evidence from facts and figures?

Filter 5 – Disprove
- How can the business get killed? If the company could kill one of its competitors, who would it be and why? If the company would go away for 5 years which competitor would they bet on and why? How resistant is the business to adversity? Assume the company paid out all its equity capital, would it still have any value? Could someone with the access to billions of dollars and talent, successfully compete with the company? How much damage could a competitor do if he doesn't care about returns? Recession sensitivity? Execution risk? Will new technology help or hurt?

Filter 6 – What are the consequences if I'm wrong?

Introduction

Page

ii   "I think that I am…" Francis Darwin (editor), *The Autobiography of Charles Darwin and Selected Letters,* Dover Publications, New York, 1958, p.55.

Part One

Page

4   "The brain is the…" Gerald Edelman, *BrainMatters,* The NeuroSciences Institute, Fall 2000.

7   "Isaac Newton might have…" Ralph Greenspan, *Nature Reviews,* Volume 2, May 2001, p.386.

13   "Even if fishes hone…" Stephen Jay Gould, *Wonderful Life: The Burgess Shale and the Nature of History*, W.W. Norton & Company, New York, 1989, Norton paperback 1990, p.48.

16   "As things get…" Steven Pinker, *How the Mind Works,* W.W. Norton & Company, New York, 1997, p.392.

19   "But it may be…" Charles Darwin, *The Descent of Man,* Second edition, Murray, London, 1874, Chapter five (On the Development of the Intellectual and Moral Faculties During Primeval and Civilised Times)

22   "At the moment…" Charles Darwin, *The Descent of Man,* Second edition, Murray, London, 1874, Chapter four (Comparison of the Mental Powers of Man and the Lower Animals)

27   "Inasmuch as every act…" Frans De Waal, *Good Natured: the Origins of Right and Wrong in Humans and Other Animals*, Harvard University Press, Cambridge, Massachusetts, 1996, Fourth printing, 1997, p.115.

27   "At a small dinner gathering…" Lee Alan Dugatkin, *Cheating Monkeys and Citizen Bees: The Nature of Cooperation in Animals and Humans,* The Free Press, Simon & Schuster, New York, 1999, p.101.

27   "Fear of disapproval is…" Garrett Hardin, *The Ostrich Factor: Our Population Myopia*, Oxford University Press, New York, 1998, p.77.

28   "Throw a bunch of…" Robert Wright, *The Moral Animal: Evolutionary Psychology and Everyday Life,* Abacus, Little Brown and Company, London, 1994, Abacus edition 1996, p.239.

Part Two

Page

77   "His [Jones] masterstroke was…" Robert Cialdini, *Influence: The Psychology of Persuasion*, Quill William Morrow and Company, New York, 1984,1993, p.156.

77   "In a country like…" Robert Cialdini, *Influence: The Psychology of Persuasion*, Quill William Morrow and Company, New York, 1984,1993, p.154.

77   "Have the courage…" Benjamin Graham, *The Intelligent Investor: A Book of Practical Counsel*, Harper & Row, Publishers, New York, 1973, Fourth Revised Edition, p.287.

83   "If one could open…" Herbert Simon, *Models of My Life,* The MIT Press, Cambridge, Massachusetts, 1996, p.226.

91   "The status of…" Matt Ridley, *Genome: The autobiography of a species in 23 chapters,* Fourth Estate Limited, London, 1999, pp.155-156.

Part Three

Page

107   "A complex system…" Gerald Edelman, *BrainMatters,* The NeuroSciences Institute, Fall 2002.

112 "As a colony grows…" Garrett Hardin, *Living Within Limits: Ecology, Economics, and Population Taboos,* Oxford University Press, New York, 1993, Oxford University Press paperback 1995, pp.266-267.

132 "It is said to be…" Henry Howard Harper, *The Psychology of Speculation: The Human Element in Stock Market Speculations*, Fraser Publishing Company, Burlington, Vermont, 1966, p.44.

141 "A general surgeon left…" Atul Gawande, *Complications: A Surgeon's Notes on an Imperfect Science*, Metropolitan Books, Henry Holt and Company, New York, 2002, p.55.

144 "Occasionally, a vegetable…" Carl Sagan, *The Demon-Haunted World: Science as a Candle in the Dark,* Ballantine Books, New York, 1996, First Ballantine Books Edition March 1997, p.46.

155 "Cancer is now more…" Horace Levinson, *Chance, Luck and Statistics*, Dover Publications, Mineola, New York, 1939, 1950, 1963, Dover edition 1963, p.259.

Part Four

Page

168 "If, in some cataclysm, all…" Richard Feynman & Robert Leighton & Matthew Sands *The Feynman Lectures on Physics*, Addison-Wesley Publishing Company, Reading, Massachusetts, 1963, Sixth printing, 1977, p.1.2.

174 "See that bird?…" Richard Feynman as told to Ralph Leighton, *What Do You Care What Other People Think?: Further Adventures of a Curious Character*, W.W. Norton & Company, New York, 1988, Bantam edition, 1989, pp.13-14.

174 "There is a picture…" Richard Feynman, "What is Science?", *The Physics Teacher*, volume 9, 1969, pp.313-320.

175 "the soles of your…" Richard Feynman, "What is Science?", *The Physics Teacher*, volume 9, 1969, pp.313-320.

175 "Without using the…" Richard Feynman, "What is Science?", *The Physics Teacher*, volume 9, 1969, pp.313-320.

178 "If earnings not paid…" John Burr Williams, *The Theory of Investment Value*, Fraser Publishing Company, Burlington, 1997, pp.57-58.

186 "You can't believe…" Noel Tichy and Ram Charan, "Speed, Simplicy, Self-Confidence: An Interview with Jack Welch," *Harvard Business Review*, September-October 1989, p.112.

190 "In nearly every detective…" Albert Einstein & Leopold Infeld, *The Evolution of Physics: The Growth of Ideas from Early Concepts to Relativity and Quanta,* Cambridge University Press, Cambridge, 1938, Reprinted 1978, p.4.

211 "It does not make any…" Richard Feynman, *The Character of Physical Law*, The Modern Library, Random House, New York, 1965, 1994 Modern Library Edition, p.150.

211 "About thirty years ago…" Charles Darwin to Henry Fawcett (18 September 1861), Letter No. 133 in Francis Darwin (editor), *More Letters of Charles Darwin*, Vol. 1 D. Appleton, New York, 1903.

214 "I had also…" Francis Darwin (editor), *The Autobiography of Charles Darwin and Selected Letters*, Dover Publications, New York, 1958, pp.45,52-53.

225 "I rejoice that…" Francis Darwin (editor), *The Autobiography of Charles Darwin and Selected Letters,* Dover Publications, New York, 1958, pp.46,279.

Source notes – Charles Munger and Warren Buffett
Introduction
Page

i "All I want to…" Berkshire Hathaway Inc., 1996 *Annual Report*, p.9.

i "I believe in the…" Lecture by Charles T. Munger to the students of Professor William Lazier at Stanford Law School, *Outstanding Investor Digest*, March 13, 1998, p.63.

iii "I think it's a huge…" Lecture by Charles T. Munger to the students of Professor William Lazier at Stanford Law School, *Outstanding Investor Digest*, March 13, 1998, p.63.

Part One

32   "It's ego. It's greed…" *Adam Smith's Money Game*, Transcript #105, Air Date: May 15, 1998.

32   "I always look at…" *Buffett & Gates on Success*, KCTS/Seattle, May 1998 transcript p. 4.

Part Two

Page

35   "I came to the…" Andrew Kilpatrick, *Of Permanent Value: The Story of Warren Buffett*, Birmingham: AKPE, 2000, p.873.

35   "If you want to…" Berkshire Hathaway annual meeting, 1991, *Outstanding Investor Digest*, May 24, 1991, p.32.

40   "We only give…" Berkshire Hathaway annual meeting, 1995, *Outstanding Investor Digest*, August 10, 1995, p.4.

41   "The iron rule of nature…" Wesco Financial annual meeting, 2001.

42   "The worst abuses…" Wesco Financial annual meeting, 1994, *Outstanding Investor Digest,* June 23, 1994, p.15.

43   "From all business…" Lecture by Charles T. Munger to the students of Professor Guilford Babcock at the University of Southern California School of Business on April 14, 1994, *Outstanding Investor Digest*, May 5, 1995, p.59.

43   "The food value…" Lecture by Charles T. Munger to the students of Professor William Lazier at Stanford Law School, *Outstanding Investor Digest*, December 29, 1997, p.27.

44   "Well, the customer…" Lecture by Charles T. Munger to the students of Professor William Lazier at Stanford Law School, *Outstanding Investor Digest*, December 29, 1997, p.29.

44   "As you occupy some…" Wesco Financial Inc., 1990 *Annual Report,* (Berkshire Hathaway Inc., *Letters to Shareholders*, 1987-1995, p.203.)

44   "Goals should be…" Berkshire Hathaway Inc., 1996 *Annual Report*, p.10.

45   "It's very hard to change…" Berkshire Hathaway annual meeting, 1998, *Outstanding Investor Digest,* September 24, 1998, p.55.

45   "An example of a…" Berkshire Hathaway annual meeting, 1993, *Outstanding Investor Digest,* June 30, 1993, p.29.

46   "without the help of…" Berkshire Hathaway Inc., *Letters to Shareholders*, 1994, p.149.

46   "All commissioned salesmen…" Wesco Financial annual meeting, 1988, *Outstanding Investor Digest*, April 30, 1988, p.21.

47   "They were paid…" Wesco Financial annual meeting, 1992, *Outstanding Investor Digest*, June 22, 1992, p.8.

47   "Mark Twain used to say…" Berkshire Hathaway annual meeting, 1995, *Outstanding Investor Digest*, August 10, 1995, p.11.

48   "I have no use…" Berkshire Hathaway annual meeting, 1995, Andrew Kilpatrick, *Of Permanent Value: The Story of Warren Buffett*, Birmingham: AKPE, 2000, p.1074.

48   "I do not understand…" Berkshire Hathaway annual meeting, 1994, *Outstanding Investor Digest*, June 23, 1994, pp.23-24.

48   "When they make…" Berkshire Hathaway Inc., *Letters to Shareholders*, 1989, p.60.

48   "I would say that…" Berkshire Hathaway annual meeting, 2002.

49   "I'd say that…" Berkshire Hathaway annual meeting, 2001, *Outstanding Investor Digest*, Year End 2001 Edition, p.24.

50   "We want the manager…" Berkshire Hathaway annual meeting, 1998, *Outstanding Investor Digest,* September 24, 1998, pp.55-56.

53   "we do have a…" Berkshire Hathaway Inc., *Letters to Shareholders*, 1995, p.162.

53   "We have very much…" Wesco Financial annual meeting, 1989, *Outstanding Investor Digest*, July 26, 1989, pp.6-7.

53   "I think it was…" Berkshire Hathaway annual meeting, 1998, *Outstanding Investor Digest,* September 24, 1998, p.40.

55 "We've done a…" Berkshire Hathaway annual meeting, 2000, *Outstanding Investor Digest*, Year End 2000 Edition, p.60.

55 "The most important…" Berkshire Hathaway Inc., *Letters to Shareholders*, 1990, p.74.

56 "Berkshire extracted a…" Wesco Financial annual meeting, 1989, *Outstanding Investor Digest*, July 26, 1989, p.9.

56 "What the human being…" Berkshire Hathaway annual meeting, 2002.

57 "Charlie and I believe…" Berkshire Hathaway annual meeting, 1998, *Outstanding Investor Digest,* September 24, 1998, p.40.

57 "Heavy ideology is…" Lecture by Charles T. Munger to the students of Professor William Lazier at Stanford Law School, *Outstanding Investor Digest*, March 13, 1998, p.47.

58 "(A) You're facing deprival…" Lecture by Charles T. Munger to the students of Professor William Lazier at Stanford Law School, *Outstanding Investor Digest*, March 13, 1998, p.53.

59 "The deprival super-reaction…" Lecture by Charles T. Munger to the students of Professor William Lazier at Stanford Law School, *Outstanding Investor Digest,* March 13, 1998, p.52.

59 "One reason why…" Lecture by Charles T. Munger to the students of Professor William Lazier at Stanford Law School, *Outstanding Investor Digest,* March 13, 1998, p.52.

60 "Buffett: A very important …" Berkshire Hathaway annual meeting, 1995, *Outstanding Investor Digest*, August 10, 1995, p.6.

61 "In Captain Cook's…" Lecture by Charles T. Munger to the students of Professor William Lazier at Stanford Law School, *Outstanding Investor Digest*, March 13, 1998, p.50.

67 "Techniques shrouded in…" Berkshire Hathaway Inc., *Letters to Shareholders*, 1987, p.12.

69 "Three quarters of…" 1994 Lecture of The E. J. Faulkner Lecture Series, A Colloquium with University of Nebraska-Lincoln Students by Warren E. Buffett, pp.15-16.

73 "This friend, who ran…" Berkshire Hathaway Inc., *Letters to Shareholders*, 1995, p.148.

74 "Most managers have very…" Berkshire Hathaway Inc., *Letters to Shareholders*, 1984, p.96.

74 "Grown-up people…" Wesco Financial annual meeting, 1995, *Outstanding Investor Digest,* August 10, 1995, p. 62.

77 "We derive no comfort…" Letter to partners, January 18, 1965.

80 "Any investor can…" Berkshire Hathaway Inc., 1997 *Annual Report*, p.3.

80 "It is remarkable…" Wesco Financial Inc., 1989 *Annual Report,* (Berkshire Hathaway Inc., *Letters to Shareholders*, 1987-1995, p.196.)

80 "We won't do anything…" Lecture at Stanford Law School, March 23, 1990, *Outstanding Investor Digest*, April 18, 1990, p.14..

83 "Good character is…" Charles Munger, Berkshire Hathaway annual meeting, 1993, *Outstanding Investor Digest,* June 30, 1993, p.29.

83 "I'm not saying that…" Berkshire Hathaway annual meeting, 1998, *Outstanding Investor Digest,* September 24, 1998, p.54.

84 "His rule for all…" Lecture by Charles T. Munger to the students of Professor Guilford Babcock at the University of Southern California School of Business on April 14, 1994, *Outstanding Investor Digest*, May 5, 1995, p.50.

87 "What happens is that…" Wesco Financial annual meeting, 2000, *Outstanding Investor Digest*, December 18, 2000, p.52.

87 "Predicting rain…" Berkshire Hathaway Inc., 2001 *Annual Report*, p.9.

88 "The sad fact…" Berkshire Hathaway Inc., *Letters to Shareholders*, 1994, pp.147-148.

89 "We hear a great…" Berkshire Hathaway Inc., *Letters to Shareholders*, 1979, pp.20-21.

89 "We've got great…" Wesco Financial annual meeting, 2000, *Outstanding Investor Digest*, December 18, 2000, p.60.

89 "There's no use…" Berkshire Hathaway Inc., *Letters to Shareholders*, 1993, p.129.

91 "I have no stress…" Berkshire Hathaway annual meeting, 2001, *Outstanding Investor Digest*, Year End 2001 Edition, p.46.

91 "All the businesses…" Warren Buffett interview, *Outstanding Investor Digest*, June 23, 1989, p.12.

92   "When you get two…" Berkshire Hathaway annual meeting, 1991, *Outstanding Investor Digest*, May 24, 1991, p.32.

92   "A very significant…" Lecture by Charles T. Munger to the students of Professor William Lazier at Stanford Law School, *Outstanding Investor Digest,* March 13, 1998, pp.51-52.

93   "I don't want to…" Lecture by Charles T. Munger to the students of Professor William Lazier at Stanford Law School, *Outstanding Investor Digest,* March 13, 1998, p.55.

94   "I've gotten so that…" Lecture by Charles T. Munger to the students of Professor Guilford Babcock at the University of Southern California School of Business on April 14, 1994, *Outstanding Investor Digest*, May 5, 1995, p.51.

94   "Take all the main…" Lecture by Charles T. Munger to the students of Professor William Lazier at Stanford Law School, *Outstanding Investor Digest*, March 13, 1998, pp.48-49.

95   "One of the things…" Wesco Financial annual meeting, 1998, *Outstanding Investor Digest,* December 29, 1998, pp.46-47.

Part Three

Page

102   "They had all…" Wesco Financial annual meeting, 2001, Wesco Special Report, *Outstanding Investor Digest*, OID.COM Edition, 2003, p.10.

103   "An excess of what…" Charles T. Munger, speech at Miramar Sheraton Hotel, Santa Monica, CA, on October 14, 1998 to a meeting of the Foundation Financial Officer Group, *Outstanding Investor Digest*, 1998 Bonus Edition, p.2.

107   "I'm all for fixing…" Wesco Financial annual meeting, 1998, *Outstanding Investor Digest*, March 13, 1998, p.57.

108   "We try and predict…" Wesco Financial annual meeting, 2001, Wesco Special Report, *Outstanding Investor Digest*, OID.COM Edition, 2003, p.1.

108   "We believe the…" Berkshire Hathaway Inc., 1996 *Annual Report*, p.9.

112   "Both we and our…" Berkshire Hathaway Inc., 2001 *Annual Report*, p.14.

117   "For years it was…" Lecture by Charles T. Munger to the students of Professor William Lazier at Stanford Law School, *Outstanding Investor Digest*, March 13, 1998, p.48.

125   "Catastrophe insurers…" Berkshire Hathaway Inc., *Letters to Shareholders*, 1992, p.113.

125   "Even if perfection…" Berkshire Hathaway Inc., 1996 *Annual Report*, p.9.

125   "Given the risks…" Berkshire Hathaway Inc., *Letters to Shareholders*, 1994, p.153.

125   "We do, though,…" Berkshire Hathaway Inc., *Letters to Shareholders*, 1995, p.169.

125   "In setting prices and…" Berkshire Hathaway Inc., 2001 *Annual Report*, p.8.

126   "No one knows…" Berkshire Hathaway Inc., 2001 *Annual Report*, p.8.

136   "Here were 16 extremely…" Warren Buffett, Berkshire Hathaway annual meeting, 1999, *Outstanding Investor Digest*, December 31, 1999, pp.55-56.

138   "How many of those…" Berkshire Hathaway annual meeting, 1999, *Outstanding Investor Digest*, December 10, 1999, p.56.

139   "You may consciously…" Berkshire Hathaway Inc., *Letters to Shareholders*, 1993, p.136.

139   "We expect all…" Berkshire Hathaway Inc., 2000 *Annual Report*, p.7.

154   "People like to look…" Berkshire Hathaway annual meeting, 1989, *Outstanding Investor Digest,* June 23, 1989, p.9.

154   "Conditions relating to…" Berkshire Hathaway annual meeting, 1992, *Outstanding Investor Digest,* June 22, 1992, p.45.

154   "The same mistake…" Berkshire Hathaway Inc., *Letters to Shareholders*, 1988, p.23.

154   "In the future…" Berkshire Hathaway Inc., 2001 *Annual Report*, p.4.

155   "The water system…" Wesco Financial annual meeting, 1990, *Outstanding Investor Digest*, June 28, 1990, pp.20-21.

157   "It is assumed by…" Wesco Financial Inc., 1989 *Annual Report,* (Berkshire Hathaway Inc.,

Letters to Shareholders, 1987-1995, p.193.)

162 "You tend to forget…" Wesco Financial annual meeting, 1998, *Outstanding Investor Digest,* December 29, 1998, p.50.

162 "Managers tend to…" Berkshire Hathaway annual meeting, 1999, *Outstanding Investor Digest,* December 31, 1999, p.60.

162 "Berkshire is basically…" Berkshire Hathaway annual meeting, 1994, *Outstanding Investor Digest,* June 23, 1994, p. 31.

Part Four
Page
165 "If you ask not…" Wesco Financial annual meeting 1999, *Outstanding Investor Digest,* December 31, 1999, p.37.

166 "Another model that…" Lecture by Charles T. Munger to the students of Professor William Lazier at Stanford Law School, *Outstanding Investor Digest,* December 29, 1997, p. 25. And March 13, 1998, pp.55-56.

167 "The models that come…" Lecture by Charles T. Munger to the students of Professor Guilford Babcock at the University of Southern California School of Business on April 14, 1994, *Outstanding Investor Digest,* May 5, 1995, pp.50-51.

167 "In most messy human…" Wesco Financial annual meeting, 2000, *Outstanding Investor Digest,* December 18, 2000, p.52.

167 "Suppose you want…" Lecture by Charles T. Munger to the students of Professor William Lazier at Stanford Law School*, Outstanding Investor Digest,* December 29, 1997, p.26.

168 "If you don't…" Wesco Financial annual meeting 1999, *Outstanding Investor Digest,* December 31, 1999, p.40.

168 "You get *lollapalooza*…" Lecture by Charles T. Munger to the students of Professor William Lazier at Stanford Law School, *Outstanding Investor Digest,* December 29, 1997, p.25.

174 "Bad terminology is…" Berkshire Hathaway Inc., 2001 *Annual Report,* p.10.

176 "We use the…" Berkshire Hathaway annual meeting, 1997, *Outstanding Investor Digest,* August 8, 1997, p.18.

177 "In the end…" Berkshire Hathaway annual meeting, 2001, *Outstanding Investor Digest,* Year End 2001 Edition, p.37.

177 "These numbers routinely…" Berkshire Hathaway Inc., *Letters to Shareholders,* 1986, p.142.

177 "When companies or…" Berkshire Hathaway Inc., 2001 *Annual Report,* p.10.

178 "Trumpeting EBITDA…" Berkshire Hathaway Inc., 2002 *Annual Report,* p.21.

178 "If somebody's reinvesting…" Berkshire Hathaway annual meeting, 1998, *Outstanding Investor Digest,* September 24, 1998, p.36.

178 "Intrinsic value is an…" Berkshire Hathaway Inc. 2001 Annual Report, *An Owner's Manual,* p.67.

179 "Using precise numbers…" Berkshire Hathaway Inc., 2000 *Annual Report,* p.13.

179 "What you're trying to…" Berkshire Hathaway annual meeting, 2002.

179 "Growth can destroy…" Berkshire Hathaway Inc., 2000 *Annual Report,* p.13.

179 "First, we try to…" Berkshire Hathaway Inc., *Letters to Shareholders,* 1992, p.117.

180 "We try…to keep…" Berkshire Hathaway Inc., 2000 *Annual Report,* p.14.

180 "You'd try to…" Berkshire Hathaway annual meeting, 1994, *Outstanding Investor Digest,* June 23, 1994, p.26.

180 "For our discount…" Berkshire Hathaway annual meeting, 1996, *Outstanding Investor Digest,* August 8, 1996, p.28.

180 "And that discount…" Berkshire Hathaway annual meeting, 1998, *Outstanding Investor Digest,* September 24, 1998, p.36.

180 "We love owning…" Berkshire Hathaway Inc., 2002 *Annual Report,* p.16.

180 "We believe that…" Berkshire Hathaway annual meeting, 1995, *Outstanding Investor Digest,* August 10, 1995, p.12.

181   "We are very inexact…be obvious" Berkshire Hathaway annual meeting, 1990, *Outstanding Investor Diges*t, May 31, 1990, p.25.

181   "When we look…" Berkshire Hathaway annual meeting, 1998, *Outstanding Investor Digest,* September 24, 1998, p.37.

182   "If you and I…" Berkshire Hathaway annual meeting, 1999, *Outstanding Investor Digest,* December 10, 1999, p.48.

183   "One friend of mine…" 1994 Lecture of The E. J. Faulkner Lecture Series, A Colloquium with University of Nebraska-Lincoln Students by Warren E. Buffett, p.6.

183   "My conclusion from…" Berkshire Hathaway Inc., *Letters to Shareholders*, 1985, p.108.

186   "We have a passion…" Wesco Financial annual meeting, 2002.

186   "Charlie and I decided…" Berkshire Hathaway Inc., *Letters to Shareholders*, 1993, p.134.

187   "I'm a follower…" Wesco Financial annual meeting, 2002, *Outstanding Investor Digest,* December 31, 2002, p.38.

188   "There are things…" Wesco Financial annual meeting, 2002, *Outstanding Investor Digest,* December 31, 2002, p.26.

188   "Easy does it…" Berkshire Hathaway Inc., *Letters to Shareholders*, 1989, p.62.

188   "We basically have…" Berkshire Hathaway annual meeting, 1995, *Outstanding Investor Digest,* August 10, 1995, p.20.

188   "I've heard Warren…" Charles Munger, Berkshire Hathaway annual meeting, 1997, *Outstanding Investor Digest,* September 24, 1998, p.38.

189   "A serious problem…" Berkshire Hathaway Inc., 1996 *Annual Report*, pp.15-16.

189   "I love focused…" Berkshire Hathaway annual meeting, 1996, *Outstanding Investor Digest,* August 8, 1996, pp.24-25.

189   "There are two questions…" Berkshire Hathaway, press conference, May 2001.

191   "In allocating capital…" Berkshire Hathaway Inc., 1998 *Annual Report*, p.12.

191   "If you feel like…" Berkshire Hathaway annual meeting, 1996, *Outstanding Investor Digest,* August 8, 1996, pp.23-24.

191   "A few major opportunities…" Wesco Financial Inc., 1996 *Annual Report*, p.6.

192   "Any time anybody…" Lecture by Charles T. Munger to the students of Professor Guilford Babcock at the University of Southern California School of Business on April 14, 1994, *Outstanding Investor Digest*, May 5, 1995, p.62.

192   "What counts in this…" Berkshire Hathaway Inc., 2001 *Annual Report*, pp.7-9.

193   "We really can…" Berkshire Hathaway annual meeting, 1998, *Outstanding Investor Digest,* September 24, 1998, p.48.

193   "Generally speaking…", Wesco Financial annual meeting, 2002, *Outstanding Investor Digest,* December 31, 2002, p.26.

197   "Our definition of…" Berkshire Hathaway annual meeting, 2000, *Outstanding Investor Digest,* December 18, 2000, pp.39-40.

198   "If you've got two…" Berkshire Hathaway annual meeting, 1997, *Outstanding Investor Digest,* August 8, 1997, p.16.

200   "All of the advantages…" Lecture by Charles T. Munger to the students of Professor Guilford Babcock at the University of Southern California School of Business on April 14, 1994, *Outstanding Investor Digest*, May 5, 1995, p. 56.

201   "If you're a captain…" Lecture by Charles T. Munger to the students of Professor William Lazier at Stanford Law School, *Outstanding Investor Digest,* March 13, 1998, pp.60-61.

203   "Leaving the question…" Berkshire Hathaway Inc., *Letters to Shareholders*, 1992, p.116.

203   "While an increase…" Berkshire Hathaway Inc., *Letters to Shareholders*, 1985, p.109.

203   "Return on beginning…" Berkshire Hathaway Inc., *Letters to Shareholders*, 1980, p.27.

203   "Over the long term…" Lecture by Charles T. Munger to the students of Professor Guilford Babcock at the University of Southern California School of Business on April 14, 1994, *Outstanding Investor Digest*, May 5, 1995, p.61.

204 "Examine the record…" Berkshire Hathaway Inc., 2000 *Annual Report*, p.18.

204 "Finally, be suspicious…" Berkshire Hathaway Inc., 2002 *Annual Report*, p.21.

204 "A few years ago…" Berkshire Hathaway Inc., *Letters to Shareholders*, 1991, pp.94-95.

206 "Of one thing, however…" Berkshire Hathaway Inc., 1997 *Annual Report*, p.15.

208 "When we buy a stock…" Berkshire Hathaway annual meeting, 2000, *Outstanding Investor Digest*, December 18, 2000, pp.34-35.

209 "Value is destroyed…" Berkshire Hathaway Inc., 2000 *Annual Report*, p.14.

209 "There's plenty of magic..." Berkshire Hathaway annual meeting 1993, *Outstanding Investor Digest,* June 30, 1993, p.37.

211 "…you have to have…" Wesco Financial annual meeting, 1998, *Outstanding Investor Digest,* December 29, 1998, p.47.

212 "The best judgment…" Warren Buffett from a speech at the Emory Business School as reported in, "Track record is everything", *Across the Board*, October 1991, p.59.

215 "The mental habit of…" Lecture by Charles T. Munger to the students of Professor William Lazier at Stanford Law School, *Outstanding Investor Digest*, December 29, 1997, p.24.

216 "A lot of success…" Wesco Financial annual meeting, 2000, *Outstanding Investor Digest*, December 18, 2000, p.60.

216 "If you were hired…" Lecture by Charles T. Munger to the students of Professor William Lazier at Stanford Law School, *Outstanding Investor Digest,* December 29, 1997, p.24.

217 "Let's say you have…" Lecture by Charles T. Munger to the students of Professor William Lazier at Stanford Law School, *Outstanding Investor Digest*, March 13, 1998, pp.51-52.

220 "The simple fact…" Robert Lenzner and David S. Fondiller, "The not-so-silent partner," *Forbes Magazine,* January 22, 1996, p.83.

220 "When we look at…" Warren Buffett, Berkshire Hathaway annual meeting, 2000, *Outstanding Investor Digest*, December 18, 2000, p.43.

220 "In stocks, we expect…" Berkshire Hathaway Inc., 2002 *Annual Report*, p.16.

221 "I had a relative…" Wesco Financial annual meeting, 2002, *Outstanding Investor Digest,* December 31, 2002, p.28.

221 "If we can't…" Berkshire Hathaway Inc., 1996 *Annual Report*, p.9.

222 "We try to arrange…" Wesco Financial annual meeting, 2002, *Outstanding Investor Digest,* December 31, 2002, p.33.

222 "If you understand…" Berkshire Hathaway annual meeting, 1997, *Outstanding Investor Digest,* August 8, 1997, p.17.

222 "Charlie drummed in…" Janet Lowe, *Damn Right: Behind the Scenes with Berkshire Hathaway Billionaire Charlie Munger*, John Wiley & Sons, New York, 2000, p.54.

223 "You have to stick…" Berkshire Hathaway annual meeting, 1993, *Outstanding Investor Digest,* June 30, 1993, p.24.

224 "We'd rather deal…" Lecture by Charles T. Munger to the students of Professor William Lazier at Stanford Law School, *Outstanding Investor Digest*, March 13, 1998, p.55.

224 "I'm proud to be…" Margie Kelley, "In the Money: Alumni financiers take stock of the market and careers spent trying to beat it," *Harvard Law Bulletin*, Summer 2001.

225 "I do think enthusiasm…" *Buffett & Gates on Success*, KCTS/Seattle, May 1998 transcript p. 20.

226 "Whenever you think…" Wesco Financial annual meeting, 2001, Wesco Special Report, *Outstanding Investor Digest*, OID.COM Edition, 2003, p.20.

Adams John, *Risk,* UCL Press, London, 1995

Allison Graham & Zelikow Philip, *Essence Of Decision: Explaining the Cuban Missile Crisis,* Addison-Wesley Educational Publishers, New York, 1999

Aronson Elliot, *The Social Animal,* W.H. Freeman and Company, New York, 1996

Asimov Isaac, *Asimov on Physics,* Avon Books, New York, 1976

Ayer A.J., *The Problem of Knowledge,* Penguin Books, Middlesex, England, 1956

Baars Bernard J, *In the Theater of Consciousness: The Workspace of the Mind,* Oxford University Press, New York, 1997

Badcock Christopher, *PsychoDarwinism: The New Synthesis of Darwin & Freud,* Flamingo, HarperCollins, London, 1995, 1994

Bak Per, *How Nature Works: The Science of Self-organized Criticality,* Oxford University Press, Oxford, 1997

Baron Jonathan, *Thinking and Deciding,* Cambridge University Press, Cambridge, 1988, 1994

Barrow John D., *Impossibility: The Limits of Science and the Science of Limits,* Oxford University Press, Oxford, 1998

Bazerman Max H., *Judgment In Managerial Decision Making,* John Wiley & Sons, New York, 1998

Bell E.T, *Men of Mathematics,* A Touchstone Book, Simon & Schuster, New York, 1937, 1965

Belsky Gary & Gilovich Thomas, *Why Smart People Make Big Money Mistakes – and How to Correct Them: Lessons From The New Science of Behavioral Economics,* Simon & Schuster, New York, 1999

Beltrami Edward, *What is Random: chance and order in mathematics and life,* Springer-Verlag, New York, New York, 1999

Bennett, Deborah J., *Randomness,* Harvard University Press, Cambridge, Massachusetts, 1998

Bernstein Peter L., *Against the Gods: The Remarkable Story Of Risk,* John Wiley & Sons, New York, 1996

Blank Robert H., *Brain Policy: How the New Neuroscience Will Change Our Lives and Our Politics,* Georgetown University Press, Washington, D.C., 1999

Bloom Howard, *The Lucifer Principle: A Scientific Expedition into the Forces of History,* The Atlantic Monthly Press, New York, 1995

Boole George, *An Investigation Of The Laws of Thought on Which are Founded The Mathematical Theories of Logic and Probabilities,* Dover Publications, New York, 1958, (Macmillan 1854)

le Bon Gustave, *The Crowd: A Study Of The Popular Mind,* Cherokee Publishing Company, Atlanta, 1982

Boyd Robert and Silk Joan B, *How Humans Evolved,* W.W. Norton & Company, New York, 1997

Brian Denis, *Einstein: A Life,* John Wiley & Sons, New York, 1996

Brian Denis, *The Voice of Genius: Conversations with Nobel Scientists and Other Luminaries,* Perseus Publishing, Cambridge, Massachusetts, 1995

Brown Andrew, *The Darwin Wars: How Stupid Genes Became Selfish Gods,* Simon & Schuster, London, 1999

Brown Laurie M. and Rigden John (editors), *Most of the Good Stuff: Memories of Richard Feynman,* Springer-Verlag, New York, 1993

Browne Janet, *Charles Darwin Voyaging: Volume I of a Biography,* Pimlico, Random House, London, 1995

Buss David M., *Evolutionary Psychology: The New Science of the Mind,* Allyn & Bacon, Boston, 1999

Calne Donald B., *Within Reason: Rationality and Human Behavior,* Pantheon Books, New York, 1999

Calvin William H, *How Brains Think: Evolving Intelligence, Then and Now,* Basic Books, HarperCollins Publishers, New York, 1996

Capen E.C., Clapp R.B. and Campbell W.M., *Competitive Bidding in High Risk Situations, Journal of Petroleum Technology,* 23, June 1971, pp.641-653.

Carroll Lewis, *The Best of Lewis Carroll*, Castle, New Jersey

Casti John L, *Paradigms Lost: Images of Man in the Mirror of Science,* William Morrow and Company, New York, 1989

Casti John L, *Searching for Certainty: What Science Can Know About the Future,* Abacus, Little, Brown and Company, London 1993

Casti John L. *Complexification: Explaining a Paradoxical World Through the Science of Surprise,* Abacus, Little, Brown and Company, London 1994

Casti John L, *Five Golden Rules: Great Theories of 20th-Century Mathematics – and Why They Matter,* John Wiley & Sons, New York, 1996

Casti John L., *Paradigms Regained: A Further Exploration of the Mysteries of Modern Science,* Harper Collins Publishers, New York, 2000

Caudill Edward, *Darwinian Myths: the Legends and Misuses of a Theory,* The University of Tennessee Press, Knoxville, 1997

Cavalli-Sforza Luigi Luca, *Genes, Peoples, and Languages*, North Point Press, New York, 2000

Chernoff Herman & Moses Lincoln E., *Elementary Decision Theory,* Dover Publications, New York, 1959, 1986

Cialdini Robert B., *Influence: The Psychology of Persuasion,* Quill William Morrow and Company, New York, 1984,1993

Cialdini Robert B., *Influence: Science and Practice,* Harper Collins College Publishers, New York, 1993

Claxton Guy, *Hare Brain, Tortoise Mind: Why Intelligence Increases When You Think Less,* The Ecco Press, New Jersey, 1997

Damasio Antonio R., *Descartes' Error: Emotion, Reason, and the Human Brain*, HarperCollins Publishers, New York, 2000

Darwin Charles, *The Origin of Species*, Gramercy Books, New York, 1979

Darwin Charles, *The Expression of the Emotions in Man and Animals,* Third Edition, Oxford University Press, New York, 1998

Darwin Charles, *The Descent of Man*, Second Edition, Murray, London, 1874

Darwin Francis (editor), *The Autobiography of Charles Darwin and Selected Letters,* Dover Publications, New York, 1958

David F.N., *Games, Gods and Gambling: A History of Probability and Statistical Ideas*, Dover Publications, Mineola, New York, 1998

Dawes Robyn M., *Rational Choice in an Uncertain World*, Harcourt Brace College Publishers, Orlando, 1988

Dawkins Richard, *The Selfish Gene,* Oxford University Press, Oxford, 1976, 1989

Dawkins Richard, *The Blind Watchmaker,* Penguin Books, London, 1986, 1991

Dawkins Richard, *Climbing Mount Improbable,* Viking, Penguin Books, London, 1996

Dawkins Richard, *River out of Eden: A Darwinian View of Life,* Weidenfeld & Nicolson, London, 1995

Dawkins Richard, *Unweaving the Rainbow: Science, Delusion and the Appetite for Wonder,* Allen Lane, Penguin Books, London, 1998

Deci Edward L, *Why We Do What We Do: Understanding Self-Motivation,* Penguin Books USA, New York, 1995

Dennett Daniel C, *Kinds of Mind: Toward an Understanding of Consciousness,* Weidenfeld & Nicolson, London, 1996

Deutsch David, *The Fabric of Reality: The Science of Parallel Universes – and Its Implications,* Penguin Books, New York, 1997

Diamond Jared, *The Rise and Fall of the Third Chimpanzee,* Vintage Books, Random House, London, 1991

Diamond Jared, *Why is Sex Fun?: The Evolution of Human Sexuality,* Basic Books, HarperCollins Publishers, New York, 1997

Diamond Jared, *Guns, Germs, and Steel: The Fates Of Human Societies,* W.W. Norton & Company, New York, 1998

Dineen Tana, *Manufacturing Victims: What the Psychology Industry is Doing to People*, Constable and Company, London, 1999 van Doren Carl, *Benjamin Franklin,* Penguin Books USA, New York, 1938, 1966

van Doren Charles, *A History of Knowledge: Past, Present, and Future,* Ballantine Books, New York, 1991

Doyle Arthur Conan, *The Adventures and Memoirs of Sherlock Holmes,* The Modern Library, Random House, New York, 2001

Dozier W. Rush, *Fear Itself: The Origin and Nature of the Powerful Emotion That Shapes Our Lives and Our World*, St. Martin's Press, New York, 1998

Dreifus Claudia, *Scientific Conversations: Interviews on Science from The New York Times*, Times Books, Henry Holt and Company, New York, 2001

Dugatkin Lee, *Cheating Monkeys and Citizen Bees: The Nature of Cooperation in Animals and Humans*, The Free Press, Simon & Schuster, New York, 1999

Dugatkin Lee, *The Imitation Factor: Evolution Beyond The Gene,* The Free Press, New York, 2000

Durant Will and Ariel, *The Lessons of History*, Simon and Schuster, New York, 1968

Eccles John C., *The Human Mystery: The GIFFORD Lectures University of Edinburgh 1977-1978*, Routledge & Kegan Paul, London, 1984, 1979

Edelman Gerald, *Bright Air, Brilliant Fire: On the Matter of the Mind,* Penguin Books, London, England, 1992

Edelman Gerald M., and Tononi Giulio, *A Universe of Consciousness: How Matter Becomes Imagination,* Basic Books, New York, 2000

Einstein Albert and Infeld Leopold, *The Evolution of Physics: The Growth of Ideas from Early Concepts to Relativity and Quanta,* Cambridge University Press, Cambridge, 1938

Ekeland Ivar, *Mathematics and the Unexpected,* University of Chicago Press, Chicago, 1988.

Eldredge Niles, *The Pattern of Evolution*, W.H. Freeman and Company, New York, 1999

Ehrlich Paul R., *Human Natures: Genes, Cultures, and the Human Prospect,* Island Press, Washington, DC, 2000

Fabian A.C. (editor), *Evolution: Society, Science and the Universe*, Cambridge University Press, Cambridge, 1998

Feynman Richard & Leighton Robert & Sands Matthew, *The Feynman Lectures on Physics*, Addison-Wesley, Reading, Massachusetts, 1963, 1964, 1965

Feynman Richard P, *Six Easy Pieces: Essentials of Physics Explained by Its Most Brilliant Teacher,* Helix Books, Addison-Wesley, Reading, Massachusetts, 1963, 1989, 1995

Feynman Richard P, *Six Not-So-Easy Pieces: Einstein's Relativity, Symmetry, and Space-Time,* Helix Books, Addison-Wesley, Reading, Massachusetts, 1963, 1989, 1997

Feynman Richard, *The Character of Physical Law*, The Modern Library, New York, 1965, 1994

Feynman Richard P & Leighton Ralph, *"Surely You're Joking, Mr. Feynman!": Adventures of a Curious Character,* W.W. Norton & Company, New York, 1985

Feynman P Richard, *QED: The Strange Theory Of Light And Matter*, Princeton University Press, Princeton, New Jersey, 1985

Feynman Richard P & Leighton Ralph, *"What Do You Care What Other People Think?": Further Adventures of a Curious Character,* W.W. Norton & Company, New York, 1988

Feynman Richard P, *The Meaning of it All: Thoughts of a Citizen Scientist,* Helix Books, Addison-Wesley, Reading, Massachusetts, 1998

Feynman Richard & Weinberg Steven, *Elementary Particles and the Laws of Physics: The 1986 Dirac Memorial Lectures*, Cambridge University Press, Cambridge, 1987

Feynman Richard P, *The Pleasure of Finding Things Out: The Best Short Works of Richard P. Feynman,* Helix Books, Perseus Books, Cambridge, Massachusetts, 1999

Fishman Scott, *The War on Pain: How Breakthroughs in the New Field of Pain Medicine Are Turning the Tide Against Suffering*, HarperCollins Publishers, New York, 2000

Foster Kenneth R. and Huber Peter W., *Judging Science: Scientific Knowledge and the Federal Courts*, The MIT Press, Cambridge, Massachusetts, 1997

Garnham Alan and Oakhill Jane, *Thinking and Reasoning,* Blackwell Publishers, Oxford, UK, 1994

Gawande Atul, *Complications: A Surgeon's Notes on an Imperfect Science*, Metropolitan Books, New York, 2002

Gazzaniga Michael S. (editor), *Conversations in the Cognitive Neurosciences*, The MIT Press, Cambridge, Massachusetts, 1997

Gazzaniga Michael S., *The Mind's Past*, University of California Press, Berkeley and Los Angeles, 1998

Gigerenzer Gerd, Todd M. Peter and the ABC Research Group, *Simple Heuristics That Make Us Smart*, Oxford University Press, New York, 1999

Gigerenzer Gerd, *Adaptive Thinking: Rationality in the Real World*, Oxford University Press, New York, 2000

Gigerenzer Gerd, *Calculated Risks: How To Know When Numbers Deceive You*, Simon & Schuster, New York, 2002

Gilovich Thomas, *How We Know What Isn't So: The Fallibility of Human Reason in Everyday Life,* The Free Press, New York, 1991

Gilovich Thomas, Griffin Dale, and Kahneman Daniel (editors), *Heuristics and Biases: The Psychology of Intuitive Judgment,* Cambridge University Press, Cambridge, United Kingdom, 2002

Glassner Barry, *The Culture of Fear: Why Americans Are Afraid of the Wrong Things*, Basic Books, New York, 1999

Gleick James, *Genius: The Life and Science of Richard Feynman*, Vintage Books, New York, 1992

Goldratt Eliyahu M., *What is this thing called theory of constraints and how should it be implemented?*, North River Press, Great Barrington, Massachusetts, 1990

Goldsmith Timothy H., *The Biological Roots of Human Nature: Forging Links between Evolution and Behavior,* Oxford University Press, New York, 1991

Goldstein William M and Hogarth Robin M (editors), *Research on Judgment and Decision Making: Currents, connections, and controversies*, Cambridge University Press, Cambridge, 1997

Goodstein David L. & Goodstein Judith R., *Feynman's Lost Lecture: The Motion of Planets Around the Sun,* Vintage, Random House, London, 1997

Gould Stephen Jay, *Wonderful Life: The Burgess Shale and the Nature of History*, W.W. Norton & Company, New York, 1989, Norton paperback 1990

Gower Barry, *Scientific Method: An historical and philosophical introduction*, Routledge, London, 1997

Graham Benjamin, *The Intelligent Investor: A Book of Practical Counsel*, Harper & Row, Publishers, New York, 1973

Greenfield Susan A, *The Human Brain: A Guided Tour,* Basic Books, HarperCollins Publishers, New York, 1997

Gribbin Mary & John, *Richard Feynman: A Life In Science,* Penguin Books, London, 1997

Gribbin Mary & John, *Being Human: Putting people in an evolutionary perspective,* Phoenix, Orion Books, London, 1993

Gribbin Mary & John, *Ice Age,* The Penguin Press, London, 2001

Griffiths Paul E, *What Emotions Really Are: The Problem of Psychological Categories,* The University of Chicago Press, Chicago, 1997

Gullberg Jan, *Mathematics: From the Birth of Numbers*, W.W. Norton & Company, New York, 1997

Haigh John, *Taking Chances: Winning with Probability,* Oxford University Press, Oxford, 1999

Hallowell Edward M, *Worry: Controlling It and Using It Wisely*, Pantheon Books, New York, 1997

Hamer Dean and Copeland Peter, *Living with Our Genes: Why They Matter More Than You Think,* Bantam Doubleday Dell Publishing Group, New York, 1998

Hardin Garrett, *Filters Against Folly: How to Survive Despite Economists, Ecologists, and the Merely Eloquent,* Penguin Books USA, New York, 1985

Hardin Garrett, *Living Within Limits: Ecology, Economics, and Population Taboos,* Oxford University Press, New York, 1993

Hardin Garrett, *The Ostrich Factor: Our Population Myopia,* Oxford University Press, New York, 1998

Harper Henry Howard, *The Psychology of Speculation: The Human Element in Stock Market Speculations*, Fraser Publishing Company, Burlington, Vermont, 1966

Hardy, G.H., *A Mathematician's Apology*, Cambridge University Press, Cambridge, 1940, 1967

Hazen Robert M. and Trefil James, *Science Matters: Achieving Scientific Literacy*, Bantam Doubleday Dell Publishing Group, New York, 1991

Hock R. Roger, *Forty Studies that Changed Psychology: Explorations into the History of Psychological Research*, Prentice-Hall, New Jersey, 1999,1995,1992

Hoffer Eric, *The True Believer: Thoughts on the Nature of Mass Movements,* Harper & Row, New York, 1951

Hoffman Paul, *The Man who Loved only Numbers: The Story Of Paul Erdos And The Search For Mathematical Truth,* Hyperion, New York, 1998

Horgan John, *The End of Science: Facing the Limits of Knowledge in the Twilight of the Scientific Age*, Broadway Books, New York, 1996, 1997

Horgan John, *The Undiscovered Mind: How the Human Brain Defies Replication, Medication, and Explanation,* The Free Press, Simon & Schuster, New York, 1999

Horner John R. and Dobb Edwin, *Dinosaur Lives: Unearthing an Evolutionary Saga*, Harcourt Brace & Company, New York, 1997

James William, *The Principles of Psychology,* Dover Publications, New York, 1890, 1918

James William, *Selected Writings,* Everyman, J.M. Dent, Orion Publishing Group, London 1995

Jeans James, *Physics and Philosophy*, Dover Publications, New York, 1981

Johnson Phillip E., *Defeating Darwinism by Opening Minds,* InterVarsity Press, Downers Grove, Illinois, 1997

Jones Steve, *Almost Like A Whale: The Origin Of Species Updated,* TransWorld Publishers, London, 1999

Joyce James M., *The Foundations of Causal Decision Theory*, Cambridge University Press, Cambridge, 1999

Kahneman Daniel, Slovic Paul and Tversky Amos (editors), *Judgment under uncertainty: Heuristics and biases,* Cambridge University Press, Cambridge, 1982

Kahneman Daniel and Tversky Amos (editors), *Choices, Values and Frames*, Cambridge University Press, Cambridge, 2000

Keynes Randal, *Annie's Box: Charles Darwin, his Daughter and Human Evolution*, Fourth Estate, London, 2001

Kilpatrick Andrew, *Of Permanent Value: The Story of Warren Buffett*, AKPE, Birmingham, 2000

King Jerry P., *The Art of Mathematics*, Ballantine Books, New York, 1992

Klemm William R., *Understanding Neuroscience*, Mosby-Year Book, St. Louis, 1996

Kline Morris, *Mathematics for the Nonmathematician*, Dover Publications, New York, 1967

Krauss Lawrence M., *Fear Of Physics: A Guide for the Perplexed,* Vintage, Random House, London, 1994, 1996

Kuhn Harold W. and Nasar Sylvia (editors), *The Essential John Nash*, Princeton University Press, Princeton, New Jersey, 2002

Landes David, *The Wealth and Poverty of Nations: Why Some Are So Rich and Some so poor,* W.W. Norton & Company., New York, 1998

Laplace Marquis de, *A Philosophical Essay on Probabilities*, Dover Publications, New York, 1951.

LeDoux Joseph, *Synaptic Self: How Our Brains Become Who We Are*, Viking Penguin, New York, 2002

Lee Jeffrey A, *The Scientific Endeavor: A Primer on Scientific Principles and Practice,* Addison Wesley Longman, San Francisco, 2000

Levinson Horace C, *Chance, Luck and Statistics*, Dover Publications, New York, 1939, 1050, 1963

Lewis H.W, *Why Flip a Coin: The Art and Science of Good Decisions,* John Wiley & Sons, New York, 1997

Lightman Alan, *Great Ideas In Physics: The Conservation of Energy, The Second Law of Thermodynamics, The Theory of Relativity, and Quantum Mechanics,* McGraw-Hill, New York, 2000

Lorenz Edward, *The Essence Of Chaos*, UCL Press, London, 1993, 1995

Lowe Janet, *Damn Right!: Behind The Scenes With Berkshire Hathaway Billionaire Charlie Munger*, John Wiley & Sons, New York, 2000

Lynch Peter, *One up on Wall Street,* Simon & Schuster, New York, 1989

Lowenstein Roger, *Buffett: The Making of an American Capitalist*, Random House, New York, 1995

Lowenstein Roger, *When Genius Failed: The Rise and Fall of Long-Term Capital Management*, Random House, New York, 2000

MacKay Charles, *Extraordinary Popular Delusions & the Madness of Crowds*, Crown Publishers, New York, 1980

Mahoney David and Restak Richard, *The Longevity Strategy: How to Live to 100 using the Brain-Body Connection,* John Wiley & Sons, New York, 1998

Mandler George, *Human Nature Explored,* Oxford University Press, New York, 1997

Manktelow Ken, *Reasoning and Thinking,* Psychology Press, Hove East Sussex, England, 1999

Mayr Ernst, *This Is Biology: The Science of the Living World,* The Belknap Press of Harvard University Press, Cambridge, Massachusetts, 1997

Mayr Ernst, *What Evolution Is*, Basic Books, New York, 2001

McConnell James V. and Philipchalk Ronald P, *Understanding Human Behavior,* Harcourt Brace Jovanovich College Publishers, New York, 1992

Mehra Jagdish, *The Beat of a Different Drum: The Life and Science of Richard Feynman*, Clarendon Press, Oxford, 1994

Milgram Stanley, *Obedience to Authority: An Experimental View,* Harper and Row, New York, 1974

Minsky Marvin, *The Society of Mind,* Touchstone, Simon & Shuster, New York, 1985, 1986

Von Mises Richard, *Probability, Statistics and Truth*, Dover Publications, New York, 1957

Murphy Michael P. and O'Neill Luke A.J (editors), *What is Life? The Next Fifty Years: Speculations on the Future of Biology,* Cambridge University Press, Cambridge, 1995

Myers David G., *Social Psychology,* The McGraw-Hill Companies, New York, 1983, 1987, 1990, 1993, 1996

Nesheim John, *High Tech Startup: The Complete How-To Handbook for Creating Successful New High Tech Companies*, 2000

Nesse M.D. Randolph M and Williams Ph. D. George C, *Why We Get Sick: The New Science of Darwinian Medicine,* Vintage Books, Random House, New York, 1994, 1996

Newman James R.(editor), *The World of Mathematics: Volume I-VI*, Dover Publications, New York, 1956

Newton, Roger G., *The Truth Of Science: Physical Theories and Reality*, Harvard University Press, Cambridge, Massachusetts, 1997

Newton Roger G., *Thinking about Physics,* Princeton University Press, Princeton, New Jersey, 2000

Nicholson Nigel, *Executive Instinct: Managing the Human Animal in the Information Age*, Crown Publishers, New York, 2000

Niven Ivan, *Mathematics of Choice, or How to Count without Counting,* The Mathematical Association of America, Washington, 1965

O'Hear Anthony, *Beyond Evolution: Human Nature and the Limits of Evolutionary Explanation*, Clarendon Press, Oxford, 1997

Orkin Mike, *What are the Odds: Chance in Everyday Life*, W.H. Freeman and Company, New York, 2000

Packel Edward, *The Mathematics of Games and Gambling,* The Mathematical Association of America, Washington, 1981

Pascal Blaise, *Pensèes,* translated by A.J. Krailsheimer, Penguin Books, London, 1966,1995

Paulos John Allen, *Innumeracy: Mathematical Illiteracy and Its Consequences,* Vintage Books, Random House, New York, 1988

Paulos John Allen, *Beyond Numeracy: Ruminations Of A Numbers Man,* Vintage Books, Random House, New York, 1991

Paulos John Allen, *A Mathematician Reads the Newspaper,* An Anchor Book, Bantam Doubleday Dell Publishing Group, New York, 1995

Paulos John Allen, *Once upon a number: The Hidden Mathematical Logic of Stories,* Basic Books, New York, 1998

Peterson Ivars, *The Mathematical Tourist: New and Updated Snapshots of Modern Mathematics*, W.H. Freeman & Company, New York, 1998

Peterson Ivars, *The Jungles of Randomness: A Mathematical Safari,* John Wiley & Sons, New York, 1988, 1998

Piattelli-Palmarini Massimo, *Inevitable Illusions: How Mistakes of Reason Rule Our Minds*, John Wiley & Sons, New York, 1994

Pinker Steven, *How the Mind Works,* W.W. Norton & Company, New York, 1997

Plous Scott, *The Psychology of Judgment and Decision Making,* McGraw-Hill, New York, 1993

Poincaré Henri, *The Value of Science: Essential Writings of Henri Poincaré,* The Modern Library, New York, 2001

Polya G, *How to Solve it: A New Aspect of Mathematical Method*, Princeton University Press, Princeton, New Jersey, 1948, 1988

Popper Karl R., *The Open Universe: An Argument for Indeterminism,* University Press, Cambridge, 1956, 1982, 1988

Popper Karl R., *Quantum Theory and the Schism in Physics*, Hutchinson Publishing Group, London, 1956, 1982

Poundstone William, *Prisoner's Dilemma*, Bantam Doubleday Dell Publishing Group, New York, 1992

Poundstone William, *Carl Sagan: a life in the cosmos*, Henry Holt and Company, New York, 1999

Ramachandran V.S. and Blakeslee Sandra, *Phantoms in the Brain: Probing the Mysteries of the Human Mind*, William Morrow and Company, New York, 1998

Ridley Mark (editor), *Evolution,* Oxford University Press, Oxford, 1997

Ridley Matt, *The Origins Of Virtue: Human Instincts and the Evolution of Cooperation,* Penguin Books USA, New York, 1996, 1997

Ridley Matt, *Genome: The autobiography of a species in 23 chapters*, Fourth Estate Limited, London, 1999

Rose Michael R., *Darwin's Spectre: Evolutionary Biology in the Modern World*, Princeton University Press, Princeton, New Jersey, 1998

Rota Gian-Carlo, *Indiscrete Thoughts,* Birkhäuser, Boston, 1997

Rothman Tony & Sudarshan George, *Doubt and Certainty*, Perseus Books, Reading, Massachusetts, 1998

Ruelle David, *Chance and Chaos,* Princeton University Press, Princeton, New Jersey, 1991

Russell Bertrand, *Logic and Knowledge: Essays 1901-1950,* George Allen & Unwin, London, 1956

Russell Bertrand, *Russell's Best: Silhouettes in Satire,* Routledge, London, 1958

Russell Bertrand, *The Problems of Philosophy,* Oxford University Press, Oxford, New York, 1959

Sagan Carl, *The Demon-Haunted World: Science as a Candle in the Dark,* Ballantine Books, New York, 1996

Sapolsky Robert M., *Why Zebras Don't Get Ulcers: And Updated Guide to Stress, Stress-related Diseases, and Coping*, W.H. Freeman and Company, New York, 1994, 1998

Sawyer W.W, *Mathematician's Delight,* Penguin Books Ltd., Middlesex, England, 1943

Schacter Daniel L., *The Seven Sins of Memory: How the Mind Forgets and Remembers*, Houghton Mifflin Company, New York, 2001

Schwed Fred Jr., *Where Are the Customers' Yachts?: or A Good Hard Look at Wall Street*, John Wiley & Sons, New York, 1940, 1955, 1995

Richard Schweid Richard, *the cockroach papers: a compendium of history and lore*, Four Walls Eight Windows, New York, 1999

Schick Jr. Theodore and Vaughn Lewis, *How to Think about Weird Things: Critical Thinking for a New Age,* Mayfield Publishing Company, Mountain View, CA, 1995

Segre Emilio, *Enrico Fermi Physicist*, The University of Chicago Press, Chicago, 1970

Shaw Patrick, *Logic and its Limits,* Oxford University Press, New York, 1981, 1997

Shefrin Hersh, *Beyond Greed and Fear: Understanding Behavioral Finance and the Psychology of Investing,* Harvard Business School Press, Boston, Massachusetts, 2000

Shermer Michael, *Why People Believe Weird Things: Pseudoscience, Superstition, And Other Confusions Of Our Time,* W.H. Freeman and Company, New York, 1997

Shermer Michael, *The Borderlands of Science: Where Sense Meets Nonsense*, Oxford University Press, New York, 2001

Shiller Robert J., *Irrational Exuberance*, Princeton University Press, Princeton, New Jersey, 2000

Simon Herbert A., *Models of My Life*, The MIT Press, Cambridge, Massachusetts, 1996

Singh Simon, *Fermat's Enigma: The Epic Quest to Solve the World's Greatest Mathematical Problem,* Walker and Company, New York, 1997

Skinner, B.F., *"Superstition" in the pigeon,* Journal of Experimental Psychology, 38, 1948.

Skinner B.F, *About Behaviorism,* Vintage Books, Random House, New York, 1976

Slater P.J.B. and Halliday T.R. (editors), *Behaviour and Evolution,* Cambridge University Press, New York, 1994

Slovic Paul, *The Perception of Risk*, Earthscan Publications, London, 2000

Smitley Robert L., *Popular Financial Delusions,* Fraser Publishing Company, Burlington, Vermont, 1963

Sober Elliott, *The Nature of Selection: Evolutionary Theory in Philosophical Focus,* The University of Chicago Press, Chicago, 1984

Sober Elliott (editor), *Conceptual Issues in Evolutionary Biology*, Bradford Book, The MIT Press, Cambridge, Massachusetts, 1994

Sokal Alan and Bricmont Jean, *Fashionable Nonsense: Postmodern Intellectuals' Abuse of Science,* Picador USA, New York, 1998

Sternberg Robert J., *Thinking Styles*, Cambridge University Press, Cambridge, UK, 1997

Stevens Anthony and Price John, *Evolutionary Psychiatry: A New Beginning*, Routledge, London, 1996

Stewart Ian, *Nature's Numbers: The Unreal Reality of Mathematical Imagination*, Basic Books, New York, 1995

Stewart Ian and Cohen Jack, *Figments of Reality: the evolution of the curious mind,* Cambridge University Press, Cambridge, 1997

Sulloway Frank J, *Born to Rebel: Birth Order, Family Dynamics, and Creative Lives,* Vintage Books, Random House, New York, 1997

Sutherland Stuart, *Irrationality: The Enemy Within,* Penguin Books, London, 1992

Sykes Christopher (editor), *No Ordinary Genius: The Illustrated Richard Feynman*, W.W. Norton & Company, New York, 1994.

Teger Allan I., *Too Much Invested to Quit: The Psychology of the Escalation of Conflict*, Pergamon Press, New York, 1980

Tenner Edward, *Why Things Bite Back: Technology And The Revenge Of Unintended Consequences*, Vintage Books, New York, 1996, 1997

Thaler Richard H., *The Winner's Curse: Paradoxes and Anomalies of Economic Life,* Princeton University Press, Princeton, New Jersey, 1992

Thompson W.C., Taroni F., Aitken C.G.G., *How The Probability of a False Positive Affects the Value of DNA Evidence, J Forensic Sci,* Jan 2003, Vol. 48, No.1 Paper ID JFS2001171_481. Copyright by ASTM International.

Train John, *The Money Masters*, Harper & Row, New York, 1980

Train John, *The Midas Touch: The Strategies That Have Made Warren Buffett America's Pre-eminent Investor*, Harper & Row, New York, 1987

Trefil James, *The Edge of the Unknown: 101 Things You Don't Know About Science And No One Else Does Either*, Houghton Mifflin Company, New York, 1996

Trefil James, *Are we Unique: A Scientist Explores the Unparalleled Intelligence of the Human Mind,* John Wiley & Sons, New York, 1997

Tudge Colin, *The Time Before History: 5 Million Years of Human Impact,* Touchstone Book, Simon & Schuster, New York, 1996

Vogel Steven, *Cats' Paws and Catapults: Mechanical Worlds of Nature and People*, W.W. Norton & Company, New York, 1998

Vyse Stuart A., *Believing in Magic: The Psychology of Superstition*, Oxford University Press, New York, 1997

de Waal Frans, *Good Natured: the Origins of Right and Wrong in Humans and Other Animals,* Harvard University Press, Cambridge, Massachusetts, 1996, 1997

Weaver Warren, *Lady Luck: The Theory of Probability*, Dover Publications, New York, 1963

Weiner Jonathan, *Time, Love, Memory: A Great Biologist And His Quest For The Origins Of Behavior,* Alfred A. Knopf, New York, 1999

White Michael, *Isaac Newton: The Last Sorcerer,* Helix Books, Addison-Wesley Reading, Massachusetts, 1997

White Michael, *Leonardo: The First Scientist,* Little, Brown and Company, London, 2000

White Michael and Gribbin John, *Darwin: A Life in Science,* Simon & Schuster, London, 1995

Williams John Burr, *The Theory of Investment Value,* Fraser Publishing Company, Burlington, 1997 and originally published in 1938 by Harvard University Press

Wills Christopher, *Children of Prometheus, The Accelerating Pace of Human Evolution,* Perseus Books, Reading Massachusetts, 1998

Wilson Edward O, *In Search of Nature,* Island Press, Washington D.C., 1996

Wilson Edward O, *Consilience: The Unity of Knowledge,* Alfred A. Knopf, New York, 1998

Wolf Robert S., *Proof, Logic, and Conjecture: The Mathematician's Toolbox,* W.H. Freeman and Company, New York, 1998

Wright Robert, *The Moral Animal: Evolutionary Psychology and Everyday Life,* Abacus, Little Brown and Company, London, 1994, 1996

Yoerg Sonja, *Clever as a Fox: Animal Intelligence and What It Can Teach Us About Ourselves,* Bloomsbury Publishing, New York, 2001

Zeckhauser Richard J. (editor), *Strategy and Choice,* The MIT Press, Cambridge, Massachusetts, 1991

Zimbardo Philip G, *The Stanford Prison Experiment: A Simulation Study of the Psychology of Imprisonment,* www.prisonexp.org

Berkshire Hathaway Inc., Letters to Shareholders 1977-1986, 1987-1995, Annual Reports 1996-2002

Cardozo Law Review, *The Essays of Warren Buffett: Lessons for Corporate America,* Volume 19, Sept.-Nov. 1997 Numbers 1-2

Daedalus, Journal of the American Academy of Arts and Sciences, Spring 1998, The Brain

Program on *Investment Decisions and Behavioral Finance* at John F. Kennedy School of Government, Harvard University

Mayoclinic.com

The Neurosciences Institute Scientific Report and Catalog 1981-2001

Outstanding Investor Digest 1988 – 2003.

The Royal Swedish Academy of Sciences: Advanced information on the Prize in Economic Sciences 2002, *Foundations of Behavioral and Experimental Economics: Daniel Kahneman and Vernon Smith*